PSYCHOLOGY
AS A HUMAN
SCIENCE

PSYCHOLOGY AS A HUMAN SCIENCE

A PHENOMENOLOGICALLY

BASED APPROACH

Amedeo Giorgi
PROFESSOR OF PSYCHOLOGY
DUQUESNE UNIVERSITY

HARPER & ROW, PUBLISHERS
NEW YORK, EVANSTON, AND LONDON

Psychology as a Human Science: A Phenomenologically Based Approach

LIBRARY OF CONGRESS CATALOG CARD NUMBER: 74-96229

TO MY WIFE,
ANNIE

CONTENTS

PREFACE

THIS WORK BELONGS WITHIN THE MOVEMENT OF the so-called "Third Force" psychology, but unlike many other works in this stream of thought it approaches the problems of man as a person from a point of view that comes from within science and from an academic psychological perspective. I stress this not because there have been no other such attempts, but because these attempts are definitely in the minority—and because very often, to those who are not knowledgeable about the movement, Third Force psychology seems to be a domain reserved exclusively for clinicians. This impression is obtained because most of the Third Force psychologists *are* clinicians or psychologists interested in personality theory. Also, the mistaken notion that if one is interested in the whole person then it is not possible to be scientific is still too prevalent. In truth, the impact of Third Force psychology is by no means limited to clinical psychology—its insights are relevant for the whole field. Moreover, it is precisely the prejudice that Third Force psychology must be either antiscientific or nonscientific that we would like to challenge. Consequently, both the term "human" and the term "science" are important to us. We would insist upon the relevance of the term *human* to those who want to build a psychology of the human person according to the conception of science as developed by the natural sciences and who adhere rigidly to that concept despite changes in subject matter. We would insist upon the relevance of *science* for those who want to study the humanistic aspects of man without any concern for method or rigor whatsoever. These positions are on opposite sides of an implicitly static and univocal conception of science. As I see it, the solution lies precisely in extending and deepen-

ing the very concept of science itself so that science is not committed to only one set of philosophical presuppositions. This is
what this work attempts to do.

On the other hand, I feel no special commitment to the
expression "human science" itself. Perhaps a more adequate
expression can be found. We at Duquesne University have lived
through a number of titles that have attempted to depict this
type of psychology, but none of them has been without its difficulties. However, what I mean to communicate by the term
"human science" is that psychology has the responsibility to investigate the full range of behavior and experience of man as a
person in such a way that the *aims* of science are fulfilled, but
that these aims should *not be implemented* primarily in terms
of the criteria of the natural sciences. More specifically, the
methods of the natural sciences are not criteria for how the
human sciences are practiced. If a human scientific method
turns out to be identical with one from the natural sciences, it is
coincidental and due to a spontaneous response to a genuinely
human scientific problem.

The basic question here is one of procedure. I feel that the
fundamental problems of the human sciences should be approached directly and exactly as they present themselves and
solved by whatever means the investigator deems is necessary.
In this way a body of facts and viewpoints will be built up.
Only after such a set of data have been established can dialogue,
in the proper sense of the term, i.e., between two mature sets of
disciplines, occur. In contrast, the human sciences have begun,
for the most part, by imitating the style of the natural sciences
and accepting, mostly implicitly, the world view of the natural
sciences with the additional qualification that this world view
represented the best expression of total reality possible. In this
work the latter assumption is bracketed. Perhaps most neutrally
expressed, the fundamental question raised is: Can the world
view of the natural sciences comprehend fully and adequately
the phenomenon of man as a person? In principle I can accept
either a "yes" or "no" answer to this question. However, it
seems that the bulk of the evidence both within and outside
of psychology indicates a negative answer. I realize, of course,

that both the evidence and the criteria for acceptable evidence are still in the realm of preference rather than in the domain of universally accepfable facts. Consequently, more than the answer itself, this work wishes to emphasize that there is more than a single *approach* to the answer. One way, which is the route of the natural sciences, is to take the concepts, viewpoints, techniques, etc., of the natural sciences and apply them to the phenomenon of man and then see how well they fare. Another way is to go directly to the phenomenon of man and see what concepts, viewpoints, methods, etc., emerge as a necessary result of studying him. The latter approach we would term the "human scientific perspective." The chief purpose of this book is to defend the position that such an approach is scientific and accurate, or in brief, legitimate.

My original intention was to write a book called *The Foundations of Psychology as a Human Science* in which all the problems of the approach, method, and content of human scientific psychology would be worked out. Two factors changed my mind. First of all, the original intention was naïvely ambitious. To work out all of the above-mentioned problems is more a life project than a short-term effort. Thus, the original intention is still being pursued, but my expectations are now more modest. Secondly, I had originally thought that the communication of the notion of "approach" and the problems covered therein would be less difficult. However, my experience in teaching this concept and exploring all the implications that it has for the practice of psychology indicated to me that a book setting forth its meaning and its value might prove to be a worthwhile effort in its own right. This is especially true since in most of American psychology there is still a reluctance to deal with metapsychological issues that have philosophical connotations.

Consequently, those readers who look for answers regarding specific questions of method and content will be largely disappointed. This book centers on the attempt to clarify an *approach* that will lead to specific answers regarding method and content. In other words, psychology as a human science is not so much an achievement as a project. To state that a project is being undertaken means precisely that answers are being *sought* and not that one has them already. What is necessary is that there be sufficient freedom to begin and continue the work without a constant defense of the project itself. The right to define and pursue problems in ways that are different from established ways is especially precious at the beginning of such projects for that is when they are most vulnerable and least capable of self-justification. Nevertheless, all movements must pass through this phase, and it is my hope that this book will help the project of psychology conceived as a human science to get by this difficult phase by demonstrating that it is not antiscientific or even non-scientific so much as the expression of science differently conceived.

Finally, if the intention of this work is achieved it will not mean that some psychologists will be prevented from doing what they are doing now, or that they cannot do what they want, but rather that some psychologists who are hesitant to do what they really want will have the freedom to pursue their sincerest interests in ways that they deem are worthwhile. It was with the intention of introducing an alternative for those psychologists who desire it that this book was written.

While an author may have withdrawn into solitude to put his thoughts on paper, the thoughts expressed never reflect solely the writer. I am keenly aware of this fact, so it is with pleasure that I express my gratitude to those who helped bring this book to completion. First of all, I would like to thank my colleagues at Duquesne University, both philosophers and psychologists, for their encouragement and criticism, and for their active participation in the faculty seminars in which many of these issues were discussed. I would also like to thank the students who through the years patiently listened to imprecise and awkward formulations of what I wanted to say and whose very questions helped to clarify the significant issues. I would also like to thank my colleagues from other institutions who have read and commented on earlier forms of the manuscript, especially Jean Bayard, Antos Rancurello, and Frans van Doorne. Special thanks are also due to my assistants Tom Cloonan, Paul Colaizzi, Tom Doyle, Dennie Kunz, and Emily

Mann for their perseverance in pursuing the many chores I assigned them. Anita Adlin also deserves special mention for completing the typing of the manuscript in a flawless way. Last, but far from least, I would like to thank my wife for her patience and encouragement, without which this book most assuredly would not have been completed.

AMEDEO GIORGI

INTRODUCTION

MANY ASPECTS OF PSYCHOLOGY
are controversial, but there is surely one fact upon which all must agree: Psychology is a young science. It is generally agreed that psychology, as a science, was born in 1879 when Wundt established his laboratory in Leipzig. This means that it is still less than one hundred years old, very young indeed for a science.

However, it is important to note that while the science of psychology is young, science itself is not. In fact, by the late nineteenth century, when psychology chose to adopt that particular way of viewing the world that is identified with science, there already existed, within the scientific attitude, a body of seemingly incontrovertible facts as well as concepts, theories, methods, techniques, and viewpoints that had proved their fruitfulness. Consequently, when psychology entered the domain of science, it entered into a framework of thought that had already begun its systematic exploration of the world, that had many traditions established, and that had unlocked numerous secrets about the universe. An important consequence of the "establishment" of science as opposed to the "promise" of scientific psychology was that psychology began to formulate its own problems in terms of the established "truths" of science; it began to accept as criteria for its own results the norms established by science; and lastly, it took from science, as answers to its own methodological problems, the proven methods and techniques of science. In short, scientific psychology established itself by imitating the practices and aims of science.

It is also important to realize that what constituted "established" science in the late nineteenth century was almost exclusively what are today called the physical or natural sciences—

astronomy, physics, chemistry, biology, physiology, etc. The so-called behavioral or social sciences, like psychology itself, were still struggling for existence. Thus, in imitating the practices and aims of science, psychology was, in fact, imitating the practices and aims of the *natural sciences*.

The critical question to be raised now is: Should psychology have *imitated the practices and aims of the natural sciences?* Should psychology accept uncritically the *aims* of the natural sciences, or should it articulate its own aims? Should psychology implement the methods of the natural sciences precisely in the way that the natural scientists implement them? Or, if the psychologist finds it necessary to modify these methods, what are the basis and nature of these modifications? What is the psychologist responding to when he modifies some of the methods of the natural sciences? In short, is the subject matter of psychology identical to, similar to, or radically different from that of the natural sciences? If either of the first two alternatives is the answer, then psychology is essentially correct when it proceeds along natural scientific lines. But if the last alternative is correct, ought not psychology then conceive of itself and practice its science in a way that is different from the way that the natural sciences are conceived and practiced? Our position is that if the full range of experience and behavior of man as a person is to come under scientific scrutiny, then a different conception of scientific psychology will be necessary. To be sure, natural scientific psychology does yield legitimate data about aspects of man, but there is serious question whether or not the aspects that are amenable to the natural scientific conception reveal the humanness of man in an adequate way. It is this doubt, along with the evidence of everyday experience in the life-world, that leads us to seek another conception of psychology: one that will do justice both to the phenomenon of man as a person *and* to the practice of science.

Of course, when psychology started it had no such choice, because science and the natural sciences were identical. However, today, after almost a century of experience with natural scientific psychology, one can raise the question of whether the future of psychology is served better by a more intensive effort in the direction of the established conception of psychology, or whether a new conception of psychology that implies a broader conception of science would prove more promising. To raise this question is not an automatic and outright rejection of the natural scientific conception of psychology. Buytendijk (1962) has written that psychology as a positive science has become dogmatic and lacks the radicalism of doubt. It is within this critical spirit of doubting that the question is raised. Is it not possible that psychology adopted a wrong conception of science to imitate? Is it not possible that psychology has not yet clarified its aims in its own terms? At any rate, should not psychology at least raise the question openly, and either respond in the negative, or else admit that another conception of psychology is equally feasible, or even preferable?

It is our belief that psychology should not be included among the natural sciences: reasons for this belief are outlined in the succeeding pages. By excluding itself from the *natural* sciences, however, psychology does not necessarily have to leave the domain of science. Rather, the major thesis of this book is that psychology should be conceived as a human science and not as a natural science. We realize, of course, that such an assertion depends upon the fact that it is possible to have such a phenomenon as a "human science." We hope to be able to demonstrate, however, that whatever difficulties one may have with the union of the terms "human" and "science," these difficulties are due to certain prejudicial views of science and not to the way science is in fact practiced. Furthermore, we hope to demonstrate that it is *necessary* for psychology to develop within the framework of a human science if it is to develop successfully. Psychology can no longer avoid its responsibility to investigate peculiarly human phenomena along with its traditional areas, and it can no longer blame its youthfulness for not providing an adequate frame of reference for this endeavor. Lastly, it can no longer afford the luxury of neglecting to found itself properly.

In essence, then, this book is a case for conceiving psychology as a human science. We have to begin, however, by clarifying just what psychology itself meant when it aspired to become a science.

CHAPTER 1

THE MEANING
OF SCIENCE IN PSYCHOLOGY

WHEN THE REVISED EDITION OF
the classic *History of Experimental Psychology* appeared in
1950, the status of psychology was such that Boring (1950, p. 320)
was still able to write: "Even today psychologists have not ceased
to be self-conscious about the scientific nature of psychology."
Nor has this concern with science diminished since that time.
This can be seen from the fact that practically every textbook
begins with an explanation of why and how psychology is a
science, and from recurrent articles that appear almost annually
in the *American Psychologist* about the relationship between
psychology and science.

When one becomes cognizant of this trend, the following inevitable question arises: Why is psychology so concerned about
demonstrating its scientific status? Why is it that physics and
chemistry can move directly to concrete problems without
polemical prologues about their established scientific status? Is
it only because of psychology's youthfulness, or are other factors
involved? In order to attempt an answer to this question, we
shall have to investigate the history of psychology in order to
clarify what psychology itself understood as its task when it
broke from philosophy and became an independent science.

It is not easy to trace the relationship between psychology and
science. That is because, as even a cursory glance at the history
of psychology reveals, there is not a single univocal relationship,
but rather there are many relationships and many interpretations of what science means for psychology. Nevertheless, there
are certain dominant trends that can be isolated, and we shall
cover what we believe to be the major ones.

Psychology Is a Natural Science

It is the purpose of this section to demonstrate that the idea that psychology is or should be a natural science has been with psychology, both implicitly and explicitly, from its beginnings. We shall demonstrate this by covering the history of modern psychology in four phases and showing the presence of this idea in each phase.

THE FOUNDERS AND LATE NINETEENTH-CENTURY PSYCHOLOGISTS

Since psychology is one of the latecomers among scientific disciplines, it seems that a large part of its field of interest is determined first by specifying what it is not, and only secondly by spelling out what it is. This characteristic also dominated the beginnings of modern, scientific psychology, since its primary motivation seemed to be the establishment of itself as independent from the philosophy of its time, especially from deductive and speculative philosophy. It proposed to do this by becoming a member of that other branch of critical knowledge, natural science. It is important to note that its ambition to be independent was at least as strong as, if not stronger than, its ambition to be a natural science. In a sense, its desire to be a natural science was a means of achieving its aim of independence from philosophy. That psychology was revolting against the philosophy of its time is indicated by Woodworth (1931, p.3), who talks about psychology's recent departure from the parental household of philosophy. Moreover, he indicates the revolutionary nature of our science since he states that each school of psychology in the early twentieth century began as a revolt against the established psychological order of 1900, which was itself, at the beginning, a revolt against an earlier established order. In passing, we may note that with this kind of beginning, one should not be surprised if there were still more "revolts" against the establishment within psychology.

That psychology was seeking independent status is also indicated by Boring's (1950) statement that Wundt promoted the idea of psychology as an independent science, and by Wood-worth's (1931) description of how the "new, experimental" psychologists refused to see their field as a subordinate part of philosophy, and how these psychologists simply went on to found professorships, departments, and journals until psychology's independence was in fact no longer questionable.

However, it would be erroneous to infer that psychology became a natural science *only* because it wanted to become independent. There were also strong, intrinsic reasons for choosing to become a member of the natural sciences. Our first concern will be to try to understand better this double movement: away from philospohy and toward the natural sciences. Since Wundt is the acknowledged founder of modern psychology, we can begin with him. When Wundt claimed, on many occasions, that psychology ought to be a science, he had in mind the notion of a natural science.

Perhaps the most systematic and thorough treatment, although not exclusive interpretation, of the role Wundt played in the founding of psychology is that provided by Boring (1950). In his biographical summary of Wundt's life and work, Boring reveals many facts relevant to our point. Wundt came to psychology from a background in medicine and physiology. In the 1860s Wundt lectured at Heidelberg on both experimental physiology and medical physics, and these courses later became books. Boring (1950, p. 319) makes an interesting observation about these early works. He interprets Wundt's stress on medical physics as meaning that it was still necessary in those days to emphasize that physiology was a science in the sense of a physical science. Boring then reasons that if Wundt felt this need with respect to medical physics, it would only be natural to assume that he felt the need to stress that psychology too, as physiological psychology, is a science. For our purposes, it is important to note that the sense of science that Wundt was arguing for was that of the physical sciences.

Further on, Boring (1950, p.321) notes that from 1862 until 1866 Wundt offered a course of lectures on "Psychology from the standpoint of the natural sciences," and then in 1867 he continued the course but he changed his title to "Physiological Psychology." Boring states that the course had been described as the naïve psychology of the physiologist, but that it nevertheless contained an indication of many problems that were to make up the body of experimental psychology for many years. Heidbreder (1933) also notes that in Wundt's *Physiological Psychology* much that had been vaguely implicit in the psychology of the physiological laboratories was treated explicitly and systematically. Thus, this is another indication of the fact that from its very beginnings psychology was becoming scientific in the sense of the natural sciences, because much of its content was being formulated initially in a physiological lab.

Wundt himself was explicit on this point in a number of places. For example, in speaking about the methods of psychology prior to the advent of experimental psychology, Wundt (1961) applied the yardstick of natural scientific criticism, and he declared that the shortcomings could be easily discovered. In arguing for the utility of physiology for psychology Wundt (1912) stressed that it was qualified with respect to *method*, thus rendering the same help to psychology that it (physiology) itself received from physics. In still another place, Wundt (1961, p. 70) wrote the following with respect to justifying an extreme application of experimentation:

The importance which experimentation will eventually have in psychology can hardly be visualized to its full extent as yet. We do have, surely, many noteworthy beginnings in the field of psychological investigations, but as a coherent science, experimental psychology still awaits its foundations. These beginnings relate predominantly to the borderline areas where physiology and psychology touch each other, in the area of sensation and perception. It has often been held that the area of sensation and perception is the only one wherein the application of the experimental method remains a possibility, because this is the very area where physiological factors always play a role; whereas— so holds this view—it is a futile attempt to try to penetrate into the realism of the higher psychic activities by experimental methods. Surely, this is prejudice. *As soon as the psyche is viewed as a natural phenomenon, and psychology as a natural science,* the experimental methods must also be capable of full application to this science. (My emphasis.)

Wundt was not a naïve man, so naturally he did not argue for a rigid annexation of the methods of the natural sciences. In his own words:

. . . psychology, in adopting the experimental methods of physiology, does not by any means take them over as they are, and apply them without change to a new material. The methods of experimental psychology have been transformed—in some instances, actually remodelled —by psychology itself, to meet the specific requirements of psychological investigation. Psychology has adapted physiological, as physiology adapted psychical methods to its own ends. (Wundt, 1912, p. 688)

However, in referring to psychophysics, which Wundt considers to be an aspect of psychology and not the whole field, Wundt (1912) writes: "In execution it (psychophysics) will be predominantly physiological, since psychophysics is concerned to follow up the anatomical and physiological investigation of the bodily substrate of conscious processes. . . ."

Consequently, Wundt's own writings unmistakably reflect the impact of the natural scientific attitude on psychology. This influence made itself present primarily through Wundt's physiological leanings, but also because of the importance of the experimental method for Wundt. It should be mentioned here that natural scientific psychology is not an exclusive conception of psychology and its methods on the part of Wundt, but these points will be discussed later, along with the reasons for the emphasis that we have given Wundt.

It is not difficult to establish that the same aim of making psychology a natural science existed among some of Wundt's precursors and contemporaries. Fechner, for example, was a marvel to his contemporaries precisely because he was able to "measure" mental processes and present them in a quantitative manner (Heidbreder, 1933). Indeed, according to Heidbreder (1933), the significance of Fechner for psychology is precisely his attempt to treat psychological processes in the manner of the exact sciences, and in the fact that he succeeded in developing exact, quantitative experimental procedures. Similarly, Helmholtz's significance for psychology lies in the fact that he succeeded in demonstrating the possibility of studying the processes of seeing and hearing by the methods of natural sciences. This fact takes on an added significance when it is recalled that in his day, these processes were regarded as constituting the groundwork of mental life, so that, in effect, the meaning of Helmholtz's work to his contemporaries was that the methods of exact observation and experimentation were applied to specifically psychological material (Heidbreder, 1933). It is also important to note that Heidbreder (1933) lists Helmholtz's achievements as belonging to three fields: physics, physiology, and psychology. Lastly, to complete the German influence, we may note that Ebbinghaus is noted more for the fact that he was able to experiment with the "higher processes" than for the specific findings (Heidbreder, 1933). However, this means that he achieved fame by being able to "experiment" with the mind, or if we translate this fact into terms that are relevant to our point, we might say that Ebbinghaus was able to experiment on memory in a way that met the demands of the natural scientific method.

The best known psychologist in the United States prior to 1900 was, of course, William James. Although he defined psychology as the science of mental life, both of its phenomena and their conditions (James, 1890), James leaves no doubt that by science he meant natural science. James clearly states this in his *Principles* (1890, I, p. 183), and he devotes an article to this end (James, 1892). James's own motives for this seem to be to safeguard the right of psychologists to engage in concrete work without having to answer all of the questions concerning man raised by many metaphysical assumptions (James, 1890, I, p.184).

Lastly, the titles of some other publications of the time indicate that this trend was a long time in developing. Rand (1912), for example, lists a book written by Beneke published in 1833, entitled *A Textbook of Psychology as a Natural Science,* and one by Drobisch published in 1842, called *Empirical Psychology According to the Methods of Natural Science.*

FROM 1900 TO WORLD WAR I

During this period there were not so many strong assertions about the necessity of psychology to be a natural science—but there were some, and there were also many that communicated the message by implication. From hindsight, it seems that this was a lull before the storm of behaviorism.

However, to show that the idea of psychology as a natural science was sustained during this period of psychological history, we can point to the following authors. Cattell (1923), for example, argued that psychological work should be as independent of introspection as work in the natural sciences of physics or zoology. Angell (1923) stated that experiment in psychology has precisely the same merits and involves precisely the same kind of procedure that it does elsewhere in the natural sciences. He argued against the reproach to psychology that it could never become a true science, partly because it was alleged it could never employ mathematics and could not therefore attain real accuracy, and partly because it was regarded as being outside the range of experiment. For Angell, by 1912, both of those assertions were conclusively disproved. Yerkes (1923) stated that just as physical science teaches us how to predict and prepare for or control events in the objective world, so psychology teaches us how to foresee and modify events in consciousness. And in his textbook, Ebbinghaus (1923) wrote that in order to understand correctly the thoughts and impulses of man, we must treat them just as we treat material bodies, or as we treat the lines and points of mathematics. Munsterberg (1908) in discussing the spread of laboratories across the world remarked that "hardly a university . . . has not opened a workshop for this youngest of natural sciences." Titchener (1904) said that psychology was a science in the sense of biology and physiology, because psychology, like them, was based upon the solid work of fact. Titchener, of course, also differentiated psychology from these other sciences, but here it is important to point out that he also thought that it was like them in some sense. In what sense are they similar? In the sense that the natural scientific method is applicable. Psychology is scientific because, like science, it is analytic (Titchener, 1910).

Lastly, we can see that the same influence pervaded even some more practically oriented books. King (1906), for example, described the following factors as being the lesson of the growth of the natural sciences: unwearied study of minute details, patient search for the law underlying the phenomena investigated and for the exact conditions involved, and precise and persistent fulfillment of these conditions. Then he reasons that because the problem of life is complex, we must attack it as the scientist attacks his problem. That is, King (1906) argued that success in understanding life will result if we attack its problems the way the natural sciences attack their problems. Hence, the natural scientific approach in psychology was not only present in this particular period, but it was also being articulated and, in some instances, defended as the only possible route for psychology.

FROM WORLD WAR I TO WORLD WAR II

This period includes the birth of behaviorism and of course the point we want to establish is easy to demonstrate among the behaviorists. However, as we have already noted, the attitude preceded the behaviorists and it extends beyond them. For the sake of completeness, however, we can give one sample of Watson's views. According to Watson (1935a, p. 810), "psychology is that division of natural science which takes the behavior of people as its subject matter"; and "the data of science are common property and the methods of science are the same in principle however much they may vary in form" (Watson 1935b, p. 810). An even more succinct formulation can be found in Weiss (1935) who saw as one of behaviorism's major innovations "the repudiation of causal factors in human behavior that are not accepted by the natural sciences." Or again, Weiss (1930) stated his belief that it was possible to start with the fundamental assumptions of physics, and with these only, and to show that man and the social organization of which he is a part are the resultant of the static and dynamic interrelations between the fundamental elements of physics (whatever these may be found to be).

However, the same sentiments can also be found outside the strict behavioristic camp during this period. Jastrow (1930), for example, wrote that modern psychology is naturalistic, and that he saw the actual development of psychology as consistently moving toward a naturalistic view of human behavior. Also, Kantor's (1924) whole position is centered around the idea that psychology is a natural science. Kantor noted the difficulty psychology has had in being accepted as a natural science, and the main reason for its lack of success in this respect was due, according to Kantor, to the fact that psychologists were still conceiving of their data in animistic terms. Kantor, however, was careful to distinguish psychology from biology and physiology as well as from "animatistic psychology." What then is the domain of psychology? Kantor's (1924) aim "is to study psychological phenomena as actual, observable events consisting of the responses of psychological organisms on the one hand, and the stimulus objects or conditions which interact with them on the other" (p. xv). The advantages of this approach, for Kantor (1924), consist in the fact that "the study of stimuli factors provides us with materials for understanding psychological phenomena in terms of correlated conditioning factors" (p. xv), and the fact that the necessity "of finding in an acting thing the causes of its own behavior" (p. xvi), is precluded. Kantor views the rejection of self-determining principles of action in favor of interacting organisms and stimuli as an attempt to model psychology after a Galilean model. Thus, in spite of his effort to walk a narrow line between "animism" and other natural sciences, Kantor's efforts almost exclusively err on the side of natural science in the sense that he precludes the possibility of self-determining principles of action; he actively seeks a model built upon Galileo's; he desires to understand psychological phenomena in terms of correlated conditioning factors; and lastly, the environment is to be understood in terms of stimuli as specified by physics.

Very often the introspective school causes some confusion because it explicitly professes to deal with consciousness or experience, and thus one may be tempted to think that its approach is something other than natural-scientific. However, we have already quoted from Titchener, the leading U.S. exponent of this school, and we saw that he felt that he was being scientific in his approach despite the fact he defined psychology as the study of consciousness. This interpretation is reinforced by Murphy's (1935) analysis; Murphy pointed out that introspective psychology in fact makes many of the same assumptions as behaviorism. Included are assumptions such as these: that psychology should be a natural science; that it should break up complex states and processes into simple ones; that it should analyze wholes into parts; and that to understand each whole, psychology must study the relations existing between the parts, and this can be done by studying the parts in isolation. The difference is that introspective psychology is concerned with experience rather than behavior. However, from the above listing of attributes, it is clear that introspective psychology attempts to study experience in terms of the attitude of the natural sciences.

The fact that experience can remain the subject matter of psychology at the same time that a natural scientific approach is adopted is also demonstrated by Warren and Carmichael (1930). They define mental life in terms of the interplay between the creature and his surroundings, and they include personal experiences, but when they come to explain this interplay, they do it in terms of receptors, effectors, and the nervous system. Moreover, in their summary, they differentiate the scientific approach to mind from the naïve approach because the latter views mind as a simple unit rather than as the strikingly complex series of processes and activities that it is—and this complexity can be understood only by an *analytic* study of experience, behavior, and the nervous system. The basic difference is that naïve individuals commence with the universal instead of the atom, but psychologists must start with the elemental and work up to the complex.

The natural scientific attitude is carried over more summarily in pedagogical texts. Muse (1939), for example, states that if psychology is to be science, there must *"be an orderly presentation of the facts and laws* which underlie human behavior." How are scientific laws obtained? "The laws of psychology must be evolved just as are the *laws of any other science.* A science knows no things which are 'more or less valuable': It is concerned also only with facts." (My emphasis.) Muse (1939, p. 66) states that "the findings of psychological research become dependable to the extent that the *scientific method* can be used to study human reactions." Finally, there is also Seashore's (1925) assertion that psychology is a natural science since it considers its phenomena to be phenomena in nature, amenable to natural laws; and, insofar as it attempts to describe and explain the experience and behavior of living beings, it is a biological science.

FROM WORLD WAR II TO THE PRESENT

This last phase of our historical analysis is no different from the earlier three phases in the sense that exemplars of psychology as a natural science are readily available. However, what seems to be slightly different is that those who ascribe to this particular viewpoint seem to be more entrenched in it and therefore less explicit about it than the psychologists of the earlier periods. They seem to be confident that they are on the right track even if they are willing to revise some of their minor theories and opinions.

Examples of the persistence of the natural scientific attitude in psychology include the following authors. Wickens and Meyer (1955, p. 6), aware that even at this late date there are still some doubts about the possibility of a true science of behavior, argue for the science of psychology by stressing that "the objectors seem to imply that it is the *material* with which one is working that determines science." However, the authors stress that it is "the *method*" that is all-important, and they write that "there is nothing intrinsic in living organisms that makes it impossible to build a science of behavior." For them, it is a simple matter: the science of psychology has come into being because it is possible to use the basic methods of science in examining behavior.

Even more direct is the beginning paragraph of the second chapter of Kimble's and Garmezy's text. It reads as follows:

The general purpose of this chapter is to develop the idea that psychology is a branch of natural science. If that goal is achieved even in part, you will come from your reading of it with the most important single idea that you will get in your first course in psychology. This chapter will show that human and animal behavior . . . can be described objectively, manipulated, controlled, and studied in the same way as other natural events. In short, it is possible to view psychology as a branch of natural science. (Kimble & Garmezy, 1963, p. 15)

Since this will be the most important single idea that the student will be exposed to concerning psychology, it is obvious that Kimble does not consider this point to be a light matter.

It is also important to realize that often those who really desire psychology to be a human science, and who wish to study characteristically human phenomena, define the science of psychology first and foremost in terms of the criteria of the natural sciences, and then find that they cannot meet those criteria whenever more humanistic types of behavior are to be studied. McCall's (1959) book is a good example of this approach. He argues that psychology should study human behavior scientifically, and the distinctive feature of science is its method, which implies that there should be controlled observation, and whenever possible, measurement. In short, he argues for a method of science that includes quantification, deduction, explanation, and mathematics. But then he goes on to say that such attributes still represent only an ideal for psychology.

As far as explanations in psychology are concerned, it would be unreasonable to expect the kind of mathematical elegance and rigor that are found in physics. But we can insist that explanations be tied as closely as possible to the empirical and that they be not permitted to get out of hand scientifically in suchwise as to become vehicles for a great deal of unsophisticated (and almost unconscious) philosophizing. (McCall, 1959, p. 11)

But one could reply: if it is unreasonable to expect psychology to achieve the standards set by physics, why are the standards drawn from physics in the first place? Note, too, while psychology is permitted to be "less rigorous" than physics, it still cannot get too far out of hand. Lastly, the implication is that psychology can only choose between science, understood as natural science (acceptable), or unsophisticated philosophy (unacceptable). Needless to say, the "ideal" attributes listed above came straight from the best exemplars of the natural sciences, physics and chemistry.

Another implicit way that the natural sciences have influenced psychology is that, because of their advanced maturity, the world of the human subject has to be understood in expressions determined by the attitude characteristic of physics and chemistry. This is demonstrated by the book written by Gagné and Fleishman (1959). In their introduction they note that psychology has a significant relationship with the physical and other sciences. Then they state:

> . . . Primarily, it (psychology) often uses instruments and methods of measurement of the physical sciences in order to be able to specify what kinds of external events the individual is responding to (light waves, sound waves, etc.) and what form of reaction is being made (in terms of such variables as time, force, extent). There is, of course, no direct relationship between psychology and physical theory; no one supposes that behavior can be "explained" in terms of atoms and molecules. Nevertheless, the psychologist recognizes that his theories, along with those of various other scientists, must ultimately be compatible with those of physical science. (Gagné & Fleishman, 1959, pp. 2–3)

The fact that the relationship between psychology and physical science is indirect makes the influence all the more subtle, because compatibility with physical science often means understanding man in terms acceptable to the physical sciences. It need not necessarily mean this, but this interpretation is reinforced by the author's belief that, fundamentally, psychology employs an approach and a point of view common to all sciences.

This same indirect and subtle relation seems to pervade Miller's (1962) text. In no single place does Miller explicitly state that psychology is a natural science, yet this attitude seems to pervade the whole book, in terms of selection of topics and examples. At the beginning, Miller admits that at the time of James's *Principles* psychology was still only the "hope of a science." But then he writes that "scientific methods, however, are notoriously successful" (Miller, 1962, p. 2). And a sentence later he states (Miller, 1962, p. 2): "Today when we say that psychology is a science we support the claim with several impressive accomplishments." Thus when he wishes to demonstrate the scientific status of psychology he appeals precisely to psychology's natural scientific achievements, although he seems very careful to avoid all kinds of extremes that have been historically present, and in addition, he wishes to retain the definition of psychology as a mental science. Yet one could argue with Miller that his own book still represents only the "hope of a science." In his conclusion, Miller states that psychology is de facto partly a social science, partly a biological science, and still partly philosophy, which is to say that it is no more unified today than it was at the time of James. It is one thing to state that a discipline comprises three perspectives, for then a unity is implied; but it is quite another thing to state that a discipline consists of three other disciplines. The latter statement shows the lack of a central viewpoint that would integrate all the phenomena of a given discipline and provide it with a unique perspective. More importantly, however, Miller is content to let the de facto situation remain, for he goes on to assert that it is unlikely that we will see any more revolutions that will completely redefine what we mean by "mental life." This implies that he sees the future of psychology as one which merely increases our stock of factual information. Such a view expresses the conservative side of science, which today, in psychology, is precisely the natural scientific conception of psychology. That is, it is conservative science that believes that the fundamental world-view is settled and that the major responsibility of contemporary scientists is simply to add to the increasingly complex store of knowledge. It communicates the implicit belief that if there is going to be another scientific revolution it can only be a methodological one, and that this methodological revolution will, in principle, have to be compatible with the existing world-view being espoused by science. However important and legitimate the conservative function of science is (Polanyi, 1963), it is only *one* function; it does not exhaust science. The forward edge of science is more open-ended; it is willing to put in abeyance not only certain facts and methods, but with sufficient reason, the very *approach* of science itself. That is why, for us, even an approach as broadly conceived as Miller's still essentially reflects a natural scientific conception of psychology.

The last few examples were chosen precisely because they were not "hard-line" approaches to psychology, but neither did they reflect the thesis presented in this work. In other words, as will be seen in the next chapters, we are arguing for more than simply a liberal natural scientific approach. However, since the arguments presented above involved subtleties and are perhaps subject to doubt by the reader, let us finish this section by pointing out some unambiguous indications of psychology conceived as a natural science by authors writing in the sixth decade of the twentieth century. Lewis, for example, writes the following:

Psychologists study their subject matter in very much the same fashion that other scientists study their subject matter. They make precise observaions and they conduct experiments. Even though the object of study may be another human, the psychologist must treat this human objectively, in the same fashion that physicists, chemists and biologists treat their subject matter. As far as the science of psychology is concerned, the fact that its only subject matter is frequently the human being makes no difference. The science-wide rules of objectivity and precise measurement still apply. (Lewis, 1963, p. 12)

Equally direct statements can be found in Kantor (1963) who believes that the scientific study of psychological evolution involves the same procedures that scientists use in studying any other class of events, and he laments the fact that psychology has not enjoyed a continuous naturalistic development, and tries to blame its "dark spots" on the specific cultural, social, and political factors of the time. For Kantor, there could not be an intrinsic reason why psychology was also at one time conceived as a human science; it has to be understood in terms of the culture of the time, and, in effect, explained away. One difficulty with such a way of viewing the history of psychology is that the natural scientific approach also belongs to a *Zeitgeist* or world-view, and in turn, may also be explained away.

Lastly, this section would be incomplete unless there was some reference to psychologists in the Skinnerian tradition. Ulrich, Stachnik and Mabry (1966) state that the behavioral scientists working within the perspective of the *science* of behavioral control have adopted the premise that human behavior, like other natural phenomena, is subject to natural laws. Yet, in spite of this success—and the authors argue that because of this success —there is still resistance to the application and development of the science of behavior control. The authors are convinced that the primary reason for this is that people simply do not want to admit the possibility of being completely controlled by outside sources—a possibility which has arisen as a result of the achievements of this new science—which in turn are due to an approach that has been perfected within the perspective of natural sciences.

Psychology Is a Human Science

There is a tradition within psychology that has been attempting to define psychology as the study of the human person. Perhaps there are more psychologists today who are receptive to such an idea, but we can find in psychological literature statements that are as strong and explicit with respect to this end as those who wished psychology to be a natural science. We must also say, however, that with the possible exception of the contemporary scene, this influence has not had the effect that other movements within psychology have enjoyed. Before attempting to understand why, we should perhaps look at the men who held such a viewpoint and briefly see what they said.

One more comment is in order before we begin the actual investigation of the historical background of psychology as a human science. Very often we look upon the history of psychology as a unitary phenomenon with a clear-cut lineage and well circumscribed spheres of influence. Nothing could be farther from the truth. Psychology's history shows a variety of influences from a number of areas, and it also displays a diversity of lineages that may or may not have had mutual influences. For example, there are the histories of the psychoanalytic movement and its offshoots, of behaviorism and neo-behaviorism, of the introspectionist school of psychology, of animal and comparative psychology, of Gestalt psychology, and so on. Similarly one can trace and differentiate a history of the humanistic viewpoint in psychology as opposed to other viewpoints. Unfortunately, its horizontal influence, until very recently, was practically nil. Nevertheless, now that its influence is spreading, one can look back and see that its existence is as old as psychology itself. This survey is not meant to be exhaustive; it only intends to demonstrate that such an interpretation of psychology has been present throughout its brief history.

THE FOUNDERS AND LATE NINETEENTH-CENTURY PSYCHOLOGISTS

The first person we will consider is Wilhelm Dilthey (1833–1911). As we shall soon see, Dilthey has written extensively on psychology, always fostering the viewpoint that psychology belongs to the human sciences and not to the natural sciences. Yet, his name does not even appear in the index of Boring's (1950) classic work, nor is there a single word concerning him in the text. Perhaps that is one reason that he is so little known to American psychologists. However, he does receive some mention in later books dealing with the history of psychology (e.g., Wolman, 1960).

According to one biographer (Rickman, 1961), the outer events of Dilthey's life were unspectacular and can be stated briefly. He obtained his doctorate in philosophy at Berlin in 1864, and he taught there for two years before being appointed Professor of Philosophy at Basel in 1867. After brief tenures at Kiel and Breslau, he returned to Berlin in 1882 where he remained until his death in 1911.

Dilthey was essentially a philosopher, but his interests and writings ranged far and wide. He wrote on and about literature, music, education, psychology, religion, politics, and history. He drew most of his inspiration from aesthetics and historical studies, rather than from mathematics and the natural sciences. His main ambition was to write a critique of historical reason and establish a true philosophy of history. However, he wrote extensively about psychology because, in his opinion, psychology would play an important role for a philosophy of history. Furthermore, psychology became a topic of interest for him because he wanted to demonstrate that the human sciences or the human studies (*Geisteswissenschaften*) could be rigorous and systematic, but in a way that was different from the natural sciences; and again, he thought that by establishing a sound psychology in this vein, he could set the basis for all of the human sciences.

According to Hodges (1944), it was Dilthey who made clear, as it was never clear before, the distinctive character of the

Geisteswissenschaften, or human studies. He showed, on the one hand, that their aims, presuppositions, and methods are not those of the natural sciences; and on the other, that in spite of this, they are not a mere welter of subjective impressions, but have rigorous methods and controls of their own. Hodges summarizes in a succinct way what Dilthey's main intention was.

[Dilthey] points to the dominating position which has been held, in most periods of philosophical history, by the study of the problems presented by mathematics and the natural sciences. The reasons for this predominance are no secret. Pure mathematics in the ancient world, and it and mathematical physics in the modern, have a perennial attraction in that they offer to us exact knowledge, and latterly also a growing power over nature, and it is a matter of deep philosophical interest to inquire how this achievement is possible and what it implies. For a long period this kind of knowledge has held a dominant position among the intellectual interests of the philosopher, and it will always be important. But, says Dilthey, we are now in a position to see that it constitutes only one half of the *globus intellectualis;* the other half is composed of the study of man in society and in history. Here we meet with a different type of study. Instead of observing our object directly, we have to approach it indirectly through written testimony and other similar evidence; instead of clearly formulated theories which can be tested by experiment, we have an attempt to analyze and describe the concrete complexities of life; instead of explanation of particular events and processes through general laws, we have an appreciative understanding of the meaning and value of the unique individual. There is no reason why the one sphere of knowledge should not be as thoroughly studied by philosophers as the other. (Hodges, 1952, pp. xiv-xv)

We would add, by psychologists as well, and indeed Dilthey himself makes this latter point numerous times.

Kluback (1956) gives a good summary of Dilthey's distinction between the natural sciences and the human sciences. According to Kluback, Dilthey observed that if the methods of the natural sciences could have been incorporated into the realm of the human sciences, the conflict between the two methodologies would not have arisen. Noting this, therefore, Dilthey, as early as 1859—twenty years before the official founding of psychology by Wundt—had distinguished between a "system of laws or

sciences" and a "system of significant and value-permeated ex-
istences" or world-views (Kluback, 1956, pp. 52–53). For Dilthey,
the natural sciences dealt with the nonhuman world. Therefore,
in this approach, we could

. . . take phenomena out of context, substitute symbols for them, and
mathematically manipulate those symbols to create algebraic laws of
phenomenal behavior. These algebraic laws were then known as
natural scientific laws. In this sense, the natural sciences built up a
structure of knowledge tested by experimental repetition which it called
"science." Dilthey, however, believed that the human sciences dealt with
a human world, the product of an active mind with free will; they
studied and interpreted phenomena as expressions of an inner spiritual
reality. The human sciences could not remove phenomena from their
historical context, as it was the context which gave them meaning. They
had to be studied in their historical setting as part of the pattern of
meaning and value which they formed. Human science led to a creation not of laws, but of systems of values. In this manner, the human
sciences built up a structure of knowledge based on corroborative
evidence which Dilthey called a "world-view" or *Weltanschauung*.
(Kluback, 1956, pp. 52–53)

Dilthey saw two essential defects in the psychology of his time.
The first was its inability to do justice to the higher functions of
human thought and action. He noted that it was harmless at
worst and often instructive when it talked about sensation, or
about the simpler pleasures and pains. But it really had nothing
to say about creative imagination as seen in the artist, about the
sense of obligation and value, about self-sacrifice, about religious
devotion, about understanding and sympathy. On points like
these, we learn much more from the vast but formless literature
in which keen observers have written down their experience of
life. According to Dilthey, psychology ought to take this wisdom
and the insights of the poets and give them precise expression
and a logical grounding, but the existing psychology was incapable of this.

The second defect Dilthey found in psychology was the un-
certainty of its results. According to him, it was because psychology had adopted a mistaken method. Psychology took shape
in the bosom of modern philosophy at a time when philosophy

was strongly influenced by mathematics and the natural sciences. The methods and presuppositions of atomic physics were treated as the methods and presuppositions of all possible sciences, and Hume was only giving voice to a generally accepted prejudice when he said that the way to make psychology scientific was to apply to it the procedures of physics. Those psychologists who have been following theoretical discussions of psychology within the last decade will probably be very familiar with such an argument. However, not all may know that no one said it any better than Dilthey in 1894.

Before moving to some of the reforms that Dilthey would have liked to initiate with respect to psychology, one might receive the mistaken impression that Dilthey would have preferred a literary type of psychology because of the examples he used in the preceding paragraphs. However, this is not true. In another passage, Dilthey (Hodges, 1944, p. 132) stated:

> But to this day, in all of the reflective literature which aims at grasping the full reality of man, its superiority of content is offset by its incapacity for systematic presentation . . . [it] contains no apprehensible general system of mental life. We are tired of hearing that Lear, Hamlet, and Macbeth contain more psychology than all the psychological textbooks together. If only these art-fanatics would unveil for us the psychology wrapped up in such works! If we understand by psychology a description of the regular system of mental life, the works of the poets contain no psychology at all; . . . but it is true that the way in which great writers and poets deal with human life presents psychology with a task and a material. Here is the intuitive understanding of the whole system which psychology too has to approach in its own way, by generalization and abstraction. One wishes for a psychology which could catch in the net of its descriptions that which these poets and writers contain over and above present-day psychology.

Thus it becomes evident that when Dilthey criticized the natural scientific approach to psychology, he was not suggesting that it should become an art. There is a position between natural sciences and art, and it is the position of a human science, and that is where psychology belongs.

In order to see how psychology should be reformed, Dilthey

appealed to the distinction between "descriptive" sciences and "explanatory" sciences (Hodges, 1944, p. 42).

All science must analyze its object, seeking to determine its ultimate irreducible units and the laws which express their interrelation. A descriptive science is one whose units and laws are found by empirical analysis, or close examination of what is actually given in experience. An explanatory science is one which takes its units and laws from a methodological assumption which determines their general nature beforehand. Such an assumption, and all that flows from it, is a hypothetical construction. The classic example is modern physics, and it is this influence which has led psychology to adopt its hypothesis of unit sensations and feelings, and other hypotheses which equally go behind the facts of experience. The analytic psychologists thought they were describing the mind and did not realize how far they had strayed from experience. (Muller-Freienfels, 1935)

Thus, Dilthey wished to construct a psychology without building hypotheses into its foundations, and he thought that a descriptive approach was the answer. For him:

Mental life is a functional unity which cannot be reduced to or built up theoretically out of non-functional units. . . . The real unit of mental life is not a sensation, or a feeling, or even an isolated intentional act with its content, but a total reaction of the whole self to a situation confronting it. Every such reaction [called by Dilthey an *Erlebnis*] includes elements of three main types: cognitive, affective and conative. . . . The relations among the three elements in experience are called the "structure" of the mind, and the possibility of a descriptive psychology rests on the fact that this structural system is not discovered by inference or hypothesis, but is actually experienced, or "given in lived experience." (Hodges, 1944, pp. 42–44)

Dilthey contrasted "structural" relations to causal relations; whereas causes can be inferred, structural sequences have their meaning in themselves, and in them the essence of the mind is perceived.

For Dilthey, the outstanding difference between natural and human sciences was that the latter are concerned with human beings and the human world. It may seem redundant and sim-

plistic to state such a thing, but then, we can remind ourselves
that we are off on such a venture as this precisely because our
own contemporary psychology has forgotten this fundamental
fact. In the natural sciences, we have knowledge and explanation,
but in the human sciences we have understanding and interpretation (Rickman, 1961). Understanding is, for Dilthey, the
process of grasping meaning, and it is a mental operation which
can be defined in terms of other mental operations as little as
can seeing or reasoning. For Dilthey, it is a technical term and
it means having an insight into the working of the human mind,
or as he says in another place, it is "the rediscovery of the I in
the Thou" (Rickman, 1961, p. 39). It is an inside view of human
nature that we all possess. Thus, the natural sciences may achieve
greater precision, but understanding has the incomparable advantage of moving in a world which is familiar to us. Once again,
Dilthey does not mean to imply by such statements that understanding is an obscure, unanalyzable intuition, a mystery which
"replaces disciplined intellectual work" (Rickman, 1961, p. 40).
Such a view is often held by those who wish to *explain* understanding in natural scientific terms, but that would be submitting
understanding to a wrong set of criteria.

The above sampling of Dilthey's ideas should be sufficient to
indicate what he meant by the term "human sciences" and how
he saw psychology as fitting into their context. That Dilthey's
thought is still relevant can be seen from the fact that one still
finds in psychology today parallels to arguments that he first
presented over a hundred years ago. Surely some of his language
is dated, and he often argues about problems that are no longer
of concern, but there is much in his thought and writings that
still is fresh and bears direct relevance for contemporary psychological issues. Most importantly for the point at issue, at the
very time that psychology was being founded, Dilthey was
arguing for a wholly different type of foundation, and for a very
different kind of psychology—a psychology that would be conceived along the lines of the human sciences.

The second psychologist we would like to consider briefly is
Franz Brentano (1838–1917). In 1874, Brentano wrote his most
famous work, *Psychology from an Empirical Standpoint*. In this

work, Brentano sought to systematize the psychology of his time so that there could be one psychology to replace the many that were then current (Boring, 1950).

Boring notes that Wundt also had completed his first handbook by 1874, and these two books represented attempts to formulate the "new" psychology. Boring finds the contrasts between Brentano and Wundt to be as follows: Brentano's psychology is empirical but not experimental; Brentano's method was argumentative and Wundt's descriptive, at least in intention; and lastly, Brentano organized his system about the psychical act, and Wundt built his about sensory contents.

The above contrasts indicate an important point, namely, that there is a distinction between empirical and experimental. Thus, to be empirical does not necessarily mean to follow the methods of experimental science, although it is sometimes interpreted in that light today. Brentano himself had respect for the results of experiment, but he believed that the continual stressing of experimentation led to an overemphasis upon method and a blindness to main issues (Boring, 1950). This does not mean that he was against experimentation, but only that he was against excessive experimentation. As Boring (1950) points out, the empirical psychologist is interested in certain "critical experiments" that yield information about certain dubious points. In this sense, the "critical experiment" belongs in an argument and is thus apt to be part of the empirical method.

As far as some of Brentano's own ideas go, a good many of them are based upon a revitalized scholasticism. By this is meant a scholasticism that was viewed critically and selectively. For example, one of Brentano's ambitions in developing his own psychology was to repudiate the type of psychology that treated mental faculties as the ultimate terms of psychological analysis. His insistence was that the ultimate data of psychological analysis are the particular manifestations of consciousness, and these he called psychic phenomena. These were held to be directly discernible manifestations of mental functioning as opposed to inferences or constructed mental powers (Ryle, 1932).

Furthermore, Brentano distinguished two radical kinds of inquiry into mental functioning (Ryle, 1932). The first he called empirical, meaning by this the inductive, experimental, and statistical approach to phenomena, and he maintained that the conclusions of such an approach were generalizable in terms of probability theory. The second kind of investigation Brentano did not name, but he described it as an inquiry into the concepts or presuppositions of empirical psychology. This question might be formulated: "what is it to be a case of remembering, choosing, regretting, etc.?" Or, one could ask, what ultimate forms of mental functioning are there to be exemplified in particular instances?

Brentano tried to develop two lines of inquiry proper to psychology because he was not satisfied with the direction of the psychology of his time. He was convinced that neither physiological nor association psychology was on the right track; hence he had to examine their presuppositions. He felt that explanation of conscious phenomena in terms of physiological substrata or unconscious association dynamics were not doing justice to conscious phenomena. In his own mind, he was perfectly clear that analysis or root types of mental functioning was one thing, and experimental or statistical search for laws governing the occurrence of mental acts and states was quite another (Ryle, 1932).

It is his concern with these problems that puts Brentano within the camp of human scientific psychologists. He was equally interested in studying characteristically human phenomena in a rigorous way, and for him, any characteristically human phenomenon would have to include the presence of mind. Perhaps more than anything else, Brentano is remembered for his conception of mind. Brentano believed that mental phenomena were irreducible, and that they were characterized by intentionality. By this Brentano meant that mental phenomena could be distinguished by the intentional inexistence of an object in a mental act (Sullivan, 1968). Implied in this description of mental phenomena is the notion that the psychical is characterized by directedness to an object, or reference to a content, and apparently, for Brentano, this was the more important meaning of intentionality (Spiegelberg, 1960, I, p. 40). His plan then was to differentiate psychological phenomena according to types of intentionality which could be discovered by a careful analysis of experience. Also implied in Brentano's notion of intentionality is the fact that all psychological phenomena are acts in the broad sense of the term.

Thus, Brentano is clearly aligned with the "Act" school of psychology, and for a while, a battle was raging between "Act" and "Content" for the position of primacy. The "Act" psychologists accepted activity as the essence of mind, and made this fact the cornerstone of their psychology, whereas the "Content" psycologists stressed the object toward which the mind was directed. The palpability of the content and the ability to work with it with the then known methods as opposed to the impalpable and ephemeral acts were decisive factors in determining the outcome of the struggle (Boring, 1950). Wundt was a representative of the "Content" school, and history has shown that content psychology has won the day, but the existence of this section of this book shows that the victory was not total. Indeed, there is some evidence to indicate that future developments in psychology may go in the direction of Brentano's vision rather than Wundt's (Rancurello, 1968).

While we have been contrasting Brentano to Wundt, and generally blaming Wundt for having initiated and determined many of the characteristics of psychology as a natural science, we must now balance the picture and indicate how Wundt also stands in the tradition of psychology as a human science. All historians make it clear that Wundt never believed that the method of experiment was the only method for psychology (Boring, 1950; Heidbreder, 1933), although this fact is rarely mentioned outside of the history books, and even in the history texts, Wundt's later writings where he spoke about folk psychology and tried to deal with higher mental processes are given secondary emphasis. For these latter areas of psychology Wundt believed that it was necessary to study the natural history of man.

Wundt (1916, p. 3) himself wrote:

It is true that the attempt has frequently been made to investigate the complex functions of thought on the basis of mere introspection. These attempts, however, have always been unsuccessful. Individual

consciousness is wholly incapable of giving a history of the development
of human thought . . . [The] problem of [folk psychology] relates to
those mental products which are created by a community of human life
and are, therefore, inexplicable in terms merely of individual consciousness, since they presuppose the reciprocal action of many.

Consequently, Wundt not only distinguishes the methods of
folk psychology from the method of experiment, but even from
the method of introspection, and it must be remembered that
Wundt was one of the latter's champions. In a more positive
vein, Wundt argues that man can be understood in groups only
by a modification of an historical method. Thus, by definition,
this includes the "essentially human" characteristics of man, and
thus Wundt can qualify as belonging to the human scientific
tradition. Further proof can be found by consulting Wundt's
book, *Elements of Folk Psychology*, the last section of which
deals with "The Development to Humanity," including a chapter on "The Concept 'Humanity.'"

The last psychologist to be considered in this section is William James. While James may be considered an ambiguous example in the sense that he may also be seen to be forerunner of
behaviorism, this ambiguity is in no way compromising to the
point at issue, because what matters is not so much the "purity"
of the example as the presence of a certain style of thought, or a
certain way of treating psychological problems, or even the type
of problems selected. According to the latter criteria, James
clearly fits within the human scientific perspective, and indeed,
it has recently been shown just how James is equally a forerunner
of phenomenological psychology (Linschoten, 1968).

Even a simple scanning of the *Principles* (James, 1890) shows
interest in topics such as stream of consciousness, will, experience, etc., that would seem to be archaic after the advent of
behaviorism. The fact that there may be a renewed interest in
these topics today does not alter the fact that James perceived
them to be psychologically relevant within the context of a science of psychology when others have dismissed such topics precisely in the name of science. Moreover, James always treated
these topics in such a way that their peculiarly human character

was never lost. James anticipated the notion of intentionality as employed by Husserl and even the notion of the lived-body of Merleau-Ponty although these notions did not receive from him the explicit clarity they did in the hands of the men with whom they are associated (Linschoten, 1968). It was precisely James's adoption, perhaps implicitly, of a descriptive attitude towards experiential phenomena that enabled him to uncover so many important aspects of them and reveal them as they were experienced. At the same time, this attitude probably prevented him from incorporating his descriptive findings within the scientific frame of reference that he was also trying to achieve. James never succeeded in arriving at a unified viewpoint and perhaps that is why he ultimately conceded that psychology as he knew it was only "the hope of a science" (James, 1948). Our position is that perhaps James was too influenced by his times in his understanding of science, and thus he expected his descriptive studies to meet criteria that were never intended to be standards for the kind of phenomena he was investigating. Rather, James's descriptive studies, we would maintain, contain an implicit vision about the kind of science that is necessary to study human phenomena, and it is this vision, as implied not only by James, but by all the psychologists under consideration in this section that we hope to make more explicit.

FROM 1900 TO WORLD WAR II

It seemed reasonable to make a division of the natural scientific historical survey between 1900 and World War II at the time of World War I because the advent of behaviorism in 1916 radicalized that approach, but since there was no similar movement in the human scientific lineage, we can cover the entire period as one. Again, the intention here is not to be exhaustive, but merely to indicate representatives of this tradition during this phase of psychology's history.

The first person we would like to consider very briefly is Eduard Spranger (1882–1963). Spranger became the formal successor to Dilthey when he was appointed to the latter's chair at the University of Berlin, and his own writings indicate a strong Diltheyan influence. Spranger explicitly defined his psychology

as one which took its point of departure from the cultural
sciences. As a cultural science, psychology takes the inner phenomenon as a meaningful whole belonging to a psychic situational whole. In this system, meaning always has reference to
value. Spranger admits of both subjective and objective evalua-
tions in his system, and he calls the realization of that which is
of objective value "performance" (Muller-Freienfels, 1935). With
the introduction of the term "performance" we can see that there
is a possibility for all of behavioral data to enter into Spranger's
system, although this is not patently evident from reading him
because of his terminology.

Spranger's psychology aims for understanding. Understanding,
unlike explanation, seeks no basic causality, but rather a nexus
of "meaning" relationships. For Spranger, understanding is that
complex theoretical act in which we grasp the inner, meaningful
nexus in the life and actions of individuals. To understand
means to penetrate into the specific system of values of a mental
connection. We can do so on the basis of objectifications which
always have a physical and mental side (Muller-Freienfels, 1935).
For Spranger (1928), subjectivity is always related to objective
creations. He considers the subject with his experiences and
creations as interwoven with the configurations of the historical
and social world, and because of this, we free the subject from
the isolation of purely subjective states and relate it to objective
realities. Spranger (1928) considers these realities objective for
three reasons: (1) because they are attached to physical forms,
whether these forms function as direct carriers of value, such as
signs, or as means of artistic expression; (2) because they have
been developed from the reciprocal relations of many single
subjects, and in this context he refers to them as collectively determined forms; and (3) because they are based on definite laws
of meaning which have a supra-individual validity. By this third
criterion, Spranger refers to ideal mental laws, the norms according to which the individual creates some mental fact. What
is of significance here is that there is an attempt to clarify the
meaning of objectivity in terms of the actions of human subjects.

Approaching psychology from this viewpoint, Spranger (1928)
felt that he by-passed many of the dilemmas that are found in

traditional psychology. Three significant problems that he felt he avoided are (1) the whole body-mind issue; (2) the fact that traditional psychology, because of its natural scientific leanings, relates psychic phenomena to a specific form of the objective world, namely, external nature which is in fact a correlate of a special cognitive attitude; and (3) because of the influence of physics, the whole issue of trying to understand complex mental processes in terms of their elements is avoided. To demonstrate this difference in approach, Spranger called traditional psychology a "psychology of elements" and names his own brand "structural psychology."

Of course, Spranger is most famous for his typology which we know mostly through Allport-Vernon-Lindzey's Study of Values Test. However, it should be pointed out that the basic types he created are not what Spranger calls "photographs" of real life, but rather these types are based upon an isolating and idealizing method. In other words, they are ideal types that are never found "purely" in reality. Thus we see in Spranger the direct utilization of ideals that establishment of which would presuppose an eidetic psychology similar to the kind Husserl was advocating.

Thus, the very terminology, constructs, methods, phenomena, and topics that Spranger used and discussed are very different from what one encounters in a traditional psychological text. Most of Spranger's influence—what there is of it—comes to us via personality theory. Thus there is a tendency to delimit Spranger to the area of personality and dismiss him from other aspects of psychology. Few people realize that Spranger had a system that is, in intention at least, as broad as the whole of psychology. Of course, the philosophical basis for the kind of psychology he espoused is also very different from traditional psychology, and this prohibited very much cross-fertilization. But it is precisely this different philosophical outlook that places Spranger within the human scientific perspective, and that calls for his inclusion in this section.

Another psychologist who easily qualifies for this perspective is William Stern (1871–1938). Stern called his psychology "personalism," so that from the very outset it proclaimed its dissociation from all mere analysis of consciousness, and from all systems

of psychology which strive to find some cerebral process to corre-
spond with introspective experience (Muller-Freienfels, 1935).
For him the idea of person was meant to be psychophysically
neutral; it is the substratum of mind and body; it is that something that has existence going beyond or prior to differentiation
into mental and physical. He defined the person as a living
whole, unique, individual, striving towards goals, self-contained,
yet open to the world around him. That is, openness refers to
the fact that the person is capable of having experiences. Thus,
for Stern (1938), psychology was the science of a person having
experiences, or capable of having experiences. Experience in his
system is understood as a matrix which is unified by a goal-
directed person. The human personality is a self-determining,
purposive, meaningful totality. Furthermore, the personality is
not completely independent of the environment because they
are "convergently" related to each other (Muller-Freienfels, 1935).

Stern is primarily concerned with the inner structure of personality.
The personality develops in "convergence" with the environment and
by means of the "introception" of supra-individual goals; but the individual brings his personality into the world in the form of tendencies
or dispositions which in the beginning are only vague. In the course of
existence these dispositions shape themselves, in convergence with the
environment, into more definite characteristics. (Muller-Freienfels, 1935,
p. 327)

An "existential" theory and a system that is broad enough to
allow for both nature-subject interactions and culture-subject
dialectics are implied by these notions.

Stern is generally considered an integrationist. He wanted to
leave nothing out that he thought could help us understand the
person. Thus, he thought that psychology should always pre-
serve the correlation between part and whole, figure and ground,
analysis and totality, and the methods of explanation with the
methods of understanding. He was also critical of one-sided approaches. He rejected behaviorism because it closed off introspection; and he was not a psychoanalyst because that system closed
off the study of conscious phenomena; and he turned away from
experimental psychology because it closed off experiential data.
Stern held that the life of personality presents itself in a

dual aspect: as expression and impression. The body is expressive and the psyche is impressive. Experience occurs as expression or expressive action; but as consciousness, it is simultaneously an impression. Hence, expression and impression are two forms of the same experience, but they are not to be understood as parallel since they can enter into diverse combinations in a unitary personality (Muller-Freienfels, 1935). Moreover, by limiting the role of consciousness, Stern forces us towards the notion of behavior as subject matter for psychology, and makes us aware of the other dimensions of the person that may not have been given with full clarity. Undoubtedly, Stern's psychology is as much programmatic as it is factual, but, in our opinion, it is a workable program and one that is worthy of much more attention than it is receiving.

Lastly, I would like to mention William McDougall (1871–1938). McDougall agreed with the twentieth-century notion that psychology should deal with more than consciousness, and that it should be concerned with behavior, but he disagreed with Watson and Pavlov on the meaning of behavior. Behavior was not elementistic and it could not be conceived as consisting of a bundle of reflexes. McDougall (1923) listed seven marks of behavior that made it necessary to conceive of it as purposive: (1) spontaneity of movement, (2) persistence of activity independently of the continuance of the impression which may have initiated it, (3) variation of direction of persistent movement, (4) end of animal's movements as soon as they have brought about a particular kind of change in its situation, (5) preparation for new situation toward the production of which the action contributes, (6) some degree of improvement in the effectiveness of behavior when it is repeated by the animal under similar circumstances, and (7) the totality of reactions of the organism. McDougall concludes that a reflex does not meet these criteria; only purposive behavior does. Thus, McDougall's system came to be know as "purposive behaviorism."

McDougall (1928, p. 268) quoted Driesch as giving the psychological problem its most succinct expression: "In acting then, there may be no change in the specificity of the reactions when the stimulus is altered fundamentally, and again there may be the most fundamental difference in the reaction where there is almost no change in the stimulus." That is, a simple knowledge of causal relation between a subject and his environment cannot render fully intelligible the behavior of any subject. It is precisely the problem of psychology to understand how this is possible, and it can only do so by viewing behavior in a way that does not tie it to its environment in an exclusively cause-effect relationship.

McDougall was keenly aware of how students get introduced to certain *attitudes* as well as certain methods and contents, and he also knew that the attitudes into which the students were introduced were more significant because they usually were not explicit, and they remained effective all the longer for not being so. Thus he tried desperately to combat this factor, although it seems that he was not able to prevail against the *Zeitgeist*. For example, in the Preface of his psychology text, McDougall (1923, p. vii) wrote as follows:

. . . there will still be need for the book which will introduce the student to his science, which will aim at giving him at the outset of his studies a profitable line of approach, a fruitful way of thinking of psychological problems, and a terminology as little misleading as possible. The need of such a book is greater in psychology than in any other science. . . . In physical sciences the student needs only to refine upon the methods of observation and reasoning which he has learned to apply in dealing with the physical world about him, regarding all events as links in a mechanical chain of cause and effect. Most students have begun, by the time they approach psychology, to regard this as the true and only way of science. And many of the books on psychology encourage them in this belief. Having begun in this way myself, and having slowly and painfully extricated myself and found what seems to be a much more profitable attitude toward psychological problems, I held that the path of the student may be made smoother by setting clearly before him at the outset the alternative routes. . . . The two principal alternative routes are (1) that of mechanical science, which interprets all its processes as mechanical sequences of cause and effect, and (2) that of the sciences of mind, for which purposive striving is a fundamental category, which regard the process of purposive striving as radically different from mechanical sequence.[1]

[1] Reprinted with the permission of Charles Scribner's Sons from *Outline of Psychology*, pages vii, xi, 36, and 39–40 by William McDougall. Copyright 1923 Charles Scribner's Sons; renewal copyright 1951 Ann A. McDougall.

Today we might say that all psychological phenomena are intentional, and intentional analyses are very different from cause-
effect analyses. It seems to be equally significant that McDougall
stressed the importance of the attitude of the psychologist as
being responsible for which route to psychology is adopted.

Undoubtedly, McDougall was having difficulty in putting
across his viewpoint. Further on in the preface, he (McDougall,
1923, p. xi) wrote:

The psychophysiology of the senses is a field rich in accumulated
observations, the fascination of which as a field of research is not unknown to me . . . the student who approaches psychology by this route
is almost inevitably led into the mechanical, atomistic way of thinking
which I would have him avoid. To begin with the study of the senses is
seductive; for this is one way of simplifying psychology and of enabling
the student to feel that he is acquiring a solid basis of facts. But it is a
simplification achieved at the cost of an abstraction from actual experience, the degree of which the young student does not easily understand . . . we do at least deal with concrete realities rather than with
abstract and artificial entities such as "the sensations" are.

Of course, he was trying to point out here that the very learning of traditional psychology already necessitated the assumption
of an attitude that implies a certain philosophy of the world
and man. The fact that the realities that McDougall wanted to
deal with were more "concrete" than "sensations" was something
McDougall had to argue for.

McDougall also anticipated the human scientific frame of
reference in the sense that he wanted to deal with behavior *as
such,* and not to explain it in terms of the central nervous system. For example, McDougall (1923, p. 36), in answering an objection that he should equate mind with brain, wrote:

I do not underrate the value of this physiological knowledge and research; but I assert that, in the present state of science, it is not profitable to substitute the brain for the mind. To do so limits unduly our
freedom of thought; it ties us down to one kind of explanation; it leads
us to absurd consequences, and worst of all, is apt to blind us to facts
of observation, and biases our interpretation of other facts.

One might say that the "bracketing" procedures of the phenomenologists were invented for the same purpose.

McDougall not only had a nonobjectivistic interpretation of
behavior, but he also felt that the study of experience was
legitimate for psychology. In speaking about experience, Mc-
Dougall (1923, p. 40) writes:

> Experience is not made up of things; it's a process and perhaps a
> train of activity. The most general and fundamental facts about expe-
> rience . . . are two. First, experience or experiencing is always an expe-
> riencing of something . . . even when, as in psychologizing, that object
> is itself an experiencing or thinking. Secondly, all experiencing . . . is
> the experiencing or thinking of *some one,* some subject, some person,
> some organism. So far as we positively know, this *some one,* this subject,
> is always a material organism, or is embodied in, and manifests itself
> only in and through the medium of a material organism. That is to say,
> experience, as we know it, is always the thinking of some subject of or
> about some object.

The above quote contains in germinal form a number of notions
that were explicitly developed by later phenomenologists. We
mean such things as the idea of reciprocal implication between
man and the world, the notion of intentional relationships with
the world, and the idea of the body-subject. Such notions are
absolutely vital for the development of psychology conceived as
a human science and here we see McDougall anticipating them.

Finally, McCurdy (1968, p. 120) cites McDougall's answer to
the question: "Does mental activity involve some form or forms
of energy other than those recognized by the physical sciences?"
as being: "In view of the purposive nature of human activity, the
positive answer to this question seems inevitable. We must
postulate some energy which conforms to laws not wholly identical with the laws of energy stated by the physical sciences."
Unquestionably, McDougall understood well the natural scientific approach to psychology, but he argued vigorously and
openly for another conception of psychology, a conception
which we feel is more acceptable by our times than it was
during his.

FROM WORLD WAR II TO THE PRESENT

This section will be brief since it overlaps with the contemporary period which will be covered in detail in a later section. Consequently, only a few references will here indicate the
continuity of the trend described above. Snygg (1941), for example, has written on the inadequacy of the objective approach
for the prediction of human behavior and has suggested as an
alternative a phenomenal system that takes the point of view of
the behaving organism rather than that of the researcher. Mac-
Leod (1947) argued for a complete changeover of presuppositions
in social psychology so that the methods adapted from physics
and sensory physiology would not be simply carried over, even
though they had achieved earlier successes. MacLeod was arguing
that psychologists should adopt presuppositions that would enable them to describe the essential characteristics of phenomena
first. Obviously, among the psychologically relevant phenomena
would be included the phenomenon of man as a person. In fact,
MacLeod (1947) makes it clear that our reference must always
be not some preestablished category which may be real for *us*,
but one that is real for the person with whom we are dealing.

Lastly, we can consider some of the writings of Gordon Allport. In discussing the problem of scientific models and human
morals, Allport (1947) has spoken of the embarrassment on the
part of a number of psychologists concerning "the scarcity of
scientific findings, and even of serviceable concepts and well-
formulated problems, that psychology has to offer *of the type
that is being sought*" (Allport's emphasis). After raising the
question of why there is such a scarcity of relevant findings, Allport (1947, p.190) sums up his answer by stating:

The designs we have been using . . . are not—to borrow Morris's
crisp term—sufficiently iconic with our subject matter. Addiction to
machines, rats, or infants leads us to overplay those features of human
behavior that are peripheral, signal-oriented, or genetic. Correspond-
ingly it causes us to underplay those features that are central, future-
oriented and symbolic.

Unlike many of his contemporaries, Allport was optimistic that a breakthrough would eventually come about. After discussing the many hopeful signs he saw, Allport (1947, p. 191) summed up his position by stating: "All these and many more signs indicate the growing dependence of modern theories upon a model that is none the less scientific for being humane." Unfortunately, the precise articulation of this "human science" has not yet emerged, and this is one of the reasons that an attempt to spell out such an approach is being made now.

The Differentiators: Psychology Is Really Two Sciences

The problem of whether psychology is a human science or natural science has been solved by some psychologists by outwardly advocating that psychology is in fact two sciences. Fernberger (1935) is such an author. He writes that he would be for the separation of the psychological discipline into two distinct and independent sciences. One would be called the "science of behavior," and the other the "science of consciousness." Both have their points of view, both have their different interpretative categories, both have their distinct materials for observation, and both have their methods. Furthermore, Fernberger believes that both may be truly experimental, and each could be consistently carried on from a single point of view.

Here is how Fernberger (1935, p. 37) describes the science of behavior:

> The materials to be studied by a thoroughgoing behaviorism are the reactions of the striated and non-striated muscles and of the glands and their integrations. . . . The method is one of simple observation, either directly or in a more refined manner with the aid of instruments, on the part of the experimenter or experimenters as with a classification of the observation into interpretative *reactive* categories. . . . Hence we would include most of the quantitative work on memory, forgetting, sensation, association, learning and the like under the behavioristic discipline.

In contrast, here is how Fernberger (1935, p. 37) describes the science of consciousness:

> The material of this science is merely the conscious middle term in the reaction chain and nothing more. In this we would include a study of the conscious elements, of their integrations and of conscious meanings. The method is systematic introspection—experimental wherever possible. Such data readily give a qualitative system of consciousness. . . . Hence the science of consciousness must be largely qualitative in form.

Fernberger even points out that the splitting of a science into two distinct sciences is not new and, in a sense, ought to be expected. The example he gives is chemistry, which began as a branch of physics, and which itself has spawned such offshoots as mineralogy and metallurgy. Fernberger concludes by saying that because the present data treated under the term psychology cannot be treated from a single point of view or from a single set of interpretative categories, that it would be better to simply frankly recognize the independence of the sciences of consciousness and of behavior. In his judgment, the two are so different in point of view, in interpretative categories implied, in materials to be studied and in methods to be used that a reconciliation under one science would seem impossible.

Fearon (1937) devoted a whole book to the "two sciences of psychology," and while he believed that both were necessary for a full understanding of man, he treated them as separate disciplines and also stated that that was the way they were usually treated. Fearon (1937, pp.25–26) sketches out the relative spheres of the two disciplines in the following manner:

> The physical psychologist, who may be compared in his aim to the physicist, the astronomer, the biologist, the chemist, and to others who study the manifestations of material substances, confines his field of endeavor to the study of the immediate phenomena and causes of life. He observes vital facts through his senses aided often by instruments; and he interprets these facts with his intellect. The metaphysical psychologist, who studies human life from the philosopher's point of view, confines himself to interpreting the deeper reasons for human behavior.

In a sense, Fearon gives each of the warring partners his due and then cuts them adrift. Physical psychology is psychology from the natural scientific viewpoint, and metaphysical psychology is a branch of philosophy which interprets the data of physical psychology and analyzes the deeper motives of human life. For both Fearon and Fernberger the fact that two apparently disparate sets of methods existed was an important factor in differentiating these two sciences. However, as we shall soon see, we take a little more seriously Fearon's own admission that the "two sciences" still need each other.

The Synthesizers: Psychology Is One Complex Science That Is Difficult to Classify

Since psychology has been struggling between two conceptions of science, it is not surprising that people have tried to put them together as well as sever them. Perhaps the first attempt at such a synthesis was the one performed by Messer (Boring, 1950), who made his approach most explicit in a book written in 1914. Messer's attempt was to integrate what was at that time in Germany known as the difference between "act psychology" and "content psychology," and according to Boring (1950) it comes very close to being simply a bipartite psychology dealing with two kinds of very different materials, impalpable acts and palpable contents, although Boring believes that Messer achieved something more than a mere juxtaposition of incompatibles. Apparently, Messer organized his psychology around intentional experiences, "acts" in a broad sense, but he felt that such impalpable acts also contained palpable contents, and thus it was the responsibility of psychology to investigate both acts and contents.

In the late twenties, Calkins (1930) also thought that she detected signs of a rapprochement in psychology, but this time not just between two types of psychology, but among a plurality of schools. What Calkins perceived to be common to several different systems are the following: (1) opposition to atomism, (2) that psychology should not concern itself with states or "contents" but with integrating conscious wholes, (3) that every conscious existent should be studied in its relation to the environment, and (4) that psychology is a social science. Calkins thought that while each of four schools had to give a little, they could also communicate around these four central points. The four schools she referred to were behaviorism, Gestalt psychology, introspectionism, and self-psychology.

Heidbreder (1933), after reviewing seven schools of psychology and stressing their differences, concludes that it would have been equally possible to write an account of the schools of psychology that would stress their underlying similarities and that would show, despite their differences, that they are all directed towards the same class of facts. She gives examples of agreements between behaviorists and Gestalt psychologists, and between Külpe and Binet, and between Watson and McDougall, etc., as demonstrations of her point. She also demonstrates agreements among schools towards the mind-body problem, in spite of superficial differences, and she demonstrates a communality with respect to the definition of psychology. She even points out how in polemical argumentation between the schools, the various representatives point to the same fundamental facts, which, of course, implies a ground of agreement against which the differences can be focused. In the last analysis then, Heidbreder thinks that there is a continuity of development in psychology that will become clearer as psychology matures and that this continuity will assimilate the best of all schools, even though the latter may not disappear altogether. Woodworth (1931) makes the identical case for psychology, arguing that there are more "middle-of-the-roaders" in psychology than there are adherents of all the schools put together. One of the arguments Woodworth uses to support his case is the fact that psychology did not split up during the decades between 1910 and 1930, and he attributes this unity partly to the fact that all psychologists were cultivating the same general field. Hence, he feels that there is more solidarity among psychologists than outsiders would suspect. The main problem, as Woodworth sees it, is to define the science of psychology broadly enough to cover the positive findings and emphases of all the schools.

Some Reflections on the Relationship
Between Psychology and Science

It should be fairly clear to the reader by now that from the brief history of psychology that we have covered, one can show a precedent for practically any position one wants to establish. One can "prove" that psychology should be a natural science, or a human science, or two sciences, or a bipartite science, or a science that integrates vastly different kinds of material, and so on. Undoubtedly, this range of attitudes and interpretations is due partly to psychology's youth, but it cannot be brushed off as being due *only* to psychology's youth.

Philosophers have been indicating weaknesses in psychology's ground or frame of reference for some time. For example, Kockelmans (1967) shows how Husserl had written that psychology developed in the absence of clearly formulated philosophical premises and that it lacked a systematic framework of basic concepts. Sartre (1962) also writes that the disorder within psychology arises from the very principles of the science of psychology itself. Nor is this type of criticism limited to philosophers within the phenomenological approach. For example, Gustafson (1964, p. xiv) quotes Wittgenstein as saying:

The confusion and barrenness of psychology is not to be explained by calling it a "young science"; its state is not comparable with that of physics, for instance, in its beginnings. . . . For in psychology there are experimental methods *and conceptual confusion."* (My emphasis.)

Thus, from the above points of view, the other difficulty concerning psychology is conceptual confusion or problems of frame of reference. The two are not unrelated, since a system of concepts is a frame of reference. Moreover, since Wittgenstein already admits that there are experimental methods, then the confusion can only refer to psychology's nature, or definition, or subject matter or the viewpoint one adopts towards it. Surely the historical survey we have just conducted justifies this interpretation. And we would add further, if there is such a conceptual confusion concerning the frame of reference or subject matter of psychology, how can we be so sure of the experimental methods we are employing? Our answer is that we cannot be, and if the frame of reference of psychology and its basic concepts must be changed, then its methods and its content must be equally reevaluated. Critical to this reevaluation, however, is an examination of why psychology developed in the way it did, and we shall now return to our historical survey and look at it in this light.

NATURAL SCIENTIFIC PSYCHOLOGY

The reason for conceptual confusion concerning subject matter is related to the reason for the difficulty of specifying just what kind of science psychology is. If we reexamine the four periods within the stream of natural scientific psychology, we find that the initial break from philosophy meant something more specific than just breaking from philosophy. It meant a breaking away from a *certain kind* of philosophizing, i.e., turning away from the method of deduction and speculation and turning towards the method of induction and the establishing of facts based upon experience. This was Wundt's mission, as well as those of his followers who essentially participated in his vision. At this stage of psychology's development, there was still full belief in the method of introspection and in the delimitation of psychology to the "contents" of consciousness. It was during the period between 1900 and World War I when the greatest tension between the dictates of science and the subject matter of psychology defined as the science of consciousness reached its peak. Earlier, there were enough new phenomena to investigate, and the application of the introspective method initially yielded enough facts on previously uninvestigated phenomena to support the belief in its utility. However, after some twenty years of effort, the limits of the method were emerging even for those who were solidly convinced of its utility and the experience of the Würzburg School began to shake its adherents of its feasibility, and this set the stage for the ready acceptance of its dismissal by Watson. In any event, the attempt to retain as the subject matter of psychology states of consciousness, or mental phenomena in general, the increasing difficulty being experienced with the method of introspection, and the awareness of the intangibility of psychology's own data as compared to the solidity of the facts of the natural sciences, all set the stage for the next phase of psychology's development.

In the period between World War I and World War II, perhaps the greatest influences were the arrival of Gestalt psychology and behaviorism as rivals for the dominant model for psychology. It is probably because of the fact that the implications of the fundamental insight of these two schools were initially diametrically opposed that so much energy went into arguments pro and con their respective merits. But during this period, the very radicality of behaviorism kept alive the opposite viewpoint, so that one could still find expressions in the texts of the times of the fact that psychology was the study of both experience or consciousness and behavior (e.g., Murphy, 1935). However, the greater acceptance of the behavioristic approach already began to appear during this time because the behaviorists could at least *do something*—and, more importantly, do something according to the expectations of the time concerning science. That is, by means of research with animals and the use of "objective" procedures on humans, they were accumulating data on learning and motivation, etc. Furthermore their data could be expressed quantitatively and it was not confused by more esoteric "introspective reports." Hence, even though there were objectors to the extremes of behaviorism, it seems that the behaviorists were busier proving that they could *do* the science of psychology better than their objectors and according to the expectations of what most psychologists thought was scientific. On the Gestalt side, the adoption of psychophysical parallelism helped make them theoretically acceptable and it also freed them to turn their attention toward concrete problems.

Then, in the last phase, the general trend seems that psychology shifted to becoming the science of behavior, and it meant by "science" a natural science. Curiously, the position of this last phase is more entrenched in the natural scientific posture than any of the others, and perhaps that is why the reaction to present-day psychology has come so strongly, and from areas that are tangential, in a sense, to the field. Thus, the humanistic and existential movements of the late fifties and sixties receive the majority of their support from clinical psychologists, and to some extent, from social psychologists and anthropologists. Thus, we are almost back to the bipartite position, rather than to the pluralism of the schools, but this time the differences, as in the days of act and content, are more clearly centered in the attitudes of the psychologists. Either their commitment is to science, and thus meeting the criteria of science becomes the privileged position; or they are committed to man, with special emphasis on the essentially human characteristics of man, and they thus render to a secondary place the concern for meeting the standards of science understood as a natural science. It is clear, however, that psychology conceived as a natural science has almost always been in the ascendant or dominant position, whereas other psychologists have almost always had to fight for their place in the sun. The reasons for this are revealing.

In the first place, psychology conceived as a natural science has more continuity than its objectors or rivals, because this type of psychology was launched *first*. And, since the objectors to it did not object to the same things during the course of its history, their only communality was a negative one—objection to the status quo psychology—and there was little positive agreement among them. This is clearly pointed out by Boring (1950, p.430). Moreover, Boring states that the "new" psychology established by Wundt was linked with a systematic position that has never been given a generally accepted name. Boring explains that this is because the school that took its origin from Wundt never regarded itself as a *school* of psychology, but simply as the whole of experimental psychology. Consequently, orthodox experimental psychology, even in its systematic tenets, was a self-conscious school only as against philosophy. It never felt the need of any other name than "psychology" (Boring, 1950). Thus, the main thrust of psychology was differentiated in intent only against philosophy and not against the subsequent objections that would arise against its systematic expositions. De facto, however, this main thrust was only one approach, and one view-

point, although an important one, among a number of viewpoints concerning psychology during the years of psychology's
birth and infancy. However, we must now understand how it got
this early jump over all other approaches and how it was able to
keep the ascendant position.

There is no doubt about the answer to the last question.
Practically all historians agree that the reason that early psychology took the form, approach and definition that it did was due
to the extraordinary powers of Wundt. Boring (1950) states that
as opposed to his contemporaries, who were teachers, or theorists,
or experimenters, etc., Wundt was an institution. Boring (1950)
also states that while many other labs were springing up in the
late nineteenth century, the *character* of the "new" psychology
was already determined by Wundt, even for America. The sheer
abundance of his output, and the fact that he was a good polemi-
cist (Boring, 1950), also contributed to his stature as the primary
molder of the new psychology. Murphy (1929) states that it
would not be an exaggeration to say that the conception of an
experimental psychology was practically Wundt's own creation.

Heidbreder (1933) makes the same point, noting that Wundt
imparted an influential system to enthusiastic students who were
proud to carry on his work. But his role as founder and primary
determiner of the nature of psychology can be seen by Heidbreder's comment that he was not unaware of the debt psychology owed him, and not altogether indifferent as to whether or
not it was recognized. As a founder, Heidbreder notes that Wundt
was inclined toward the patriarchal—almost toward the papal—
and he reserved the right to speak with authority, to pronounce
ex cathedra on psychology, and to draw a distinct line of demar-
cation between "authentic" psychology and psychology of which
he did not approve. Thus, there was a de facto orthodox psychology, even if it did not receive any other official name, and
Heidbreder (1933) notes that this initial imprint always left an
influence on Wundt's students no matter how they developed
on their own subsequently.

Thus, opposed to the institution of Wundt, other psychologists within the natural scientific perspective were mere mortals,
and those outside that perspective were mere passing actors with

bit parts on the psychological stage. Surely, one has usually *heard* of the humanistic psychologists listed earlier in this chapter, but one rarely knows what they said explicitly, and only slightly more frequently does one know what general opinions they represented.

Primarily because of Wundt, then, a natural scientific conception of psychology took the lead and developed more quickly and more fully. Undoubtedly, the approval of the *Zeitgeist,* which was justifiably impressed by the legitimate achievements of science, and the ready availability of a method that permitted immediate execution were factors that sustained the early thrust provided by Wundt. The fact that by adopting the natural scientific approach the early psychologists were able "to do" things other than "speculate" or "merely think" about their problems, especially in America, played no small role in establishing the character of psychology as an independent science. Nor is this attitude *wholly* wrong, but it is not *wholly* right either. The time, we feel, has come to balance the equation and to devote more attention to *what* we are doing, and *how* we are doing as well as to the sheer fact of doing something.

Therefore, psychology conceived as a natural science was the type of psychology that took the initiative and sprang loose from philosophy, and while there is no decade of psychology's modern period in which this type of psychology has not been challenged, or no decade in which, no matter how great its prestige, it has been the exclusive representative of psychology, it is also true that it has always been in the lead and in the dominant position. Perhaps around the time of World War I it may have tottered just a bit, or was losing its momentum, but just then Watsonian behaviorism came along and gave it a new impetus. And just when naïve behaviorism was waning, Skinner arrived on the scene and gave this type of psychology its second boost. So, it has been able to maintain its dominant and central, if not exclusive, position concerning the idea of science that psychology ought to be. However, it is important to note that not only was this idea taken over uncritically, but the founders undertook the project of psychology as a natural science with more caution and tentativeness than later writers seem to imply. For example, even while he was arguing for a natural scientific psychology, Wundt (1961) cautioned that so far there were only beginnings, and that "as a coherent science, experimental psychology still awaits its foundations." We have also seen how James saw psychology as the "hope of a science" rather than as an already existing science. In that same work, James makes it very clear that the early psychologists were both open to other possibilities, and anything but very sure of their own direction. No place is this expressed more clearly than in the very last paragraphs of his book. James's (1948, p. 467) conclusion contains the following sentiments:

> When, then, we talk of "psychology as a natural science" we must not assume that that means a sort of psychology that stands at last on solid ground. It means just the reverse; it means a psychology particularly fragile, and into which the waters of metaphysical criticism leak at every joint, a psychology all of whose elementary assumptions and data must be reconsidered in wider connections and translated into other terms. It is, in short, a phrase of diffidence, and not of arrogance, and it is indeed strange to hear people talk triumphantly of "the New Psychology" and write "Histories of Psychology," when into the real elements and forces which the word covers not the first glimpse of clear insight exists. . . . The matter of a science is with us. . . . But at present psychology is in the condition of physics before Galileo and the laws of motion, of chemistry before Lavoisier and the notion that mass is preserved in all reactions. The Galileo and the Lavoisier of psychology will be famous men indeed when they come. . . . Meanwhile the best way in which we can facilitate their advent is to understand how great is the darkness in which we grope, and never to forget that *the natural science assumptions* with which we started *are provisional and revisable things.* (My emphasis.)

By way of summing up this section, we may say that in desiring to break from philosophy and establish itself as an independent discipline, psychology wanted to get away from a particular *style* of scholarly investigation, viz., speculative and deductive philosophy and an almost exclusive utilization of reasoning and argumentative processes, in order to participate in another *style* of investigation, i.e., a careful and detached approach that was cautious in the establishment of its facts, that followed inductive

reasoning and would accept nothing that was not publicly veri-
fiable. Thus, psychology joined the natural sciences. It should
be noted, however, that in doing so, psychology went from one
existing style of scholarly investigation to another *already existing style* of investigation, and while the switchover was justified
on many occasions, it never followed a fully critical and reflective
study of just what psychology needed in terms of methodology
in order to become a science. We do not question its decision to
leave the style of speculative philosophy. What we do question is
whether psychology's interests are better served by the style of the
natural sciences, or by creating a style that is indigenous to itself.

HUMAN SCIENTIFIC PSYCHOLOGY

The reader undoubtedly will have noticed that the human
scientific authors considered above turned away from a natural
scientific approach to psychology just as strongly as those who
adopted a natural scientific approach turned away from speculative philosophy. The big difference, however, is that the natural scientific psychologists had something to turn *to,* whereas
the human scientific psychologists did not. They did not want to
return to speculative philosophy, but on the other hand they
could not agree with the attempts to make psychology a natural
science; consequently, the only alternative they had to fill the
void they were perceiving was to attempt to create the kind of
science they thought psychology ought to be. In other words, they
perceived the need for a different conception of psychological
science, a different frame of reference in order to conduct their
investigations in ways they thought to be adequate. The obvious
question at this point is to ask why these men were looking for
a new frame of reference or a different style of scholarly investigation. The excerpts quoted above supply the answer. Over and
over again the belief is expressed that phenomena such as experience, consciousness, meaning, purpose, significance, etc., simply
could not be studied by means of the available procedures of the
natural sciences. However, since man, at least in terms of everyday behavior and interaction, constantly participated in and expressed such phenomena, it was clear that there could be no
psychology worthy of its name that did not include an adequate

study of precisely these phenomena. Consequently, they launched efforts to try to understand these phenomena in a scientific way.

It must be appreciated that the primary effort of the early human scientific psychologists was a double one: first, an adequate way of conceiving science so that human phenomena could be studied, and secondly, a testing of this conception in a concrete way. The struggle to achieve both aims was more than any single one of them could handle completely, but of the two, the conception was accomplished more adequately than the testing, although all conceptions were far from being complete systems. But this means that the execution aspects of these systems, i.e., the actual carrying out of concrete studies, were subordinated to the theoretical effort, and thus, in a sense, the human scientific psychologists had little "data" to show for their efforts. This is especially true when one considers that the criteria for acceptability during these times was "empirical data." In other words, not only did these psychologists not provide data —one of the major alleged criteria for being scientific—but they also tried to supply a new conceptual frame of reference for psychology, and to many of their contemporaries, it seemed like a return to the very philosophy they were trying to get away from. From hindsight, of course, we can distinguish very clearly between speculative philosophy and the attempt to construct a tentative conceptual frame of reference, but it seems that the contemporaries of the human scientific psychologists were still too close to the break from philosophy to see this distinction. In any event, the very contribution that the human scientific psychologists wanted to make was almost diametrically opposed to the expectations of the *Zeitgeist,* and this is undoubtedly one big reason that this movement did not spread as rapidly as the natural scientific approach to psychology.

It is important to note that very few, if any, of these psychologists wanted to do away with science as such; they simply wanted a different conception of science for psychology. The reason for desiring a different conception of science for psychology was that they refused to consider many of the everyday phenomena of human life—such as experiences, feelings, laughter, meanings, misunderstandings, etc.—to be psychologically irrelevant.

On the other hand, they also maintained that in order to be studied adequately, rigorously and *as they were experienced,* these phenomena required conceptions, techniques, and procedures that the natural scientific approach could not provide. Implicitly, these authors were saying that in order to be faithful to the phenomenon of man, either a new type of science had to be invented or the meaning of science as it was understood had to be considerably broadened.

The last two points should be made before we leave the human scientific psychologists, or rather, what we would prefer to call "precursors" to a human scientific psychology. The term *"precursors"* is preferred because we feel that none of these men actually *achieved* a proper theoretical foundation for psychology. Their communality is due to their agreement that a foundation other than a natural scientific one was necessary, and in their *intention* to create such a foundation. Their lack of success was, in our opinion, also partly responsible for their relative lack of influence. Moreover, since they were writing during different periods of psychology's history, there are many differences among the different systems, despite their common intention. Because of these two factors (and this is our first point) we do not wish to defend the specifics of any of the systems of the precursors to human scientific psychology—and we prefer to call them precursors.

The second point is related to the first. Since the term "human science" has already been used extensively by Dilthey, and has been generally accepted in Germany and other parts of western Europe, we wish to emphasize our understanding of this term. Literally speaking, *Geisteswissenschaften* means "sciences of the mind, of culture or of the spirit" and to translate it as "human science" is a somewhat looser expression. Some users of the term therefore wish to restrict its meaning to the study of mind, consciousness or experience alone. For us this usage is too narrow. We prefer a more comprehensive and more neutral meaning. In our usage the term "human" always refers to an *embodied,* concrete person which is prior to the distinction between body and mind as well as that of subject and object, and which includes reference to the phenomenon of behavior. This difference in interpretation undoubtedly accounts for some of the differences between Klüver's (1929) discussion of this problem and our own.

THE DIFFERENTIATORS AND INTEGRATORS

The differentiators took the most direct approach to the knotty problem of the science of psychology by simply cutting it into two sciences. They saw the same problem as the human scientists did, but their main distinction was that they were equally concerned with keeping the natural scientific approach viable, so they gave each approach its due and simply created two sciences of psychology. They legitimized both conceptions of science and did not worry too much about the interaction between them.

The integrators, on the other hand, were more concerned with the problem of the unity of psychology, and they tried hard to discover the similarities rather than the differences between the two conceptions of science. However, it must be admitted that their unity, too, was more of a hope than an actual synthesis of viewpoints. They tried to point out common problems, or emphasized similar solutions to problems, even though the language of the two viewpoints differed, etc., but in the last analysis these efforts were not successful. The so-called syntheses were either simple juxtapositions of the opposing viewpoints in a side-by-side manner, or the complete subsumption of one viewpoint by the other, or a listing of the common concerns of a number of viewpoints with reference to a future unified psychology without specifying the exact nature of this futuristic psychology. The important point is that the two separate conceptions of scientific psychology were explicitly acknowledged; these men were just not content with the division and they attempted to bridge the gap between them.

Some Conclusions Regarding Psychology and Science

While our discussion of science is not complete, it may be worthwhile to pause here and present some conclusions concerning the analyses completed thus far.

1. It is clear that at least one unambiguous meaning of science in psychology is that it is a natural science, and that it should as much as possible participate in the approach, methods, concepts, and frames of references of the whole spectrum of the natural sciences.

2. It is also clear that there has always been some tension between the purported subject matter of psychology and the attempt to deal with it in a natural scientific way. Even those who accept fully the natural scientific conception of psychology always feel somewhat compelled to justify that psychology *is* a science, and in addition, they always find it necessary to modify and transform, often in basic ways, the methods of the natural sciences. If psychology were obviously a natural science, why would the justification be necessary, and why could the methods not be taken over with only minor modifications?

3. Other psychologists have interpreted the tensions between the subject matter of psychology and the attempt to understand it in a natural scientific way as indicating that the assumptions of the natural scientific approach are not appropriate for the unique subject matter of psychology and thus another conception of science for psychology is necessary. Thus, this group wishes to broaden the understanding of science so that it can incorporate human phenomena in a psychologically relevant way, but they must sacrifice precise articulation, at least initially, in order to do so. The natural scientific conception of science, they admit, has precision, but it is not the type of precision that is required for the phenomena they deem to be the most relevant. Thus, they argue, there must be another meaning of science, a deeper one that would not exclude the presence of the human person in psychology. It is this conception that they have tried, with varying degrees of success, to make articulate.

4. The most striking overall conclusion from the historical analysis is that all of the psychologists we have covered recognized the tension between the simple application of a strict natural scientific approach to psychology and the ability to study adequately all of the phenomena that have been considered to be psychologically relevant. This perception of the tension is explicit with the human scientific psychologists, the differentiators,

and the integrators. It is mostly implicit with the natural scientific psychologists, but it can be seen in the way they find it necessary to modify methods, in their defense of the natural scientific vision, and in their selection of topics. The four groups differed mostly with respect to the meaning and relevance that they assigned to this tension or discrepancy between the natural scientific approach and the phenomena of psychology.

It is time now to look more closely at the characteristics of natural scientific psychology in order to see whether or not these conclusions are essentially correct. We must try to identify the characteristics of the natural scientific approach and see to what extent they are fruitful for studying psychological phenomena. Ultimately, we shall want to know whether the natural scientific approach to psychology can actually do justice to human phenomena, or whether the distortion of the latter, as the human scientists maintain, must be the price for being included among the natural sciences.

CHAPTER 2

INVESTIGATION OF PSYCHOLOGY CONCEIVED AS A NATURAL SCIENCE

WE WOULD LIKE TO BEGIN WITH an analysis of some of the characteristics of psychology conceived as a natural science. As with the historical survey, it is difficult to tease out exactly what these characteristics are because of the differences between what psychologists have *said* and what they *did,* and again, because of what psychologists have *said* in order to be scientists (of a particular conception) and how they *lived.* The following observations of Woodworth (1931, p.11) are highly relevant to this point:

... in either way of looking at the matter, psychology was limited by definition to the study of consciousness, and to the individual as an experiencer.... In the lab, however, psychology declined to be limited by the formal definition. The subject in an experiment was not always treated as an experiencer, but often as a performer. The question up for investigation might be how quickly he could react, or how accurately he could perceive, or how completely he could recall material which he had memorized: and he was not asked to report his experience during the performance, but simply to perform his task. How well he performed it was observed by the experimenter. Again, in studying the feelings and emotions, a common practice was to harness the subject into recording apparatus which would give a tracing of his breathing or pulse. In theory, these objective methods were justified in the psychological laboratory simply as throwing some light, indirectly, upon feelings and other conscious experiences: but as the researches worked out, the real interest was found to lie in the performance itself. If the subject did report any incidental introspections, they were used to throw light on his performance, rather than the other way around. Psychology was finding its job and how to do it by the process of exploring its field, rather than from the dictates of theory and formal definition.

. . . In theory, the psychologists of 1900 subscribed to the definition of psychology as the science of consciousness, but in practice they were studying performance as well as experience. In theory, they were for an analytical psychology patterned after chemistry, with elementary sensations, images, and feelings, and with complex thoughts and emotions composed of these elements in varying combinations; but in practice they often disregarded this scheme. In theory they were mostly associationists, but not dogmatically so. . . . In theory, they were strong for a physiological psychology, but in practice they made a profound bow to the brain and passed on their way, since cerebral processes were still too obscure to afford much insight into mental processes.

The above description gives a fairly good feel for the type of things that were going on during the first two decades of modern psychology. In passing we may note that early psychology was *practically* oriented, i.e., working on concrete problems took precedence over theoretical embarrassments, and secondly, that the performance of the early psychologists broke away from both types of theory—those who were defining psychology as the study of consciousness actually measured performance, and those who believed that psychology should be analytic actually spoke of synthetic wholes or meaningful units. Thus, the de facto goings on of these early psychologists were almost as varied as the persons doing the work, so if we are to look for some kind of unity, it must come from the *approach* of the psychologist, which, in spite of what he said and did, is still revealed by him in his saying and doing. We have already indicated how, even though consciousness and experience were defined as subject matters for psychology, the approach of the psychologist often revealed the framework of the natural sciences. It is necessary to show now that this same approach in fact guided what they did.

The Natural Scientific Approach to Psychology

Because of historical differences we will deal first with the founders, and then with the psychology from the period of the schools, and finally with the most contemporary period. In this section, all of the emphases that this writer has singled out in the accompanying quotes are meant to indicate characteristics of the natural scientific approach.

First, we shall get some descriptions from Wundt (1912, pp. 689–690):

As an experimental science, physiological psychology seeks to accomplish a reform in psychological investigation comparable with the revolution brought about in the natural sciences by the introduction of the experimental method . . . it is the essence of experiment that we can vary the conditions of an occurrence at will and, if we are aiming at exact results, in a *quantitatively* determinable way . . . even in the domain of natural science, the aid of the experimental method becomes indispensable whenever the problem set is the analysis of transient and impermanent phenomena, and not merely the observation of persistent and relatively constant objects. But conscious contents are at the opposite pole from permanent objects; they are processes, fleeting occurrences, in continual flux and change. In their case, therefore, the *experimental method* is of cardinal importance; it and it *alone makes a scientfiic introspection* possible. For all *accurate* observation implies that the object of observation can be held fast by the attention, and any changes that it undergoes attentively followed. And this fixation by the attention implies, in its turn, that the *observed object is independent* of the observer. . . . The psychological experiment proceeds very differently (from direct self-observation). In the first place, it creates *external conditions* that look towards the *production of a determinate* mental process at a given moment. In the second place, it makes the *observer* so far master of the general situation, that the state of consciousness accompanying this process remains approximately unchanged. The great importance of the experimental method, therefore, lies not simply in the fact that, here *as in the physical realm,* it enables us *arbitrarily to vary the conditions* of our observations, but also and essentially in the further fact that it makes observation itself possible for us. The results of this observation may then be fruitfully employed in the examination of other mental phenomena, whose nature prevents their own direct experimental modification. (All emphases mine.)

We can see in this passage the paradox noted above, viz., that in spite of retaining mental phenomena as the subject matter of psychology, the intention to pursue this subject matter within the perspective of the natural sciences is dominant. We will mention the emphases and summarize the characteristics of this approach when we have completed all of our presentation. However, a very close corroborative description of what a psychological experiment was like in these days is given by Heidbreder (1933, pp. 73–74), along with a brief prefatory comment as to why psychology turned to experiments:

Before psychology could speak with the accent of science, before it could even pretend to produce results that bear the hall-mark of knowledge as distinguished from opinion, it had to acquire new methods of collecting and elaborating its data. *It had,* in short, *to learn the scientific method* and in doing so to move from its armchair to the laboratory. . . . It is the distinguishing mark of a scientific **experiment** that it is a means of **acquiring** just the information that is relevant . . . and of acquiring it in circumstances that rule out as completely as possible the accidental and private factors in observation. Therefore, the experimenter begins by *formulating his question definitely,* and *proceeds by arranging* that particular *set of conditions* which is *best calculated* to bring out the pertinent facts. He *repeats* his observations carefully, both to *increase accuracy* and to minimize chance; *he varies* the conditions *systematically,* both to broaden his view and to check his hypotheses; and *he controls* the whole situation as rigorously as possible in order that, knowing precisely what *he has put into the experiment,* he may not be misled as to what has come out of it. Whenever possible, he *reduces* his *results to quantitative terms* and submits them to statistical treatment, scrupulously taking account of negative as well as positive cases . . . in a very real sense, the scientific method is a device for protecting the investigator from the influence of his own interest in his own research. The conditions are arranged so that the *facts will emerge as clearly impersonal* as possible. . . . *Scientific psychology is but the extension of the scientific method* into a region where disinterested observation has been peculiarly difficult. (My emphasis except "experiment" and "acquiring.")

In another place, Heidbreder (1933, p. 93) summarizes Wundt's idea of an experiment in the following terms:

The psychological experiment is plainly *patterned after the physiological experiment:* it is a procedure in which the process to be studied is kept very *close to a controllable stimulus* and very *close to an objec-*

tive response, and in which introspection is an intensive, short range, carefully prepared act of observation. (All emphases mine.)

It might strike some as archaic to read such descriptions now, but one can find these *only* in the older texts, precisely because such attitudes have become so much the way of life in most of contemporary psychology that few people ever bother to spell them out in such a precise manner.

The one time that one finds a plurality of guiding lines for how psychology should be conducted is during the time of the "schools" which arose in the early 1900s and lasted until the late thirties. Most of the schools centered around a particular view or approach to psychology, which in turn were related to methods, although there are also some approaches that never got crystallized into "schools" as such (Woodworth, 1931). The reaction of psychology to the schools has also run the whole gamut, from considering them as embarrassments and a nuisance to the new science of psychology (Rubin, 1930) to seeing them as necessary "tools" for the development of any new science (Heidbreder, 1933). It is interesting how the idea of a "school" as a "tool" for the development of the science of psychology has recently been emphasized once again by Watson (1967), who has commented on the fact that thus far in its history psychology has been a *prescriptive* science. In this sense, each school laid down the prescriptive principles that it thought psychology should follow. It was perhaps a time of confusion but the natural scientific approach we are describing was safely preserved and communicated by introspectionism and behaviorism, to mention only two.

This brings us to the modern period, and while one could document the contemporary meaning of science in psychology in a detailed way, since it is the dominant trend, and since this documentation has already taken place (Giorgi, 1965; 1966), we will avoid redundancy by merely listing the attributes of the natural scientific approach to psychology. Moreover, one can see that most of these characteristics are already contained in the emphases we noted in the passages by and concerning Wundt. In essence, the approach of psychology conceived as a natural science is characterized as being empirical, positivistic, reductionistic, quantitative, genetic, deterministic, predictive, and posits the idea of independent observer. We shall now turn to the type of psychology that this particular approach sired.

Consequences of Natural Scientific Psychology

Since the consequences of natural scientific psychology differed for what we can call academic psychology and for clinical psychology, these two aspects will be discussed separately.

ACADEMIC PSYCHOLOGY

This theme has certainly been discussed before by contemporary writers, e.g., Bonner (1965), van Kaam (1966), and Straus (1966); but it is still fruitful to delve into this issue to a limited extent so that we can understand clearly the implications of psychology as a natural science.

As we have just indicated, when psychology explicitly set out to imitate natural scientific methodology, it never realized that it implicitly also accepted the assumptions underlying that methodology, or the philosophy behind the methods of the natural sciences, or in our own terminology, the *approach of* the natural sciences (Giorgi, 1965). Once the approach and the method of a science are established, the content is also established by implication. What is significant with respect to psychology is that the above description is precise with respect to the *order* in which the various aspects of the scientific endeavor entered into psychology's ideological structure. That is, the method with its implied approach received top priority and primary concern, and the phenomena that were to be investigated, or the contents of psychology, were seen in the light of the already established methodology. There was, therefore, a certain privileged position that was assigned to methodology, and any conflict that ensued between method and content was resolved in favor of the former. It was more a matter of making phenomena fit the method than vice versa and thus psychology became overconcerned about methods and means (Maslow, 1954). It should also be kept in mind that while psychology thought it was merely joining the ranks of science, it was in fact joining the ranks of the natural sciences because those were the only kind of science in existence at that time. Perhaps now we can understand a little better Koch's (1959) comment that psychology's institutionalization preceded its content; its methods presented its problems; and its commitment to science was stronger than its commitment to man. Psychology was going to remain faithful to the scientific method, as it understood it, at all costs.

While traditional psychologists still speak as though the privileged position in their view of psychology is methodology (e.g. Postman and Egan, 1949), the fact remains that the true privileged position is the semiarticulated *approach* of the natural sciences (Giorgi, 1965). This is easily demonstrated because if the priority were really with methodology, there would be all sorts of debates raging over whether the "method of limits" was the best one, or the "method of constant stimuli," or the "method of adjustment," etc., but rather reference is always made to "The Method," i.e., a generic method, of which all of the other specific methods are particularizations. And this generic method itself is nothing other than a concrete specification of the approach of the natural sciences.

In order to understand how the natural scientific conception of psychology is restricting, we have to look a little more closely at the characteristics of the natural scientific approach that we described above. We indicated that this approach is characterized as being empirical, positivistic, reductionistic, quantitative, deterministic, and predictive among other things. This means that the method to be employed by a scientific psychology must meet these criteria. Once again, it is imperative for us to bear in mind that these criteria were not posited as being intrinsic to science as a result of a special analysis; rather they represent the results of centuries of experience of dealing with the subject matter of the natural sciences, and during the course of time, they were articulated with more or less clarity, and with varying degrees of emphasis. But at the time psychology came on the scene, they were fairly well known, and psychology had merely to implement them in a way that would be fruitful for its own purposes. Thus, with proper modifications, one could get data from human beings that conformed to these criteria. In fact, one could argue that what slowed up the whole humanistic movement for at least a half a century is the fact that the application of natural scientific techniques to man worked! If these criteria were wholly inapplicable, the offspring would have been stillborn. Thus to argue for a human science does not necessarily mean that there is no sense in which natural scientific psychology is legitimate. However, what is equally true but less well advertised is that it is also limited. At the moment we are interested in understanding the limits of serving such criteria.

The chief way these criteria limit psychology is that in their status of privileged position, they not only limit the phenomena that are investigated, but they also condition the kinds of questions that psychologists ask about these phenomena. All of the above criteria interact in such a way that in effect they culminate in the measurement question. "How do you measure . . ." has become the key psychological question. Journals are replete with techniques for measuring all sorts of phenomena. It is significant that in almost all American universities, "Statistics" and "Experimental Psychology"—courses dealing with measurement and methods—are required courses, but no one is really required to study Freud or James, the so-called giants of psychology. The design of almost every dissertation, whether M.A. or Ph.D., has to include a measurement phase as a minimum requirement, if the measurement aspect itself is not the very basis of the whole dissertation. We have forgotten how to ask nonmeasurement questions. Why do we ask *only* measurement questions? What is the reason for this emphasis? Are there such things as nonmeasurement questions that are psychologically relevant?

We believe that there are, but here we are only interested in pointing out the unchallengeable priority of the measurement question in contemporary psychology. Practically all psychological phenomena are known only insofar as they are measurable. What happens when a particular phenomenon cannot be measured? Well, it is merely avoided until someone comes along with a technique for measuring it. This, of course, explains why so many peculiarly human phenomena—like crying, laughing, friendship, love—have not as yet made psychological textbooks in depth; they have not as yet been rigorously measured.

Thus, it can be seen that within the framework of most of academic psychology, the root question, the fundamental perspective, has been that of measurement. Indeed, one could say with justice that for academic psychology *measurement precedes existence*. This expression is not meant to be a slogan but simply a description of how most psychologists come to determine data. That is, a phenomenon *is* to the extent that it is measurable. If it is not measurable then it does not enter the psychological domain. It remains prescientific and therefore psychologically irrelevant. The measurement perspective has become the giant filter through which all phenomena must pass if they are to be psychologically relevant. In other words, the status of the phenomenon under investigation is due at least as much to the operations of the psychologist as it is to the way the phenomenon appears prior to psychological consideration.

We are aware, of course, that exceptions to the stand we have just described have been made before, and perhaps the most eloquent of these is the case made by Koffka (1935). He rightly acknowledged that in psychology we need both quantity and quality because psychological phenomena possess both attributes and there is no reason to limit our techniques to just one of these attributes. In addition, Koffka realized that the use of quantitative procedures in psychology was often excessive and that exaggerated claims for them were constantly being made. He rightly tried to correct these excesses by pointing out the inevitable presence of quality in physics and other natural sciences and how these sciences actually employed quantitative procedures in a more even-handed way. We agree with all of these points.

However, we feel that Koffka still retained, even if only implicitly, one subtle quantitative bias. All of his discussions on the relationship between quality and quantity led Koffka to conclude that quantitative expressions were simply one accurate way of representing quality, although he added the caution that a description may be quantitative without necessarily being the most adequate one. Then Koffka draws out the implications for psychology in the following way:

And we can now draw a lesson for our psychology: it may be perfectly quantitative without losing its character as a qualitative science, and on the other hand, and at the present moment even more important, it may be unblushingly qualitative, knowing that if its qualitative descriptions are correct, it will some time be possible to translate them into quantitative terms. (Koffka, 1935, p.15)

The bias we spoke of above can be seen in Koffka's ultimate ideal: if the qualitative descriptions are correct, then it may be possible to translate them into quantitative terms. All the way through his discussion the relationship between quality and quantity is assumed to be unilateral: quantitative expressions can represent qualitative ones. We agree. But is it not equally possible that qualitative expressions can represent quantitative dimensions? Is it not equally possible that a rigorous system of relationships among qualities can be invented that will also express primordial qualitative dimensions more precisely? Granted that such systems do not as yet exist; but ignoring these possibilities will certainly not bring them into existence. The sheer presence of existing quantitative procedures guarantees their ready use. One does not really have to worry about the development of quantitative methods and mathematical psychology, for these fields have a momentum of their own. What we are trying to do is simply awaken psychologists to the fact that other possibilities might exist. The relation between quantity and quality is *bilateral;* yet only one side of this relationship has been exploited. Whatever the reasons for this one-sided development may be, it is time to restore the balance. Moreover, quantitative expressions can also represent quantitative dimensions; can not qualitative expressions also represent qualitative dimensions in a precise manner? Must one turn to quantitative expressions? Nor would the development of effective qualitative methods, if they came into being, be a mere academic exercise. We feel that substantial progress in human scientific psychology will be made when such qualitative methods and systems come into being because peculiarly human phenomena are more adequtely comprehended by qualitative perspectiveness. Progress with respect to the problem of meaning will undoubtedly be helpful to the development of such qualitative systems.

While the usual intention is that quantitative terms should be accurate expressions of qualitative dimensions, it is often difficult to see just how and why they should be, and frequently one gets the impression that something is missing, especially with respect to human phenomena. Yet, despite these difficulties, the tendency is still to define science primarily in quantitative terms, and the bias of the unilateral development still persists. These factors can be seen even among those who are sympathetic to our position and who recognize such characteristics in science as the qualitative nature of questioning, the role of human decisions in the creation of facts, and the involvement of man in the project of science, but who still insist on quantitative operations as the sine qua non of science. Taylor (1968), for example, argues for the awareness of the qualitative aspects of scientific research and he tries to do justice to both the quantitative and the qualitative aspects of science. However, from his manner of relating quantity and quality, it is clear that science cannot exist without the presence of quantitative methods. Taylor (1968, pp. 86–87) writes as follows:

If one is engaged in research which appears to begin and end in quantitative or numerical terms, it is probably naive. Behind the quantities there must be a clearly defined qualitative problem. Good research begins with good questions, and ends with careful decisions; both are qualitative and both involve the exercise of common sense. The quantitative "middle" of research does not produce a decision. It merely indicates the probability of *a qualitative hypothetical proposition being incorrect once that proposition has been represented in quantitative terms.* . . . The quantitative "middle" however is the crucial element in making the decision a scientific decision. Well-defined qualitative questions are the beginning of both science and common sense. Qualitative answers emerge from both. With the quantitative middle the answer is scientifically justifiable and the process is rightly called research; without the quantitative middle, or with misuse of the same, the answer is at best non-science, or worse, uninformed opinion or misrepresentation. (Taylor's emphasis.)

Thus, while science begins and ends qualitatively, it must have a quantitative middle. The only other alternative is nonscience. These remarks reveal the embeddedness of the quantitative perspective in science even more strongly, because Taylor sees the very problem we are raising. Earlier in the same article Taylor (1968, p. 86) writes:

There is a very great leap of faith, and in a sense a great leap in logic, that must take place at this point. *It must be assumed that some quantitative variable, or group of such variables, fairly represents these qualities.* The fairness of this assumption must be determined principally by enlightened common sense; it seldom can be determined scientifically. . . . Why it can be assumed that a quality is fairly represented by a quantity, or any number of quantities, is a thorny question —thorny in a practical sense as well as philosophically—and can only be resolved by the common sense of the scientist. (Taylor's emphasis.)

Thus, Taylor sees the gap between qualitative variables and their quantitative expression, but he feels that the gap must be bridged by an assumptive leap if one is to be scientific. Thus the necessity arises not from the phenomena but from the desire to be scientific. But again we would point out that a specific conception of science is implied here. Unfortunately, Taylor stopped short in his pursuit of the problem. He does not pursue to the "quantitative middle" the qualitative presence that he so lucidly brought out in the other phases of scientific research. He considers the sheer presence of quantification as sufficient reason for calling research scientific. We would rather point to the *function* of quantification in the *context* of the natural sciences and relate that function to the questions that the natural scientists ask of their phenomena. In this line of reasoning the procedure for the human sciences becomes analogical, viz., what perspective must one employ in the human sciences, given its context, that will do for it and its problems what quantification does for the natural sciences? It is not a matter of directly employing quantification but of identifying the function that quantification serves for the natural sciences, and then raising the question of whether or not the same function is desirable within the context of the human sciences. Actually, quantification or measurement within the context of the natural sciences meets the requirement for rigor that science would demand, but we would maintain that it is only *one* way of being rigorous. Whether or not rigor is best served by a quantifying perspective depends upon the nature of the phenomenon and the questions that the scientist puts to it. We would agree that the human sciences should also accept the responsibility to be rigorous, but we feel that ways of being rigorous other than quantification have to be explored, invented and refined. In principle, for us, to be scientific means to implement, or to be concerned about implementing, rigor—but not necessarily a quantitative definition of rigor.

We wish to emphasize that we are not saying there is no place for the measurement perspective; we are simply stating that the tendency or the trend in academic American psychology has been almost exclusively in the direction of adopting *only* this perspective. This is the fundamental impact of psychology conceived as a natural science on traditional academic psychology.

CLINICAL PSYCHOLOGY

At first blush, it might seem odd that one even attempts to speak about the influence of the natural scientific approach on clinical psychology. After all, is not clinical psychology precisely that part of psychology that deals with man as a person? Is it not the most unscientific aspect of psychology? In what sense can we speak about the influence of the natural sciences on clinical psychology?

As a matter of fact, however, the existential movement had its first impact on psychology in the area of clinical psychology, and the cry for a more humanistic psychology came initially from the clinicians themselves. Indeed, there is far more resistance to this movement on the part of academicians than on the part of clinicians or those working in the area of personality theory. What then can account for this fact? What can it mean that precisely those psychologists who are most concerned with the whole human person clamor for a type of psychology that will do justice to the human person? Our position is that it demonstrates that there has been a strong influence of the natural

scientific approach on clinical psychology, and it is to justify
this claim that the following analysis will be undertaken, as well
as for the purpose of elucidating the specific nature of the influence. We will do this by examining what certain therapists
have said about traditional clinical psychology.

According to May (1958), a growing dissatisfaction with the
traditional explanations of therapy was being experienced by an
increasing number of psychologists and psychiatrists. More specifically, there was an awareness that serious gaps existed in the
psychologist's understanding of human beings. It seemed that
these psychologists, if they were honest with themselves, could
not really state why certain cures occurred, nor why others did
not occur, nor were they even able to explain what was actually
happening to, or within, the client during the therapy session.
Furthermore, these therapists refused to indulge in some of the
more common ways of quieting these doubts. They did not
double their effort to perfect their conceptual systems; nor did
they engross themselves in refining their techniques; nor did
they set about postulating unverifiable agents like "libido" or
"censor" to help them out of their difficulties. Of course, such
activities need not always be "escapes," but it would be naïve to
think that they cannot be. At any rate, May (1958) was referring
to them in the former sense. The important point is that these
therapists considered their doubts and uncertainties to be as
important as their theories, and they lived with them until they
were able to describe them more accurately and to find out just
what their meanings were. When these doubts were spelled out,
it became evident that the difficulties were not with any specific
techniques of therapy, but with the theory of man behind these
techniques. These therapists no longer wanted to understand
particular neuroses or psychoses as deviations from some theoretical conception of man, but rather as deviations in the
structure of that particular patient's existence. Thus, the realization finally grew that in order to quell the doubts and anxieties
that they had been living with, these therapists would have to
turn their attention away from specific techniques and specific
dynamisms, concentrate their efforts instead on the analysis of
the underlying assumptions about human nature, and try to

arrive at a structure on which all specific therapeutic systems could be based. Since the fundamental problem had to do with an understanding of man as a person, only an approach that took such an aim seriously could hope to be successful.

It is perhaps apparent that when a handful of psychologists and psychiatrists begin to tell the majority of their colleagues that the best thing that psychology needs is a better theory of man, or that it needs to understand the fundamental reality underlying all human situations, or that the next decade of research should be directed towards analyzing the structure of human existence, one can rest assured that objections and resistance will emerge. May (1958), of course, was not unaware of this, and he realized that not all of the criticism would be constructive and directed to the proper issues. He felt that the fundamental reason for the wrong type of resistance would be in the attitude of the objectors, and he classified the types of resistance as follows: (1) the attitude, not necessarily limited to psychology, that all the basic discoveries have already been made, and all that is left for the rest of us is to fill in the details; (2) the attitude whereby one shies away from broad questions and direct dealings with holistic phenomena because of the fear of the reencroachment of philosophy on psychology; and (3) the fact that most American psychologists are technique-oriented and tend to become impatient with any endeavor that tries to search for the foundations upon which the techniques can be properly based.

If we try to understand the last two sources of resistance, i.e., the fear of philosophy overtaking psychology again, and the predilection for methodology, we can see that they are closely correlated with the philosophy behind the natural sciences. The stress on the distinction between philosophy and science is based on the presupposition that sciences are autonomous, and this presupposition rests on the privileged position assigned to methodology. Sciences are believed to be autonomous because their methods differ from philosophical methods. But we have already seen that the privileged position of methodology is in reality the privileged position of *approach*, which in turn is really a philosophical viewpoint. Thus, sciences may have methods that are different from philosophical methods, but they are not thereby divorced from philosophy. In addition, even if it were true, the very choice to make methodological concerns the privileged position implies a philosophical position. Even though psychology may be ignorant of its philosophical rootedness, these very resistances imply a certain attitude on the part of traditional clinical psychologists that already reflects the influence of the natural scientific approach. They expect new breakthroughs in knowledge to be expressed in natural scientific terms, and they expect the new knowledge to be related to methodology. Thus any new movement that does not fit these expectations, such as the movement to conceive psychology as a human science, can expect resistance, and will take some time to be understood, let alone accepted. Again, not that the humanistic viewpoint is antimethodological, but it is much broader than mere methodology.

However, the influence of the scientific approach on clinical psychology is not limited to the attitudes and expectations of the clinicians. We know that psychoanalysis is an integral part of clinical psychology; and there are, and have been, frequent statements about the influence of the scientific approach on Freud. We refer, of course, to the familiar distinction that Freud's techniques were good, but that his view of man was limited. Bonner (1965), e.g., in speaking about the limitations of psychoanalysis, cites three major drawbacks. The first is its mechanistic bias, the second is its deterministic dogma, and the third is its hedonistic fallacy which is really based on the genetic bias.

With respect to this critique of Freud, we can see that it parallels very much what May (1958) was saying about clinical psychology in general. There is not a single word about techniques or methods, but there is an almost total rejection of Freud's theory of man. Secondly, if we look at the nature of these critiques, we find that they are based upon the philosophical view of man that Freud held. That is, Freud was being criticized for being mechanistic and deterministic, and for relying on the genetic bias. But these are precisely the characteristics of the natural scientific approach that we listed above. Hence, this is another way that the viewpoint of the natural sciences entered into the domain of clinical psychology; it is the cornerstone of a good deal of theorizing about psychological man.

Needleman (1963) explains in a more detailed fashion how the approach of the natural sciences influenced psychoanalysis. He points out how the natural sciences are one explanatory system among many in the history of thought. Needleman further asserts that it is characteristic of any explanatory system to cover something less than the entire universe of knowledge and experience, and that in addition, what is permitted to enter into an explanatory system is usually limited and well defined. For the natural sciences, one aspect of phenomena, processes, or things is given the privileged position of primitive facts: their spatio-temporal aspect. But the general notion of objective space-time is itself a result of another presupposition of the natural sciences considered as an explanatory system, and this more fundamental presupposition is the definition of corporeality, understood as pure corporeality. The Cartesian influence is obvious here.

However, as Needleman demonstrates, in biology the concept of corporeality was tranformed again. Instead of things, we find organisms, which are a peculiar kind of thing, but nevertheless still a thing, i.e., a phenomenon considered in objective space-time. An organism is a complex thing; and where in physics there are forces, in biology there are tropisms, instincts, and drives; where in physics there are elementary particles, in biology there are genes, etc. Needleman concludes as follows: Biology is a modification of physics in this sense—irreducible reality for the purposes of biology is spatio-temporal thinghood insofar as its functions in a living organism, itself a highly complex spatio-temporal thing. Needleman is equally perceptive in pointing out that the concept, of pure corporeality that results in such a viewpoint of biology is the product of a frame of mind, or attitude, or, if you will, if a methodological dictate: to keep the self out of its world as it investigates "the" world. Or, as Needleman (1963, p. 42) expresses it elsewhere: science demands the reduction of phenomenon to fact, fact being understood as a phenomenon devoid of consciousness and human selfhood. Obviously, as Needleman goes on to observe, psychology, the science of human consciousness and behavior, is in a strained position.

Needleman (1963) then goes on to make more explicit how this difficulty is resolved. Psychology, conceived as a natural science, is faced with the apparently absurd and self-contradictory task of investigating consciousness as part of the realm of *res extensa,* or of things. This is self-contradictory because it is of the essence of the Cartesian *res extensa* that it is what appears to consciousness, or what exists independently of consciousness. In brief, psychology must strip consciousness of consciousness in order to investigate consciousness scientifically. But, surprisingly enough, Needleman shows that that is precisely what Freud accomplished! The doctrine of the unconscious is the attempt to view consciousness as that which is essentially in the realm of *res extensa.* Thus Needleman concludes that psychoanalysis is the science that explains psychic phenomena by the reduction of these phenomena initially to their instinctual components. Or to say the same thing differently, psychoanalysis transforms phenomena as it encounters them into their function in relation to drives and needs (Needleman, 1963). To understand the full impact of this statement, we should not forget that drives and needs are related to organisms, which are more or less complex things.

On the other hand, Needleman (1963) claims that while Freud reduced phenomena to drives and needs, he did not eliminate all traces of intentionality, although it was a kind of intentionality in which no essential reference is made to a self as agent. Apparently, Freud was one of the first thinkers to propound a theory with such a curious mixture. He met the primitive demand of science to remove the self of consciousness from the field of investigation, and yet he described phenomena that were instrinsically intentional in such a way that their intentional features were retained explicitly although he never used the term "intentional" himself.

It is for this reason that Binswanger (1963b) can state that Freud's concept of man was that of a *homo natura,* or natural man. To Binswanger, it is obvious that a natural scientific approach to man will end up with natural man. Binswanger

(1963a, p. 156) quotes a single sentence from Freud which reveals most succinctly the influence of the scientific method on psychoanalysis: "In our method, observed phenomena must take second place to forces that are merely hypothesized." Binswanger notes that the above sentence reflects the genuine natural scientific spirit. Hence, Binswanger (1963a) stresses that the idea of *homo natura* which is psychoanalytic man, is a genuine natural scientific, biopsychological idea of the organism. The reality of the phenomenal, its uniqueness and independence, is absorbed by the hypothesized forces, drives, and the laws that govern them (Binswanger, 1963a).

Medard Boss (1962) quotes the identical sentence that Binswanger used as the basis of his point of departure from a strict Freudian view of man. His complaint is against the mechanical and rigidly technical way in which so many psychological phenomena are being "explained." He feels that such "explanations" are in reality intellectual short-circuits, and he sees at the root of the problem the interpretation of that key term, "psychodynamics." Whatever the many meanings attributed to this word are, Boss (1962) claims that the interpretation of the term has been reduced to mean forces and energies, and he cites Freud's role in such a reduction. He states that Freud aimed at nothing less than at making the psychic phenomena quantifiable, calculable, predictable, etc. This resulted in the classical psychological theories' ambition to discover the "psychodynamic" causal connections among the different psychic formations, and especially in discovering the very first cause in each causal chain. It was assumed that the elimination of the cause would result in the disappearance of all the pathological effects (Boss, 1962). The very language that Boss uses in his critique illustrates the influence of this natural scientific approach.

We must not lose sight of our goal. Our intention is not a full-fledged critique of Freud, but rather the aim is to show that even clinical psychology is conceived in terms of the natural sciences, and there is still one more influence that we feel should be mentioned. That influence is clinical psychology's early relationship with medicine, and the lasting influence that medicine had on clinical psychology.

Needleman (1963) convincingly demonstrates how medicine took over the biological concept of organism; thus viewing man as a natural man very much as did Freud. Thus, for Needleman, the irreducible reality for the purposes of medicine is spatiotemporal thinghood insofar as it functions in or has reference to the human organism, itself a highly complex organism among organisms. However, such a description is almost purely biological, and Needleman adds that medicine, conceived as the science of healing, has a special "value context" to add to that description. The "value context" to be added is that medicine is concerned with the health of the organism. Hence, in medicine, Needleman (1963) continues, phenomena as they appear are not transformed into facts as such, but into symptoms, i.e., determinants of health, disease, or malfunction. But in this sense, a symptom is simply a value-laden biological fact. It is a biological fact that has reference to the functioning of a specific organism (man), or in Needleman's (1963) terms, biological facts contain a special teleological reference, the health of the organism. However, what we would like to stress here is the assumption that a symptom is first and primarily a fact in the sense in which we have previously used it in this discussion, i.e., a phenomenon devoid of consciousness and human selfhood.

That this interpretation is correct receives some corroboration from Maslow (1954, pp.31, 32). In order to try to organize the data dealing with certain aspects of personality, Maslow wanted to use the concept "syndrome," but he notes that this concept is borrowed from medicine and hence he tries to strip it of its medical meaning precisely because in its medical sense it is a hindrance for psychology. Why is its medical connotation a hindrance? Mostly because in medicine it has been used in a merely additive sense. A syndrome is a list of symptoms (like a list of facts), rather than an organized and interdependent structure. Furthermore, in medicine, the syndrome has been used in a causal context; each symptom is caused (as is a fact) and then a group of symptoms, in turn, can be the cause of something else. That is, like natural scientific facts, symptoms have external relations with other symptoms and a syndrome is understood to consist of correlated causes. It is precisely these medical connotations that Maslow tries to get rid of, and although he keeps the terms "syndrome" and "symptom," one can see that he tries to define them differently. We could perhaps summarize this discussion by saying that in stripping the concept "syndrome" of its medical connotations, Maslow is trying to rid it of its natural scientific usage.

Thus, there can be little doubt left that the natural scientific approach has had a profound influence on clinical psychology. We needed to consider the way medicine contributed to the *natural scientific approach* to clinical psychology, because with the usage of the term "symptom" or "syndrome," or if we generalize further we could say "function," we have a clear indication of the way in which the natural scientific approach has most directly influenced clinical psychology. We can say that clinical psychology, under the influence of the natural scientific approach, operated with the implicit assertion that *function precedes existence*. The key point is that a function for an organism is the biological equivalent of a fact for physics. Binswanger (1963b) describes this process as the attempt to create a psychology that serves to bring a reified functional complex into relation with a material "organ" (e.g., brain). The important point here is that functions are reified. Thus, "function precedes existence" means that a phenomenon *is* to the extent that it meets the preestablished, but often implicit and radically unclarified, criteria of reified function. Whatever phenomenon or event is observed that cannot fit into this concept is simply not qualified to receive psychological consideration. Thus, despite the different expressions, we can see that the same fundamental attitude is behind both the academic and clinical side of psychology; and furthermore, we can trace this attitude directly to its source, viz., the influence of the natural scientific approach on psychology. We have also seen that the impact of this attitude has been both powerful and pervasive.

In order to avoid possible misunderstandings, it should be noted that we are not saying that every other psychologist except phenomenologists submits to this attitude, or that in the history of psychology there have been no other opponents of this viewpoint. Our own discussion of the historical background proved otherwise. What we are saying is that a large majority of contemporary psychologists were trained in such a way that they were introduced to this viewpoint uncritically, and with the attitude that the fundamental approach of psychology is correct, although it could undoubtedly undergo minor refinement and revision of various sorts. We are saying that the basic kind of psychology that is being taught and communicated in the mainstream of our field is essentially a natural scientific psychology that is simply presumed to be the only psychology that there is or can be. Most psychologists are simply unaware that it can be conceived another way.

A contemporary example will demonstrate the persistence of the points we have been discussing. Arnold Buss (1966) has recently published a book entitled *Psychopathology*. One does not have to read very far in this text to find the natural scientific bias we have been speaking of. The very first paragraph of the Preface to this volume reads as follows:

> Two assumptions underlie the organization and content of this book. The first is that the exposition should be rigorous and systematic. This means that observations should be separated from explanations, data from inferences, and facts from theories. We shall start with facts—the events to be explained—and then proceed to an understanding of these events. The "events" of psychopathology consist of symptoms. (Buss, 1966, p. vii)

That is, a symptom is a fact.

His second assumption is equally interesting.

> The second assumption is that progress may be marked by advances from the clinic to the laboratory. In any field, the early, crude, qualitative observations are supplanted by later, refined, quantitative data. At first the clinician's subjective observations and inferences predominate and are the basis of most knowledge. Later the laboratory researcher's objective, quantitative data predominate and are the basis of most knowledge. . . . We favor facts obtained in the controlled context of the laboratory over observations made in the less controlled context of the clinic. (Buss, 1966, p.viii)

Once again, the influence of the natural scientific approach is palpably evident.

While Buss distinguishes between objective and subjective symptoms, he still adopts a medical model to understand symptoms. He states:

A sign (an objective symptom) is any aspect of the individual's functioning that indicates abnormality. In medicine it would be biological dysfunction, which might indicate an underlying disease process. In psychopathology it would be psychological dysfunction, which might indicate an underlying "disease" process. (Buss, 1966, p. 15)

Lastly Buss defines a syndrome as a group of symptoms that occur together. The role of the medical model is apparent.

Thus our investigations have demonstrated that psychology, both clinical and academic, has indeed been influenced by the approach of the natural sciences. If we ask why this approach has had such a powerful impact, we have to answer it was precisely because psychology's ambition was to move itself ever away from its philosophical ties and to move in the direction of the positive and natural sciences because it was under the impression that this was the only way it could achieve its status as a science.

Some Current Critiques of Psychology

Thus, the dominant trend in psychology has been psychology conceived as a natural science, and it has led to the kind of restrictions that have been outlined in the previous section. Just as in other instances of narrowing or forced closure, this attempt at delimiting psychology prematurely also sparked a reaction, and it will be fruitful for us to see just what kind of reaction has set in in order to see what light it will throw upon the current interpretation of scientific psychology.

At one time there were only certain key sources where one could find expressions concerning disappointment with the trend and direction of traditional psychology, but now there are so many examples we can only select some representative statements. Other recent books dealing with such a critique of traditional psychology are: Bugental's (1965) *The Search for Authenticity,* Lyons' (1963) *Psychology and the Measure of Man,* and van Kaam's (1966) *Existential Foundations of Psychology*. However, our survey is an independent one that indicates and documents some repetitive themes critical of traditional psychology that have been appearing with increasing frequency since the mid-fifties.

PSYCHOLOGY LACKS REAL UNITY

This theme has appeared in many ways and by a number of authors. Allport (1955) has pointed out that psychology is such an amorphus subject matter that statements concerning psychology lose their meaning unless the type of psychology at which they are directed is specified. He also points out that psychology is equally hampered by a multiplicity of approaches and a scattering of only partially related facts. Sonneman (1954) spoke about the split in psychology that not only divides theories about commonly accepted subject matter and their problems, but involves such elementary points as the definition of subject matter, the conceptualization of problems, the aim of knowledge itself, and scientific method. MacLeod (1965) has spoken of the mere semblance of unity in psychology; Kahn and Santostefano (1962) have written of the identity crisis of clinical psychology; and Sanford (1965) has spoken of psychology as fragmented.

The fact that psychologists have experienced the lack of unity as a dissatisfaction can only imply that they expect psychology to be unified. It means that they expect psychology's growth to be guided; they expect various facets of its field to be interrelated. Contrary to these expectations, however, in fact, psychology's growth has been due more to proliferation than to an in-depth development of major problems; it has been opportunistic and hasty, rather than judicious and selective. Furthermore, not only are the aspects of its fields not interrelated, but members of various subdivisions are even hostile to one another, not for reasons of personality, but for stereotyped reasons of category and classification, e.g., certain experimentalists and clinicians. Thus, psychology lacks an awareness of its own unity, and hence also lacks a real unity. The correction, in terms of aims, is simple: psychology should explore, discover, and articulate the basis of its unity. The achievement of this aim is more difficult.

How does one discover the basic unity of a science? By what means is this achieved? These are key questions that psychology must start considering despite their metapsychological implications. Thus, the first theme of the critique of traditional psychology is that it lacks unity and the correction would be to provide that unity.

PSYCHOLOGY LACKS DIRECTION

Obviously, if a given discipline is experienced as lacking unity, one would not be surprised to hear that it lacks direction. This is precisely the case with psychology. Koch (1959) has written that psychology needs a recentering and that it should be assessing its goals with respect to its indigenous problems. Wolfle (1959) has explicitly stated that psychology has not one sense of direction, but rather several unsure directions. Sanford (1965) has stated that psychology needs new methods for new problems —or, in other words, it needs a change of direction.

Just as in our consideration of the lack of unity, the correction of this second critique in terms of what is needed is simple: psychology should be provided with a direction. But what is this direction? Has psychology ever articulated its goals? On what basis? Could it be that psychology is blind to its proper goal? If it is, how can it discover its proper goal? It can do this only when it resolves the problem of its direction. It can know that it is going in the right direction only if it knows *where* it is going. But the complaint is precisely that psychology is not sure of *where* it is going—so how can it know its own goal? The relation to the first problem is obvious; one can have unity only if one has a goal, and a goal if one has direction. One may object that certainly there are enough statements about psychology's scientific aspirations and about its intentions to predict and control behavior. But, then, why is there not agreement such as there is in physics? Because one has to make a distinction between what psychology today de facto is, and what it ought to be; or between what psychology actually *is* and what its potentials are. According to these psychologists, it is not all that it should be, and that is because it never was completely sure of where it was going. Thus, psychology needs to discover its true direction. Again, this is not so much a solution but simply a better way to state the problem: How does one determine the direction, or the goal, of a science? How does a science become what it is? How are the data that fill textbooks selected? Again, we merely raise the questions here and hold in abeyance the possible answers until we have covered all of the problems, for our position is that the answer to all of these questions is essentially the same.

PSYCHOLOGY SHOULD CEASE ITS STRICT EMULATION OF THE NATURAL SCIENCES

If one wants to know why psychology is what it is today, the single most comprehensive answer is that psychology developed along the lines of the natural sciences of the nineteenth century. It is precisely this de facto development that is being questioned more and more.

Bugental (1963), for example, has directly challenged the model of the natural sciences as being appropriate for psychology. Sanford (1965) has claimed that psychology has a naïve view of science. Koch (1959) has acutely observed that psychology's institutionalization preceded its content and that its methods preceded its problems, and consequently, he has suggested that we should reexamine the characteristics of our scientific objectives. Lastly, Bakan (1965) has indicated that psychology had a preconceived notion of what it ought to be.

But where did this preconceived notion come from? By now we know that it came from the approach of the natural sciences. It would seem superfluous to have to document that fact today. But what is worthy of note is that this conception of psychology is being challenged. Of that there is little doubt; and this challenge of the natural scientific conception of psychology is the third problem we would like to emphasize. What are the implications of this criticism? The proposed corrections are almost as numerous as the individuals suggesting them. If there were as much agreement on the correction as on the complaint, there would be no problem with respect to psychology's direction. At the moment, we will content ourselves with the statement that whatever it should be, or is, psychology should not be a natural science in the sense that physics and chemistry are.

PSYCHOLOGY HAS NOT BEEN INVESTIGATING
MEANINGFUL PHENOMENA IN A MEANINGFUL WAY

This critique implies that psychology has not been investigating meaningful phenomena, or, if it has, it has not been doing it in a meaningful way. Sanford (1965) has shown how psychology has accented the sheer production of knowledge rather than the relevant organization of its knowledge. Allport (1955) has suggested that psychology should enlarge its horizons so that it can encompass more relevant problems, and he has openly lamented that psychology has relatively little to offer to the major problem of human relationships (Allport, 1947). MacLeod (1965) has shown how psychology has been cluttered with little methods and little conceptual structures rather than involved with issues that have broad significance. Lastly, Koch (1959) has claimed that the main difficulty running through Study I was that an adequate theory of definition was lacking.

This complaint shows that something basic is wrong with psychology. It acknowledges that many of the problems that psychology deals with are essentially irrelevant. Or, if a problem is a relevant one, there are often no adequate means for coping with it. Too often phenomena are studied more on the basis of the availability of methods than on how the phenomena appear and what they would require. Once again, the correction in terms of overall direction is fairly obvious—psychology should deal with meaningful problems in a meaningful way—but the implementation of this aim is still problematic. How does one determine meaningful problems in science? What are the criteria whereby one knows that one is handling a problem in a meaningful way? Thus the whole question of meaningful problems and meaningful methods is raised anew. And necessarily so because the overemphasis on one approach that limits the kinds of methods that can be employed has not been fruitful for psychology.

Another way of delineating psychological phenomena has to be found. We can state it as the problem of determining the essence of psychological phenomena without implying by this terminology that these essences are eternal or immutable and so on. To discover the essence of phenomena also means that they can be distinguished from other phenomena in a meaningful way and therefore the problem of the meaning of phenomena is simultaneously being considered. Again, the main problem here is more with the execution of the aim than with the admission of its necessity.

PSYCHOLOGY LACKS HOLISTIC METHODS

This lack was made explicit by Sanford (1965) who pointed out that psychology needs a fresh approach with respect to methodology. MacLeod (1965) has demonstrated that psychology was cluttered with little methods that were adequate only for trivial problems. Allport (1955) has written that what is small and partial, and what is peripheral and opportunistic in psychology, are what have received the chief attention of the system builders. This theme indicates that psychology's strength is with part-functions and with details of analysis, and that it does not adequately cope with wholes, frames-of-reference, or syntheses. But the very existence of this complaint shows that it is proper for psychology to have such concerns and that it could well give thought to this type of problem. The execution of this aim is likewise difficult, but since when does science shirk from difficult problems? Are not the giants of science precisely those who tackled and mastered the most difficult problems? Methods whereby one can do justice to "whole phenomena" are indeed hard to come by, but can psychology advance only when it borrows methods from other sciences? Can it not develop its own methods for its own problems, and perhaps contribute to other sciences instead of merely borrowing from them? In short, psychology must take the problem of "holistic phenomena" seriously and acknowledge that techniques that are not currently at its disposal are necessary for coping with a large number of psychological phenomena.

TRADITIONAL PSYCHOLOGY DOES NOT DO JUSTICE TO THE HUMAN PERSON

This is one of the more obvious problems. Allport (1955) has mentioned that psychology left out man's becoming. Koch (1959; 1961) has written that psychology was not, but should be, adequate to man, and he has expressed the opinion that the climate of the field was such that it did not encourage development of sensibility in humanistic domains. That a new view of man that stressed his freedom and courage would be a wholesome thing for psychology has also been suggested (Pervin, 1960). It has been stated that psychologists do not have sensitivity to human experience, but that they should receive training that would provide this kind of sensitivity (Sanford, 1965). In fact, Sanford (1965) makes it clear that the main thrust of his critique is directed against a state of affairs in which the advocates of a particular kind of psychology—a psychology without a person— have been able to gain and maintain power through putting across the idea that they are the representatives in psychology of true science. Bakan (1965) reinforces this point by indicating how the muteness of animals eliminates many complications in research, and how their domestication insures mastery or control on the part of the experimenter.

In short, this theme asserts that the very concepts, methods, and approaches that psychology uses practically render impossible an adequate study of man. Moreover, these writers are clear on how to get out of the impasse: We should get concepts, methods and approaches that are adequate to man. They all affirm that this aim is consonant with the idea of psychology as a science. In other words, with respect to the impasse between existing methods and theories of psychology and the adequate study of man, these writers opt for studying man adequately, and choose to struggle with the problem of finding methods to do so.

PSYCHOLOGY'S RELEVANCE TO THE LIFE-WORLD (*LEBENSWELT*) IS DEFICIENT

While only Sanford (1965) and Allport (1947) stressed this problem, it was implied by others, e.g., Barker (1965). This theme was expressed by statements like: psychology should get closer to everyday living, and psychology should study problems people really worry about (Sanford, 1965); or by Allport's (1947, p. 183) concern over "the scarcity of scientific findings, and even of serviceable concepts and well formulated problems, that psychology has to offer *of the type that is being sought.*" (Allport's emphasis.)

The most obvious implication of such a criticism is that psy-

chology is not yet adequately dealing with the problem of everyday life. But surely, one could object, there are all sorts of ways
in which psychologists are active in everyday life, and there is
even a branch of our field that is exclusively concerned with these
problems, viz., applied psychology. Well, then, what can Sanford
and Allport mean? Obviously, they are not referring to the
human factors specialist who is working on a complex military or
space system, nor to the market analyst who is trying to find out
whether blue, horizontal boxes or red, octagonal boxes will sell
more Wheaties. These are the kinds of so-called applied problems
that psychology deals with. They are "applied" problems in the
sense that psychology can apply scientific principles and methods
to problems that do not arise primarily within the field of psychology itself. But the main point is that such endeavors still
remain within the perspective of an already established scientific psychology.

However, the point that Sanford and Allport are making, and
one that we would also stress, is that no science is completely
removed from everyday life, and some kind of *dialogue* with
everyday life must go on. The relationship is not a unilateral
one, and it is not simply a matter of applying science to the
everyday world. That is why applied psychology does not really
fill this need—because it deals with everyday problems on its own
terms, i.e., by first translating the problem into a scientific expression, and then solving it. That is one way, but it is mostly
a one-way street; scientific psychology imposing on everyday
life. Thus there is a gap between psychological facts and every-
day-living problems because psychology is not sufficiently receptive to those problems precisely as they exist in everyday life.
In other words, a completely different attitude is called for,
one that places more of a privileged position on the side of the
"everyday problems" rather than on the side of the scientific
principles of psychology. It calls for more of a dialogue between
the two "worlds." It implies that the transformation of these
problems into "scientific" terms essentially transforms the problems. Thus, the corrective implied by this theme would assert
that it is perfectly legitimate for psychology to deal with those
problems that are bothering most people in everyday life, but

it must be precisely in the way those people experience them—
i.e., as unique, living, human beings. Or again, we should be able
to cope with the problems of the life-world *(Lebenswelt)* in a
better way.

Discussion of Contemporary Critiques of Psychology

Thus, we have covered the seven themes or problems around
which the contemporary criticisms of psychology revolve. It
should be kept in mind that these criticisms have all come from
within psychology, and they have all been voiced by contemporary psychologists. However, by now the reader is surely aware
that the criticisms being voiced are not unique to the contemporary period; they have been with psychology since its inception.
Consequently, one cannot say that these difficulties are the result
of a recent change of direction of psychology. Nor are they the
consequence of a purposeless drifting that is contemporary in
origin. Psychology has always lived with these problems. This
is perhaps merely another way of saying that it is a young science,
or better still, that perhaps psychology is still struggling to
achieve its proper conception and frame of reference. We interpret the persistence of these critical themes as indicating the
latter.

This interpretation is not merely based on the persistence of
such critical themes; it arises primarily because they are of such
a vital and significant nature. Moreover, historically speaking,
it is demonstrable that the beginnings of most sciences are characterized by false starts, multiple viewpoints, and constant questioning of foundations. Nor is the critique of traditional natural
scientific psychology meant to be a condemnation of it in the
historical sense. There is probably no other way that psychology
could have begun. The only point is whether those who do see
another possibility, another way of conducting and understanding the science of psychology, have the freedom to attempt a new
beginning because, whether rightly or wrongly, they feel that
continuing in the same direction is no longer fruitful.

Another way of ascertaining the validity of our interpretation that psychology's frame of reference needs revision is by noting whether or not the de facto frame of reference of natural scientific psychology is adequate, i.e. whether it can be applied fruitfully across the board, and whether it is accepted by all. But we have already seen that this was precisely one of the critiques. As pointed out earlier, in 1892 James (p.468) said that the natural scientific assumptions were subject to revision; in 1931 Woodworth (p.3) stated that "his object [was] to bring forward unsettled questions of fundamental importance, questions on which keen debate is going on, *doubts whether psychology is on the right track,* efforts on the part of one or another *leader to steer the group in some new direction"* (my emphases); and in 1963 Bugental directly challenged the relevance of the natural scientific model. Thus, while many have accepted this viewpoint, and others have staunchly defended it, it has not been without its challengers.

Lastly, our interpretation that the thematic critiques outlined above indicate a basic flaw in the conception and frame of reference of psychology can be supported by showing the difficulties encountered by maintaining the natural scientific conception, and the fruitfulness of adopting another frame of reference. The rest of this book will deal with the latter point; here we will deal with the former one. Our position is that the adoption of the natural scientific frame of reference, or the wish to be a natural science, is not just one theme among the rest; it is the most important theme—and consequently its critique the most important critique—in the sense that it is responsible for all of the other critiques of psychology we have outlined. If it is not responsible for the sheer existence of all of the other problems, it is responsible at least for their poor formulation and for the belated attempts to take them seriously. Let us demonstrate this.

How did psychology's commitment to be a natural science come about? How carefully was it thought through? Were other factors involved? As we have already seen (e.g., Koch, 1959), the commitment to be a natural science antedated the existence of psychology itself. Thus, most of the criteria that psychology had to meet to fulfill its commitment were already in existence, and we can legitimately say that the sources of the criteria were external to psychology. We also saw that at least one other prime factor was involved, and that was an equally strong desire to break from philosophy and from its emphasis on speculation. In those times, even the hesitant ones held an attitude something like "making psychology a science may not be the whole answer, but it is certainly better than remaining with philosophy." The idea was that *after* joining the ranks of science, psychology could have the luxury of taking its time and seeing where it was headed. However, more often than not, the provisional aspect of joining the ranks of science was forgotten, and most of the theoretical effort went into demonstrating or proving how psychology was a science. Thus, the leap itself was not carefully thought through; it was presupposed. And what was being written about the science of psychology, at least among those who argued for its scientific status, was always within the context of demonstrating that *it was a science*. Obviously, this is not the same as raising the more fundamental question of *whether* psychology was a science, and if it was, what kind. For all of these reasons, we feel that psychology's commitment to be a science, which almost always was interpreted as meaning that it should be a natural science, was premature and unwarranted.

Before we continue, one brief digression is in order; we must mention one point that cannot be discussed fully nor avoided completely. We feel compelled to state the obvious fact that natural scientific psychology has been at least partially successful. If it had not, there would be no psychology at all today. Must not this success also be taken into account? Indeed it must. But even more important are questions such as: why was it successful? what are the criteria of success? and, lastly, to what extent were the successes due to psychology itself, or to related, more mature disciplines? Briefly, our answer would be that it was successful partially because there was no earlier psychology, as a separate discipline, with which to compare its own results; partially because its modes of operations met the cultural expectations of the times; and partially, obviously, because it was also doing something right. But the latter point does not necessarily mean that psychology itself understood fully just why it was doing something right. As with all sciences, this knowledge unfolds over time, and often when a discipline begins to understand its own operations better, it usually understands ways of achieving the same aim differently—i.e., that is precisely when it begins to do things differently.

We can now return to our matter at hand, which is that of demonstrating how the commitment to be a natural science is indirectly responsible for the presence of all of the other critical themes that have emerged from the writings of some contemporary psychologists. It is responsible for the lack of unity in psychology because the full range of psychology's subject matter never fit conveniently into the concepts and methods prescribed by the natural sciences. Some psychologists wanted to acknowledge that the so-called elusive phenomena (e.g., mind, consciousness, etc.) actually existed, but then found it difficult to submit such phenomena to rigorous investigation according to the prescriptions of the natural scientific approach, and proceeded to ignore the approach and tried to devise methods for the phenomena as they knew them. Other psychologists were primarily committed to the approach of the natural sciences, and when they experienced difficulty in applying the techniques of the scientific approach, they reduced or denied the relevance of those phenomena for psychology as a *science* and thus remained true to their initial commitment. Thus, there was a divisiveness in psychology right away; a psychologist had to opt either for fidelity to the phenomena, or for fidelity to science. However, such an option would not have been necessary if a commitment to the natural scientific idea of science was not present, or even if this idea was present, if these psychologists did not experience certain difficulties in applying the natural scientific idea of science to psychology. The facts, however, show that both were present; thus, psychology began with a disunity which is related to the idea of science it tried to implement.

Once unity is missing, directions are multiple. This conflict is still not basically resolved by psychology, and one of the directions still being offered is that of the natural sciences. But we have already seen that intrinsic reasons *why* psychology should be a natural science have never been able to be sustained without a concomitant reduction in phenomena. Consequently, the sheer presence of natural scientific models, which have never been fully justified except in the sense that psychology believes it should be a natural science, is sufficient to cause a tension in the directions of psychology. Again, the tension is between fidelity to the phenomena, or fidelity to a certain idea of science.

It is easily demonstrable that the natural scientific commitment is also responsible for the criticism that psychology has not been dealing with meaningful phenomena. There is no attempt to deny here that the majority of psychologists have chosen the natural scientific frame of reference for psychology. But that is also why phenomena such as mind, consciousness, experience, etc. have been relatively ignored. It is an operational proof of the inability of the methods, techniques and concepts of the natural sciences to cope with such phenomena. Even if psychologists choose to deny their relevance for psychology (very few today deny that such phenomena exist), it is clear that this is a stance that is assumed by them, and one which must be proven, not merely stated. In any event, historically, psychologists began to ignore those areas in which their techniques and methods were deficient, and they turned increasingly towards those domains in which they were successful with their methods. Note, however, the implicit assumption that is present: psychologists should work in those areas where their methods are successful! The selection is not based upon the areas that are important. It should not be forgotten that, worse still, the guiding idea of the scientific method *preceded* psychology's existence.

This is why the point that psychology has neglected the essence of its phenomena could emerge. Psychology rarely dealt with the phenomena as such; it always saw the phenomena in the light of the method to be used. Or, as we said earlier, the implicit attitude was that "measurement precedes existence," and thus psychology has essentially been dealing with "measured phenomena" which are not the equivalent of the "essential phenomena" or the phenomena as they are lived and experienced.

The same reason holds for why the lack of meaningful problems came to be a theme of our critics. If one is committed to the methods of the natural sciences, and one has to try to deal with subject matter like a living human being, something has to give, because those methods were never intended to be used on such a subject matter. The extrapolation to man was performed by the psychologists themselves. As noted earlier, in the conflict between fidelity to scientific methodology and fidelity to the phenomena (in this case man), almost all early psychologists opted for the methodology. Thus, psychology became more and more a natural science, and less and less human, and therefore less meaningful for man in general. This also explains why psychology has not done justice to the human person; it was a choice away from the human person, even if this choice was not fully explicit and its ramifications were not all seen.

Why holistic methods were not developed is also readily understandable once it is obvious that psychology committed itself in the direction of the natural sciences. The whole strength of the natural sciences is in methods that depend upon analysis and reduction, and that are directed toward elemental processes and isolated stimuli. Thus, when psychology borrowed its fundamental concepts and methods from the natural sciences, it essentially borrowed techniques of fractionation and analysis. No holistic *methods* were in the natural scientific armamentarium. Of course, the natural sciences did go through their descriptive and taxonomic phases, and it must be kept in mind that we have noted that the natural sciences that psychology wanted to initiate were already mature at the time psychology was being born. Thus, even if direct imitation were the proper course for psychology, psychology should have imitated the historical development of the natural sciences, and should not have chosen to imitate the particular phase of growth the natural sciences coincidentally happened to be in when psychology came on the scene. The wholesale takeover of natural scientific terms, expressions, methods, etc., that psychology indulged in was really the assumption of a whole world-view.

Lastly, the lack of dialogue with the life-world is also understandable since the whole movement of science is always away from things as they are in the world. Thus scientists create their own conditions in laboratories and often manipulate variables that are specifically created for the purpose, and are often non-existent in the life-world (e.g., pure tones or pure colors). Psychology also chose this mode of operation when it adopted the methods of natural sciences as models.

Thus, we feel that psychology's commitment to be a natural science, is, in a way, at the root of all the other problems raised by the contemporary psychologists. And it must not be forgotten that this very commitment was also a theme of the critics. That is, they now feel that psychology should no longer be bound by this commitment. If our analyses are correct, it means that we can now have a fresh start on many of these key problems.

The Approach Proper to the Study of Man as a Person Is Different from the Approach of the Natural Sciences

We can begin our discussion with the following questions: Will psychology's dilemmas—meaning by this the problems outlined by the contemporary critics—be resolved by a better execution of the same type of approach, or will a radically different approach be necessary? It is our judgment that a radically different approach is needed. Is this radical approach so different that one can no longer use the term "science" to describe it in a meaningful way? It is our judgment that the radical approach which psychology ought to be applying can still be conceived under the general heading of science, in some sense of that term. Our radicality consists in exchanging the adjective "human" for the adjective "natural," so that psychology becomes a human science.

We will document this transformation more fully later, but at the moment we wish merely to present some preliminary reasons for the change. First of all, we have already seen that psychology became a natural science more from desire than from fittingness. A simple reflection shows that this de facto historical occurrence is not necessarily binding. We have also seen that this approach leads to a study of natural man which does not do full justice to man as person. Man as a person is a richer, fuller, broader, and a more comprehensive concept than is natural man; in fact, the latter concept is actually subsumed under the former in our understanding of the term. We are saying that a full and detailed analysis of man as a person will reveal that he is also, from another viewpoint, a natural man, and from still another viewpoint, an object. We mention this because within certain humanistic circles there is a tendency to delimit humanistic psychology only to the more peculiarly human activities of man. Our concept of man as a person, or the human person, is comprehensive enough to include the highest forms of human activity conceivable, but it is also integrative, that is, it admits of certain prepersonal and objective modes of being as well. We are fully aware of the fact that very different attitudes on the part of investigators are necessary to see man as a person as opposed to biological man or even objectified man, but we are also aware that, concretely, all three "realities" can be found in the same existing person. Thus, since the attitude required for adopting the viewpoint of the natural sciences is more limited than the viewpoint we are describing, better refinement of that attitude will not be the solution we are seeking because the remedy necessitates involvement with precisely those aspects of man that are excluded by the natural scientific perspective. We have already met this in the complaints of therapists and clinicians with the theory of man that psychology presupposed.

It is important to appreciate the point we are making here. If one so chooses, he can conceive of psychology as a natural science, and it is a legitimate undertaking for revealing certain truths about man—especially man as a biological being or man in his determined relations with his environment, etc. We are saying that such a conception cannot do justice to man as a person. For the latter purpose a different *conception* of science is necessary (Giorgi, in press). However, those who favor a natural scientific conception of psychology do want to speak of man as a person. This is where the difficulty appears, and it is this intention to study the entire man by means of a natural scientific conception that permits us to speak of the need of psychology as a whole to be conceived along human scientific lines. If one accepted the limits of the natural scientific conception of psychology, then its findings could be understood as being relative to that frame of reference. However, too often it is presented as *the* frame of reference. But even in the case of the limited frame of reference, one would have to give the reasons for choosing the natural scientific conception of psychology over any other, and one would still be obliged to study man as a person with a different conception of psychology. Thus, we would again be led into the position of conceiving psychology as two separate sciences. For the sake of the unity of psychology and for the sake of doing justice to all of its phenomena, we choose the more comprehensive conception. Lastly, even if one were interested in the biological and determined aspects of man, we would adopt the position that it would still be necessary to stress that it is *man* that is being studied biologically or deterministically and that this knowledge would have interpretive and methodological implications.

The second factor we may note is that psychology was not only running towards the natural sciences, but it was also running away from philosophy. We feel that a new attitude should be adopted whereby psychology makes use of philosophical wisdom just as it utilizes knowledge from other disciplines. Psychology does not hesitate to borrow concepts, methods, or facts from physiology, mathematics, neurology, sociology, anatomy, physics, chemistry, etc. Of course, we know that it does so because it prefers the company of the sciences rather than that of philosophy. But that is precisely the prejudice we would like to correct. That is, there is no intrinsic reason for borrowing only from sister disciplines, except that it is fostered by a special kind of attitude that thinks being associated with other sciences makes one more scientific. This is especially ironic when one considers that contemporary traditional psychology already reflects a philosophical viewpoint. One has only to read Boring (1950) to detect the influences of Cartesian philosophy, British empiricism, and operationism on psychology. Thus, philosophical influences do pervade psychology, and they will continue to do so, and it seems far better to recognize this fact and try to deal with it openly rather than to try to insist that psychology, as a science, has nothing to do with philosophy. We would say that precisely because psychology is a science, it can relate to philosophy without fear of losing its identity or of being reabsorbed into philosophy. While there may be overlapping content, the different methods and approaches make their contributions distinct and complementary.

The reason for attempting to include philosophical knowledge as well as facts derived from other disciplines is that it is from a philosophical perspective that we hope to get an adequate frame of reference for a psychology conceived as a human science. Philosophy is precisely the discipline that is concerned with broad world-views and adequate frames of reference, and it is not surprising that psychology has been weak in precisely these areas during its phase of explicit rejection of philosophy. Thus, an attitude that will explicitly acknowledge philosophical bases and insights is necessary.

A third reason for saying that a different attitude is necessary for coping with psychological problems emerges from an examination of the nature of the problems presented by the themes we were discussing. What is consistent about all of the implied correctives to the criticisms that emerged is that these correctives are not amenable to the methods of the natural sciences. One does not do an experiment on a theory of man; we have already seen that the natural sciences' strength is not with holistic methods; the meaningfulness of a phenomenon for man cannot be determined by measurement techniques, etc. In brief, the very nature of the problems being posed, if we allow them to be described exactly as they are being experienced, (i.e., there are ways of expressing them that would hide rather than reveal them) means that the proven techniques of the natural sciences cannot be successfully employed in resolving them. This does not mean that they are insoluble, or that they should be reduced to meet the methods (the standard techniques). But rather appropriate methods should be invented, or, if they exist already, they should be applied. But this means that a different attitude will be required, and that is the only point we are stressing now.

A fourth reason for a change in attitude results from the introduction of the distinction between the aims of science and the methods whereby those aims are achieved. It is clear from our brief exposition of the history of psychology that psychology has identified the two. It has based its operations on the belief that the only way that it could accomplish its aim as a science was by using the methods of the established sciences. However, it is not difficult to see that this is not a necessary conclusion. One could also attempt the accomplishment of the aim to be a science first by examining the nature of the phenomena that one is dealing with, and then by raising the question of how to study such phenomena in a scientific way, and only then see whether there are existing methods to accomplish the aim or whether new methods have to be invented. However, to follow such a procedure would mean a change of attitude —i.e., it would require the shift from an attitude that presupposes that certain basic questions are answered already, to an attitude that questions precisely those presuppositions.

There is still a fifth reason for demanding a change of attitude on the part of psychology. Traditional psychology is so accustomed to operating under realistic assumptions, and it believes so completely that the facts it deals with are completely sound and immutable, that it never bothers to reflect on the role of the researcher or the psychologist himself, except in the vaguest sense to admit that he is somehow there. But all of our discussion about the approach of the psychologist has shown what a significant role the approach plays. Thus it is not enough merely to note that the researcher is there, but one has to know in what manner he is there, what he expects to find, how he designed the experiment, why he chose the variables he did, etc. In other words, when one wishes to cope with a psychology at the human level, it is not possible to ignore the relationships between subjects and experimenter, nor is it safe to presume that experimenters can be changed freely without affecting the results (Rosenthal, 1966). If this is true, then somehow this fact will have to be taken into account in psychological theory, and this would certainly involve a radical shift for traditional psychology because it operates mostly under the assumption of independent observer rather than participant observer (Giorgi, 1966). In brief, a new attitude that will try to clarify the relationship between the scientist and his data and the scientist and his theory will be necessary for a humanistic psychology. For as Straus (1966) never ceases to point out, science is an exquisitely human creation. And if it is humans who create science, and psychology purports to study humans, then it cannot ignore humans as they are creating science, even their own science, as Maslow (1966) has already stated. But in order to perform this task properly, psychology will have to adopt a different stance.

Very often, one hears objections that if psychology is not a science, then it must be an art. But this is true only for those who think in terms of black-white dichotomies. We are arguing that one can retain the attitude of a scientist while dealing with the subject matter of man as a person. Of course, we must be able to express what the meaning of science is when it is not specifically related to the natural sciences. This is one of the major tasks of this work, and it might take some prolonged discussions. Here we are only concerned with freeing ourselves sufficiently in order to take up the task. That is, is there any justification whatever for wishing to retain the term "science"? Certainly, if we adopt strict definitions of science, i.e., those which define it in terms of the methodology of the natural sciences, we have our hands tied at the outset, and we would have no choice but to leave the scientific attitude. However, there are also broad definitions of science. For example, Warren (1934) defines science as organized or systematic knowledge, and Lyons (1963) defines science as a way of proving that you are wrong—in other words, the deliberate experience of error. If certain phenomena resist the deliberate attempt to contradict them, then there must be something true about them. Of course, these definitions are very general and they could stand some more positive articulation, but their very generality is what gives us some room for expanding the idea of science. Thus, we feel that we are justified in retaining the term "science" even if we do not intend to follow the way it is specified in the natural sciences. We will try to spell out our meaning of science by observing how scientists actually go about their tasks.

In addition, we wish to retain the term "human" for our enterprise because human beings are the subject matter of our study.

Obviously, however, more than this is necessary since there can be many sciences that have for their subject matter human beings —e.g., medicine, anatomy, sociology, etc. Thus, we must add that we will take a human attitude with respect to our subject matter. The key problem here, of course, is to make explicit precisely how a human attitude differs from all other attitudes, e.g., objective or biological. This, too, is a major task, but at present we will state that the adjective "human" implies that we hope to consider as subject matter any activity or experience that man is capable of, and it also has the more specific connotation that there will be an emphasis on especially those activities that differentiate man from the rest of nature or from other types of living creatures.

Thus far, we have the guiding concept of a "human science," and we wish to add one more term, that of "empirical." Again, if we took a narrow definition of empirical, we probably would not be able to retain it, but we propose to take a broad interpretation of it—viz., that empirical means anything that is based upon experience. Thus, we are saying that we conceive our endeavor along the lines of an "empirical human science," and that in order to execute this endeavor, a fundamentally different attitude on the part of psychologists is necessary. Trying to understand this attempt from a natural scientific perspective is not possible. These are two very different ways of conceiving psychology. It is the fundamental aim of this work to try to articulate—obviously in a preliminary way—how a psychology conceived as an empirical human science can be established and practiced. It is an attempt to forge a position that transcends Murray's dilemma (Bonner, 1965) between the investigation of unimportant problems by means of rigorous formal techniques, or important problems by means of inadequate methodologies, by dealing with problems that are significant for humans in a scientific way.

The following conclusions may serve as a summary of what we have covered so far in this chapter:

1. There is an increasing dissatisfaction being experienced among a minority of contemporary psychologists concerning the nature and direction of psychology. In essence, this experienced

dissatisfaction has to do with the fact that full justice is not being done to man as a person.

2. The chief source of the difficulties is psychology's commitment to be a natural science. Detailed investigation of academic and clinical psychology showed the impact of this commitment to be strong and pervasive, even if it was not the only significant force.

3. In order to help correct the dilemmas psychology finds itself in, a different attitude on the part of psychologists towards science will have to be adopted. Philosophy will aid in helping to make explicit this new direction. Our own approach draws heavily from the phenomenological movement in philosophy.

4. It has been suggested that psychology conceived as an empirical human science will enable it to fulfill its implicit ambition to study man as a person, and by doing so, it will be filling a gap in man's knowledge of himself.

The Idea of Psychology as a Human Science

If the implications of the critiques we have just analyzed are true, then it seems that a very simple idea presents itself to us: why does psychology not become a human science? As May (1967) expresses it, to state that to study and understand man we need a human model almost sounds like such a truism that one hesitates to verbalize it. But the amazing thing is that it is not a truism at all. Why not? How can the naïve everyday attitude that people who study human beings ought to have a human model, along with the criticisms of psychology that indicate that psychology is not doing justice to the full human person (both with their implications that what is needed is the notion that psychology is a human science) exist side by side with the skepticism or doubt about its accomplishment? We believe that the reasons for the doubt that an idea like "human science" can be fruitful, are related to the understanding of the terms "science" and "objectivity." We shall turn now to a discussion of these two terms.

SCIENTISM AND SCIENCE

One of the major stumbling blocks to accepting the idea of a human science is the viewpoint that has come to be known as scientism. Scientism is a pejorative term used to refer to an exaggerated claim of the proper function of science. It is the conviction that science as a theory is capable of solving all the riddles of human existence, and as a praxis, that it is able to guarantee man's unlimited control of nature, including man himself (Strasser, 1963). Implicitly, of course, this position reflects a philosophical interpretation which the sciences make of themselves. Science becomes scientism when one asserts that there are no other realities than those discovered by the natural sciences (Luijpen, 1960). The essential error of scientism is the absolutizing of one determined standpoint, of one determined question that could be put to reality (Luijpen, 1960). According to Kockelmans (1966), the primary motive behind scientism was the ideal of a unitary science, that is, the fundamental assumption that there exists a single, infinite, and rational totality of being which can be known in a fully rational way by a single science by means of a single method. Since it was the natural sciences that developed first, and its method that inspired such optimism, it was assumed that the method of the natural sciences should be *the* method. However, as we know, pluralism turns out to be the rule in science just as much as in society. But, as Kockelmans (1966) points out, it does not mean that there is no bond between the different sciences. The difference is that, from a phenomenological viewpoint, one does not seek the unity of sciences in the synthesis of their ultimate results, but in their common root and starting point.

It is not difficult to point out that the scientistic attitude has also crept into psychology. Many of the natural scientific psychologists quoted above implied this attitude at least implicitly when they attempted to posit the priority of a scientific perspective over that of any other including that of the life-world. The implicit stance is that to be scientific one must use the method of science regardless of subject matter, and that is precisely what is meant by scientism.

Besides trying to absolutize one method, the scientistic attitude presupposes that science can provide its own ground for what it is doing. But this attitude forgets that there is also truth in the life-world, and that it is precisely the life-world that is the foundation for scientific truth. In order to understand how this is so, we must move on to a discussion of science proper and try to understand how psychology can belong to that class of knowledge that is called scientific.

In dealing with the topic of science, it is often customary to adopt a definitional approach. Thus one could say that science is the utilization of the methods of science, and then defend that view with examples or illustrations. Or one could take a slightly broader frame of reference and say that science is an ordered system of statements concerning objects in a definite field of knowledge, with reference to the investigations, arguments and demonstrations upon which the conclusions are based (van Laer, 1956). This statement does not necessarily limit one to the natural scientific interpretation of science, but still one would have to justify this definition in terms of examples or arguments, and so on. Or one could simply take a very broad definition of science and define it as any methodical pursuit of knowledge, such as we did earlier, and then justify that selection. These examples clearly show that a full range of definitions are available, and that the definition that is finally adopted is more often than not one that fits the investigator's predefinitional prejudices. However, regardless of whether one takes his definition of science from the narrow or broad end of the spectrum, there is almost complete agreement on one point: knowledge that is characterized as scientific depends on *how* the knowledge was obtained and not on the mere possession of it. Most of the differences come about because of disagreements over what can be accepted as a suitable method. Our approach to understanding science will be to draw from the relatively new discipline of the history of science. The reason for this choice is given best by Kuhn (1962, p. 1):

History, if viewed as a repository for more than anecdote or chronology, could produce a decisive transformation in the image of science by which we are now possessed. That image has previously been drawn, even by scientists themselves, mainly from the study of finished scientific achievements as they are recorded in the classics and, more recently, in the textbooks from which each new scientific generation learns to practice its trade. Inevitably, however, the aim of such books is persuasive or pedagogic; a concept of science drawn from them is no more likely to fit the enterprise that produced them than an image of a national culture drawn from a tourist brochure or a language text. This essay attempts to show that we have been misled by them in fundamental ways. Its aim is a sketch of the quite different concept of science that can emerge from the historical record of the research activity itself.

In spirit, this statement is very similar to a phenomenological position which Gurwitsch (1966), following Husserl, has also warned against the confusion of the end-product of an activity with its process.

For Kuhn, the accepted view of science that he calls misleading is the view that science consists in an aggregate of facts, observations, laws, theories, and techniques for getting more such results—in short, that science is a body of information which has accumulated in a linear series of discrete discoveries about how the world is made (Gillespie, 1962). Kuhn concludes that there is ground for profound doubts about the cumulative process through which individual contributions to science were thought to have been compounded.

Furthermore, Kuhn states that the new historical perspective makes it increasingly difficult to distinguish the "scientific" component of past observation and belief from errors and superstitions. The more carefully historians study Aristotelian dynamics, phlogistic chemistry, or caloric thermodynamics, the more certain they feel that those once current views of nature were, as a whole, neither less scientific nor more the product of human idiosyncracy than those current today. If these out-of-date beliefs are to be called myths, then myths can be produced by the same sorts of methods and held for the same sorts of reasons that now lead to scientific knowledge. If, on the other hand, they are to be called science, then science has included bodies of belief quite incompatible with the ones we hold today (Kuhn, 1962).

Kuhn sides with the latter interpretation, stating that out-of-date theories are not in principle unscientific because they have been discarded. However, this makes it very difficult to conceive of science as progressing in an incremental or cumulative way.

Earlier we argued against the priority of methodology in approaching psychology in a scientific way. Kuhn corroborates this viewpoint by his own approach. In speaking about one of the prominent findings of his efforts, Kuhn (1962) points to the discovery of the insufficiency of methodological directives, by themselves, to dictate a unique substantive conclusion to many sorts of scientific questions. Instructed to examine electrical or chemical phenomena, the man who is ignorant of these fields but who knows what it is to be scientific may legitimately reach any one of a number of incompatible conclusions. Among those legitimate possibilities, the particular conclusions he does arrive at are probably determined by his prior experience in other fields, by the accidents of his investigation, and by his own individual makeup. Kuhn (1962) concludes that an apparently arbitrary element, compounded of personal and historical accident, is always a formative ingredient of the beliefs espoused by a given scientific community at a given time. In effect, Kuhn is acknowledging the relevancy of the scientist's approach in addition to method and content in the pursuit of science.

Kuhn distinguishes between "normal science" and revolutions or anomalies in science. Normal science, the activity in which most scientists inevitably spend almost all their time, is predicated on the assumption that the scientific community knows what the world is like. Communities of science are able to do this by means of paradigms or models that guide the thinking of any specific community. Kuhn (1962) points out further that much of the success of the enterprise derives from the community's willingness to defend that assumption, and if necessary, at considerable cost. Normal science, for example, often suppresses fundamental novelties because they are necessarily subversive of its basic commitments. Nevertheless, so long as those commitments retain an element of the arbitrary, the very nature of normal research ensures that novelty shall not be suppressed for very long. When the profession can no longer evade anomalies that subvert the existing tradition of scientific practice, then begin the extraordinary investigations that lead the profession at last to a new set of commitments, a new basis for the practice of science. The extraordinary episodes in which that shift of professional commitment occurs are the ones known as scientific revolutions. They are the tradition-shattering complements to the tradition-bound activity of normal science.

A science, then, is how its practitioners as a highly articulated group see the ensemble of its phenomena, and this proposition takes into consideration the psychology and sociology of scientific communities, and of what factors lead them to respond to, or to resist, innovation. Consequently, science is a dialectical process between powers of conservation and powers of progress; and each phase is both an advantage and a disadvantage, and each phase is both necessary, and at the same time has to be overcome. Polanyi (1963) has demonstrated how authority is still employed as a conservative force in science even today, although the ideology of science never mentions authority. His point is not that it is wrong, but like Kuhn, he is merely stating that authority is present in scientific communities, and he even argues that such authoritative postures are indispensable to the discipline of scientific institutions. That is, Polanyi (1963) wishes to bring into the open, more than it is at present, that the process of science is, and must be, disciplined by an orthodoxy which can permit only a limited degree of dissent, and that such dissent is fraught with grave risks to the dissenter.

Our own motives for stressing the presence of authority or conservation in science are slightly different. Firstly, we would call to attention the role of the arbitrary in the establishment of any paradigm. Secondly, there is the reason that Kuhn gives for the success of any paradigm at any given time. According to Kuhn (1962), paradigms gain their status because they are more successful than their competitors in solving a few problems that the group of practitioners has come to recognize as acute. To be more successful is not, however, to be either completely successful with a single problem or notably successful with any large number of problems. Nor does it even mean that the solution is more "true." The success of a paradigm is at the start largely a promise of success discoverable in selected and still incomplete examples. Thus, if a dogmatic or authoritarian attitude is present for too long a time, it might unduly be equally protective of its arbitrary aspects, while at the same time, preventing the correct solution from becoming a part of the community of effort.

We have spent some time on Kuhn's description of the relationship between paradigms and anomalies or revolutions because we think it is very relevant for our own efforts to construct a psychology that is conceived as a human science. Traditional psychology already has a successful paradigm working for itself, and while it is aware that this paradigm does not solve everything, i.e., it is aware of the existence of anomalies, it still feels that these anomalies will eventually be explicable in terms of the already existing paradigm. Thus, traditional psychology is exercising its conservative prerogative, and it has every right to do so, for we must not forget that this is one of science's strengths. D. O. Hebb is a good example of a psychologist conserving a paradigm that, for him, has been very successful. Hebb (1961, p. xv) states:

> The great argument of the positivists who object to "physiologizing" is that physiology has not helped psychological theory. But, even if this is true, one has to add the words *so far*. There has been a great access of knowledge in neurophysiology since the twenties.

Thus, Hebb is aware that his paradigm is limited, that it does not account for everything, but it has been too successful where he has applied it for him to give it up. He would rather work with it and try to overcome its specific limits, than to run to other paradigms whose limits he knows not. In this respect Hebb is acting in a way that thousands of other scientists before him have acted.

On the other hand, we would also like to reserve the right to leave the existing paradigm and to try to work on the construction of a new paradigm that we feel will comprehend more adequately the existing anomalies that have been reported above. In doing this, we too are merely acting in a way that thousands of other scientists have acted before us. Kuhn does not reserve the term revolution for the great scientific revolutions that we all hear about, such as those of Copernicus or Einstein, but he observes that the same sort of thing happens over and over again on a smaller scale throughout science. A revolution occurs any time that a particular scientific community agrees that the existing paradigm can no longer be accepted, and they turn to a new paradigm, and when they do so, they begin to act within the perspective of normal science once again. Thus, what is important here is to realize that the practice of science incorporates both attitudes, that it is a dialectical process between conservation and progress, between closure and openness, between solidification and expansion, and that with different phases, it is proper to be doing any one of these activities. However, it is equally important to stress that this aspect of science is revealed by an historical perspective; a definitional point of view might have revealed a more static picture.

We feel that the introduction of the notion of paradigm is a significant advance for understanding science. According to Kuhn, scientific revolutions are changes of world views. When paradigms change the world itself changes with them. Led by a new paradigm, scientists adopt new instruments and look in new places. But even more important, during revolutions scientists see new and different things when looking with familiar instruments in places they have looked before. Kuhn (1962, p. 110) states:

. . . that it is rather as if the professional community had been suddenly transported to another planet where familiar objects are seen in a different light and are joined by unfamiliar ones as well. . . . paradigm changes do cause scientists to see the world of their research-engagement differently. In so far as their only recourse to that world is through what they see and do, we may want to say that after a revolution scientists are responding to a different world.

What is of significance here is that one cannot speak of scientists without speaking of worlds. Whether it is the established world view of an existing paradigm, or the visionary world view of a new paradigm, in either case, the existence of the scientist implies a particular scientific world view, and there cannot be a world view without implying some viewer. Thus, it is obvious that the mutual implication of subject and world is maintained in science. Furthermore, as the history of science indicates, there are times when these world views change radically, although it is possible for a scientist who knows both world-views to dialogue between them. This means that there must be some sense in which there is also a continuity between the two world views in spite of their radicality. This continuity is based upon a common point between these two more specific world views, which implies that there is a more comprehensive and undifferentiated way of knowing them. In this sense, at least, the world of science depends upon the life-world.

However, Kuhn (1962) goes even a step further. He gives a number of historical examples of how new paradigms were formed, and then describes some characteristics that are common to all of the examples. These characteristics include: (1) the previous awareness of anomaly, (2) the gradual and simultaneous emergence of both observations and conceptual recognition, and (3) the consequent change of paradigm categories and procedures often accompanied by resistance. Kuhn takes great pains to demonstrate that it is most difficult to say when a discovery is really made, and at what point a new paradigm actually emerges; he stresses the equal importance of facts and theory, or concepts, for detecting a new phenomenon. For example, anomalies are often present in data, but they are often considered to be part of "background noise" or "error variance" and hence not recognized. Thus, the fact of the anomaly must first be recognized as such and then a new phenomenon can emerge. On the other hand, previous knowledge is also required. Kuhn gives the example of a student who looks at a bubble-chamber photograph and sees nothing but confused and broken lines, whereas the physicist sees a record of familiar subnuclear events. Thus the attitude of the researcher and his direct involvement with the data become evident once more.

Kuhn then makes an important analogy. He states that there is evidence that the very characteristics that he describes as being important for discoveries are built into the nature of the perceptual process itself. He then refers to Bruner and Postman's (1949) classic study on the perception of incongruity and cites how its results indicated that almost all anomalous cards were identified as normal. That is, without even any demonstration or awareness of trouble, the anomalous cards were immediately fitted into one of the conceptual categories prepared by prior experience. Kuhn then uses this experiment as a model for demonstrating why in science novelty emerges only with difficulty, manifested by resistance, against a background provided by expectation. Boring (1964) has recently spoken about the role of cognitive dissonance in science, showing that a scientist, like any other human being, frequently holds views that are inconsistent with one another. But as in the case of the paradigm with Kuhn, Boring maintains that this cognitive dissonance is both an advantage and a disadvantage, although he tends to stress its advantageous aspects over its limits.

The significant point we would like to emphasize, however, is that the role of the scientist as a human being is being stressed more and more. Maybe the resistance to change comes not so much from the paradigm one holds as from the holder of the paradigm. Maybe the scientist believes he is executing the paradigm faithfully and does not see his own "dissonance." We are very close here to the distinction made by phenomenologists between thematic and operative concepts.

By thematic concepts are meant those ideas, concepts or constructs that the scientist consciously formulates and utilizes in his activities as a scientist. By operative concepts are meant those concepts or ideas that are equally vital for the scientist in his praxis, but of which he is totally unaware, or at best, only partially aware of in vague and unformulated ways. But the distinction between thematic and operative does not belong so much to man as scientist as it does to man as such. Even in prescientific life one can make a distinction between thematic and operative concepts, or in other words, man in the life-world demonstrates the same incongruity, so that this is a phenomenon pertaining to man and not just a phenomenon peculiar to science. In Kuhn's attempt to account for normal scientific activity and revolutionary scientific activity in terms of the process of perception, we see once again that how man lives is extremely relevant for how man conducts science. The irony of it all, however, is that psychology, by trying to be scientific according to the ideals of natural science, may miss making the most significant contribution it can make. If it begins its own science by trying to account for man in terms of the world as we know it through the natural sciences, it more or less ends up explaining man in terms of science. That is, man is understood only in terms of the perspective of the natural sciences, which is a more narrow perspective than the one in which we encounter man originally in the life-world. Thus, one has to end up with a reduced man. Yet, it is the historian of science who wants to understand how man can engage in such activities as scientific activity, and he turns to psychology in order to see if that discipline can shed light on how man lives and behaves. Thus, the insight that a scientific perspective is grounded upon the world as it is lived can be helpful for psychology. Psychology, as a science, is also a more limited perspective than the life-world, but it should be dialoguing with man's behavior in the life-world in order to understand just how its perspective differs from that of the life-world; rather than positing the world as natural science knows it to be the criterion against which it has to judge its own data. This is the difference between a scientistic position and a proper scientific posture. It is also a matter of understanding man's behavior in its own terms rather than in the terms of science. This means that an authentic psychology should also help us understand the behavior of scientists. This is what Strasser (1963) means when he says that instead of "explaining" man by means of the sciences, we hope to make the sciences intelligible by way of man; and what Gurwitsch (1966) means when he refers to science as a cultural accomplishment in the life-world.

There is still one more thing that we would like to discuss before leaving the topic of a science in general, and that is a discussion of some of the characteristics of science as they are described by Kuhn (1962). This topic is germane to our purpose because any clarifications that we can make regarding science will also have feedback on the science of psychology.

Kuhn (1962, p. 167) suggests that any discussion concerning the essential characteristics of the scientific communities he has investigated can only be tentative until many more deeper studies are undertaken, but he does list four characteristics that would seem to belong. These are: (1) the scientist must be concerned to solve problems about the behavior of nature, (2) though his concern with nature may be global in extent, the problems on which he works must be problems of detail, (3) the solutions that satisfy the scientist may not be merely personal but must instead be accepted as solutions by many, and (4) the scientist may not appeal to heads of state or the populace at large in matters scientific. He must recognize the existence of a uniquely competent professional group and accept its role as the exclusive arbiter of professional achievement. These statements are descriptions of the characteristics that Kuhn observed in the pursuit of normal science.

If the above statements describe in general terms of praxis of science, can psychology, conceived as a human science such as we hope to establish, meet such criteria? We feel that it can. We will consider the four points in reverse order because the latter ones are more obvious. For example, there is no difficulty with the fourth criterion, a human scientist should not appeal to heads of state, the general population, etc. Nor is there difficulty with the third criterion: a human scientist must also be in the realm of inter-subjectively valid knowledge. We can even agree in general with the second criterion, but we would add one qualification. The psychologist as human scientist is generally concerned with more detailed and concrete problems, just as his counterpart in the natural sciences is, when he is working within the context of "normal science." However, during revolutionary phases, it is quite possible for scientific thinking to get global rather than detailed. As Kuhn himself points out, revolutions occur precisely because new paradigms are in the process of being established, and such a process must entail the turning away from details toward frames of reference. Thus, there are times when scientists, as scientists, must turn away from detailed problems to deal with problems of a more global nature. In short, theorizing is a proper function of the scientist as scientist.

Meeting the first criterion is both easy and difficult, depending upon one's perspective. It is simple in the sense that the human scientist is also interested in behavior—and thus the first criterion is met—but he is interested in the behavior of *man*. For some, there is still no basic difference between man and nature as it is understood by the natural sciences (e.g., Kantor, 1963) and that is why psychology is a natural science. From our perspective, however, while man is partially nature in the natural scientific sense he is not wholly nature in that sense, and therefore the behavior of man has to be understood differently, and that is why a different approach, one that would emphasize a *human* nature and a *human* scientific perspective is necessary. This problem will be discussed more fully in Chapter 4.

Thus, psychology, to be scientific, must deal with the behavior of man in a detailed way, although at times it may need to theorize about behavior in a global way, and it must arrive at intersubjectively valid truth among a group of men who are qualified to judge the facts and data arrived at. Surely this is still not as specific a description as is needed, but this description does show that based upon criteria that have emerged from an historical analysis of the praxis of science, the conception of a human science is possible, and that is all we wished to demonstrate just now.

OBJECTIVISM AND OBJECTIVITY

The problem of objectivism can be dealt with rather quickly since it is very similar to scientism in the sense that it too is an exaggeration of a perfectly proper function. In general, objectivism refers to the meaning that the world would have in itself independently of any man as a questioner of the world. An objectivist would speak of objectivity only if a subject is completely eliminated from the encounter with the world (Luijpen, 1960). Such a position presupposes that there is one way and only one way of knowing the world, and that is to know it the way it "actually is." Obviously, this position presupposes a realistic philosophy, i.e., that the world is complete and entire as such prior to and independent of man. Furthermore, with this definition of objectivity, the term "subjective" must always be pejorative because it means speaking about the world without removing the presence of the subject.

In a more specific sense, objectivism joins forces with scientism and posits as the privileged position the *method* of obtaining data, and the implication is that objectivity can be obtained only by means of the method of the natural sciences. Thus, there is the insistence that the conceptual framework, method, and scientific apparatus to be used in acquiring objective knowledge be not essentially different from those of the natural sciences (Strasser, 1963). When this system is applied to man, of course, he is studied objectively, but the difficulty for our purposes is that in such an approach man-as-object, or objective man, becomes the focus of study, and not man as a person. Since an objectivistic attitude admits of only that approach, within that attitude one can only say that such is the price one must pay to achieve objective knowledge. On the other hand, as indicated above, such an attitude presupposes a very specific meaning of objectivity, viz., that a specific method has to be used. Must we agree with that meaning, and give up the idea of objectivity for the study of man as a person, or can there be another sense of the term "objective"? Our next discussion will be concerned with nonobjectivistic meanings of objectivity.

The term "objectivity" is still not completely univocal, and different emphases will reveal slightly different aspects of the term, so we will try to comprehend its fuller meaning by means of a number of expressions. We might well begin by noting that we stated that objectivism was an exaggeration of a proper function of objectivity, and if so, what was the proper sense of the term that objectivism exaggerated? The truth that objectivism exaggerated was the fact that to be objective, knowledge cannot exclusively be based on the "merely" personal. In order to avoid this problem, objectivism leaped to the "thing-in-itself" as the basis for "real knowledge," which is, so to speak, an equal but opposite error. To get away from the "merely" personal, one must go toward the interpersonal, or the intersubjective, and not to the "thing-in-itself." So, one of the connotations of "objective" is that the knowledge referred to must be, at least potentially, intersubjective or interpersonal.

We say "potentially" intersubjective because if what one is experiencing cannot be at least potentially intersubjective, then it must remain merely personal or subjective, and this would rule out the minimum requirement of objectivity. On the other hand, we say potentially "inter-subjective" because it is possible that not everyone can see the objective reality that one person sees (e.g., Galileo, Einstein) but with time others will come to see it. If intersubjectivity is a minimum condition, it is not sufficient in and of itself to constitute the whole of objectivity. A further positive characteristic is required and it is this: objectivity refers to a particular stance that a human subject assumes with respect to the world. For example, the attitude of natural scientific objectivity is characterized as one in which man considers what is given to him as "merely present" rather than in a concernful way. This is a Heideggerian notion (Kockelmans, 1965), and to go from a concernful attitude to an objectivating one in this sense means to go from an attitude in which the "given" is considered in a less involved and "merely present" way. Thus, in objectivating, in a certain sense, one makes an aspect of the world "stand" before one. To be ob-jected means, literally, to be placed opposite man or to be placed before man. It should be noted that the natural scientific mode of being objective is not the only way in which man is aware of a "given" or that he is present to the world. More on this later (see p. 189).

Many implications follow from the above description of objectivity. First, it can be seen that this notion of objectivity retains the mutually implicatory relation of subject and world. There is something that is given to the subject, but in order to see it objectively, the subject has to assume a certain attitude. On the other hand, the mere assumption of an objectivating attitude is not sufficient to bring about an "object," it must be directed toward something that is in some sense given. Man cannot simply posit the world, but neither is he merely the passive recipient of stimulating energy. Man is simultaneously passive and active with respect to the world. Strasser (1963, p.60) emphasizes the same thing when he states that "the object" is a discovery made by human subjects and that objectivity is the result of a certain subjective approach. But he emphasizes that the project of objectivity is a discovery and not an invention (Strasser, 1963, p.61).

Secondly, since a subject must assume a special attitude in order to perceive the world objectively, it is evident that an objectivating attitude is only one possible attitude that one may assume with respect to the world. This fact in itself can raise a host of questions: why do we assume an objectivating attitude with respect to the world? When should we assume such an attitude? What difference does it make if we do not assume an objectivating attitude? Correlatively, the assumption of a special attitude implies that an objective attitude reveals only an aspect of the world, and not the world as such. As Strasser (1963, p.61) expresses it: "knowledge always requires a certain activity of human consciousness, which we may call un-veiling or dis-covering." But only that can be unveiled which lets itself be unveiled from a certain standpoint and in a certain way; hence what is discovered in this way is not reality unqualified but an aspect of reality.

Thirdly, we can see that objective stances are adopted because by means of these stances we can unveil certain aspects of reality, or we can say that an objective attitude is one means of arriving at the truth. It is important to appreciate the full content of that sentence because it implies that objectivity is desirable because it is a means of access to the truth, and not as an end in itself. As Luijpen (1960, p.147) expresses it: "As subjectivity-in-the-world, man unveils reality and he lets things be, what they themselves are, for himself. This unveiledness or uncon-cealedness is truth, and it is made possible by means of an ob-jective stance." Thus, the desirability of an objective attitude is understandable, but the reason for its desirability should not be overlooked.

Lastly, we point out that objectivity implies that the subject is oriented toward something that is not the subject as subject, and that he is affected by, influenced by, or normalized by (Strasser, 1963, p.85) that something. By this last point we mean to say that by a proper sense of objectivity is intended the opposite of arbitrary, or prejudice, or mood, etc. The subject, when in an objective stance, allows himself to be guided by whatever appears or is given to him. Hence, the very fact that in an objective stance the subject is oriented to something else indicates that the objective attitude is an intentional activity. And when we stated that the object of the orientation could not be the subject as subject, we meant to leave room for the possibility of objectifying aspects of persons, like the body, or even the self, but that it was impossible to completely objectify one's own subjectivity.

Thus, in order to attain objectivity, a certain attitude or stance on the part of the subject is necessary. While this insight helps us to overcome some of the objectivistic difficulties, it does not eliminate all problems. For example, one could ask, how do we know when we are in an objective attitude? Does the knowledge that objectivity is the result of an attitude help us to execute that function properly? Is it not possible to intend an objective attitude and yet be deficient in execution? Indeed, it is. One can be deficient by withdrawing too much toward the subjective pole (as in certain fantasies, or with certain deep-rooted prejudices), or one can be deficient by superimposing too much on reality, as when we have certain ideas about reality and then we try to make reality conform to our idea of it (e.g., the traditional concept of sensation). What then are the guarantees for objectivity? Well, we are not sure that there are any guarantees, but there are safeguards, cross-checks, and balances. The intersubjective aspects of objectivity enter here, along with the various means of validating one's experiences. Before Copernicus, when everyone thought that the world was flat, was this an objective truth for them? Surely it was intersubjectively believed. And probably it was even fruitful for a particular frame of reference, viz., an experiential one. The world was conceived as flat because it appeared flat. However, when another frame of reference was adopted, it was possible to conceive of the world as round. The point here is that even intersubjective truth has its limits and is dependent upon the beliefs and frames of reference of the person who assumes the objective attitude.

The relevance of the frame of reference for objectivity can help us to understand another point, viz., the fact that what is objective can be vague or specific, although objectivists usually try to limit the notion of objectivity to that which is specific or highly determinate. Let us take a mundane example. In baseball, a pitcher may throw a ball right over the plate, belt high, and the umpire calls a strike, and all is fine. The next pitch hits the dirt and the umpire calls a ball, and everything is still fine. On the third pitch, the pitcher throws a ball that just nicks the outside corner of the plate at the knees, and the umpire calls a strike and there is an uproar from one team and in the stands. Was the last call by the umpire less objective than the first two? Probably not. Why then was there an uproar with the third pitch and not with the first two? Because with respect to the frame of reference in use, the first two pitches were obvious, whereas the last one was ambiguous. Therefore, the real problem can best be described by stating that with the imposition of a particular frame of reference, and a certain human category system, the space just over the plate is no longer homogeneous or neutral, but it receives a certain value from the referential system, and that there may be pitches that will be most difficult to call with respect to all-or-none criteria within certain frames of reference. That is, there may be borderline cases that will be difficult to determine with respect to the system in use, but it does not mean that what the umpire sees is less objective. For example, given sufficient freedom, the umpire could say "That was close, I'd like to see it again." Such a statement is as objective as calling a ball that hits the dirt a ball, only it is objectively doubtful, rather than decisive. Or, given sufficient freedom, the umpire may say "I simply cannot call this pitch either way." Again, such a statement is as objective as a strike right over the plate, except that it is objectively indeterminate rather than specific. Thus, while objectivity is related to frames of reference, it is not necessarily related to specificity. It depends upon the degree of freedom that the system allows. However, objectivity is often misinterpreted as having to be specific; and very often scientific objectivity demands a high degree of determinateness, but it is possible to be objective and indeterminate. We are all familiar with certain forced choice techniques that require all-or-none answers from subjects. This can be legitimate, of course, but often such procedures are introduced only for the

purpose of being "objective." Or very often we hear about investigators who say that as yet certain phenomena cannot be
investigated because they cannot be measured, and the whole
reason for wanting to measure in the first place is so they can be
"objective." In other words, a measurement standard is a highly
refined criterion, and there are ways of researching phenomena
that may be premeasurement, but still objective. To assume that
objectivity necessitates measurement is to confuse degree of determinateness with objectivity.

For the above reasons, science in general is almost always
speaking about a more refined objectivity, i.e., one that is not
primary. These are the problems of scientific or theoretical objectivity, problems that depend upon a certain distancing from
the object under consideration so that it can be seen as it is in
the sense of being "merely present." But before a thing is known
as merely present, we have stated that it is known in a more
involved and concernful way, and in knowing a thing in this
latter way there is also a certain access to truth, a certain kind
of objectivity. We refer here to the knowledge of the world
obtained by means of praxis and doxa (beliefs). Even in this
world where there is still not a certain distancing from praxis
in terms of theory, or a distancing from doxa in terms of reflection on the doxa, there is a certain stability, a certain structure, and there is communication among persons about things.
In a strict sense, a thing is not a "refined objectivity" because it
is not seen as being merely present; but from another perspective, a thing can be considered to be at a certain level of objectivity because it serves the same role for the world of praxis and
doxa that objects serve for the theoretical and scientific worlds.
The fundamental significance of things is pragmatic or utili-
tarian. Thus, when reality presents itself as a spectacle of things,
it exists as a practical field consisting of a system of instruments
(Lingis, 1964, pp.60–64).

In order to account for this minimal stability or level of objectivity, Strasser (1963, p.77) refers to the intentional achievements that are necessary to bring about the order we find in any
world, regardless of how primitive it might be. These three
fundamental intentional achievements are isolation, identifica-

tion, and naming. Isolation refers to the ability to discriminate aspects of our world sufficiently for them to become themes of cognitive or practical actions. Of course, isolation does not mean complete isolation. Perhaps a word like differentiation might be better, since we would hold that isolation does imply a figure-ground relationship. The second achievement, which implies the first, is identification. One cannot identify if he has not isolated, but identification consists of more than mere isolation. Identification implies the ability to refer to the same thing even though many acts of perception are required, or it implies that the same thing is being referred to in spite of diversified predications. Lastly, because one has isolated and identified, naming becomes possible. Naming differs from the other two processes because it pushes the referent into a new level of openness, and it always requires an explicit act. By a new level of openness is meant that the thing stands out in a radically new way and that many more possibilities with respect to the thing are now achievable.

Let us consider an example. Suppose on a camping trip you are looking for a "hammer" to hammer down the tent stakes. You look around at all the things that are lying about until you see a rock that appears to be flat on one side, but convex on the other. The process of isolation has already occurred if one rock stands out from all others. Then you begin to see if this particular rock will serve your purpose. Is it heavy enough? Is it too brittle? Is it really grippable? Will it hurt your hands as you hammer with it? All of these questions imply the process of identification. Heaviness, brittleness, grippability, hurtability, all refer to the same rock, and these references are possible because you have identified the rock; i.e., in spite of the different qualities under consideration, they all referred to the same rock. Now, suppose you used the rock and then merely threw it away; it would most probably be forgotten. Suppose, however, that you found it to work so successfully that you decided to save it and keep it for further trips, and that you liked it so much that you decided to give it a name. You might tell your camping partners that you discovered a new tool, which you will call a "palm hammer." Once it has been thus named, the possible references to the rock and the ways you refer to it increase immensely. You can now tell someone to get it for you. It appears differently to you now, even though all the other rocks are still lying around as before. Later, you can reminisce about how you invented your new tool, and you can refer to it even though it is absent, and so on. Thus, naming transforms the way a thing stands out in the world. Needless to say, naming is an act that occurs only with man.

Also, one cannot help but notice the similarities between the way things of the praxis world are named, and the way science transforms the life-world, even though there are also differences. In order to make a thing stand out in the world of praxis, one has to isolate, identify, and name. With respect to the scientific world one has to perform the same functions, except that the criteria are more refined. In both cases, however, a transformation occurs because of the attitude that a subject assumes with respect to the world.

Thus, if one does not assume an objectivist position, there should be no problems with respect to the *possibility* of achieving objectivity within the frame of reference of a human science, for within this context it simply means: (1) that the knowledge of human sciences should be intersubjectively valid, (2) that objectivity implies the assumption of a specifiable stance on the part of a human subject, and (3) that the subject is open to himself and the world in such a way that he allows what is present in his experience to be present the way it is for him. The *actual* achievement of this type of objectivity, however, may still take time, for we still have to learn how to describe and execute all the operations that would go into establishing such objectivity. This is a labor that is still ahead of us.

The third characteristic above raises the question of whether or not the very term "objectivity" ought to be retained to describe the concern for validity and reliability as they are understood within the context of the human sciences. The reason is that, historically speaking, the term "objectivity" is related to the fact that consciousness always has an "object"; and the implications came to be associated that one was being true or reliable (i.e., objective) whenever one spoke of the "object as such," and ignored whatever any particular subject thought, felt, etc., about the object. Thus, "objective" came to mean "true" and "subjective," "arbitrary," because such "subjective" feelings depended upon a particular subject and not all possible subjects. But we have already seen that it is not the sheer *presence* of another subject that makes objectivity possible but the attitude that the subject assumes. Thus, properly speaking, one should be concerned about proper and improper attitudes toward objects and the world, rather than merely objective and subjective attitudes. For example, to describe an object from the point of view of all possible subjects is still an attitude that a *particular* subject must assume. All possible subjects cannot assume an attitude that one subject cannot assume. By stressing the importance of attitude, perhaps we can get away from the confusion surrounding the fact that subjective factors can be true and that objective factors may be false.

Secondly, the use of the term "objective" implies too strongly that what must be present to consciousness is always "object-like" if it is present at all. This too flows from the expression "consciousness always has an object." True, many people state that "objects" of consciousness can be anything, and thus they broaden the meaning of the term object. We, however, would prefer to speak of "presences" to consciousness. We would change the above expression by stating that "consciousness always has presences," or perhaps better still, "by means of consciousness, we are present to a world, ourselves, and others." The reason for this emphasis is to make clear the fact that objects are merely one type of "presence" to consciousness. For example, we are aware of the spaces between objects, and they are not object-like; we are aware of silences between musical notes and they are not object-like; we are directly aware of other persons in ways that are not object-like. Thus, "presence of objects" is merely one type of presence. But because this type is so obvious, it has received exhaustive analyses, and even worse, it has dominated our thinking so much that other types of presence are understood primarily in terms of object-like presences. For example, rather than attempting to understand positively how we perceive another person we often try to understand a person as an object-that-moves, or at the very best we can say "we know other people in

ways that are different from how we know things." But that is
only a negative description. Or we can say that we know only
ourselves directly, and then through empathy, or projection, or
something similar, we know how others must feel. But the third
possibility is that other humans are a type of presence that can
be described *directly* if we are able to break from the primacy
of object-like presences—i.e., if we can see that object-like
presence is merely one type of presence among many, and that
there are many other presences that are waiting to be classified, if
we know how to look! Once again, however, a different attitude
with a different set of assumptions is necessary. This idea in and
of itself is not new, but few people have taken the notion seriously enough to explore it systematically. In any event, it may be
less confusing if one avoids using "objectivity" in such a broad
sense, and restricts it to the mode of presence to consciousness
of objects or things.

Perhaps within the context of the human sciences one should
speak about the *accuracy* with which an experienced presence
is reported. How accurately one perceives the behavior of another person, or how accurately one can express his feelings or
his experiences, might become fresh questions for determining
new and precise methods for investigating the phenomena of
behavior, feelings and experience. Such procedures may lead to
ways of being objective with objects, animate with animals, and
personalistic with persons, and yet each attitude would be serving
the cause of accuracy. In short, each type of presence would have
its specified attitude in which it could be known maximally and
most accurately. Unfortunately this too is a task the completion
of which lies in the future. However, if we can at least admit of
its necessity, solutions may come more quickly than we realize.

Conclusions with Respect to Psychology and Science

In the first chapter we saw that the relationship between psychology and science was a complex one. We would agree, however, that psychology was correct in breaking away from the

philosophy of its time in order to become a discipline in its own right. We would also agree that, given the historical situation and the spirit of the times, it is not surprising that psychology chose to become a natural science. But we feel that now, almost one hundred years later, we can reflect upon this choice and see if it was proper. Our judgment is that it was not the correct choice for psychology, and this decision is supported by the challenges that natural scientific psychology has received throughout its history, and by the criticisms (offered by some contemporary psychologists) of the value of this type of psychology for solving significant problems.

All of the above factors, we believe, point to the fact that psychology is essentially a different kind of science. It is a science, because it wants to participate in the aims of any science, i.e., to take a critical attitude toward its phenomena of interest and to investigate them in a methodical and systematic way. However, because its subject matter includes man as a person it must pursue these aims in ways that are different from the ways that the natural sciences pursue their aims. Consequently, in psychology, because man as investigator takes man as a person as subject matter, we call this type of pursuit a human science. Difficulties with accepting even the notion of a human science come mostly from those who implicitly accept either a scientistic or objectivistic position. Scientism or objectivism posit as *the* procedure the procedures of the natural sciences for establishing objectivity and conducting science. We feel that both are exaggerations of legitimate points. Both extrapolate beyond their adequate frame of reference procedures that are valid only for a limited frame of reference. Consequently, it is possible to be both scientific and objective when studying the phenomenon of man as a person, but both terms have to be understood in ways that are different from the meanings they have assumed within the context of the natural sciences. Consequently, rather than being antiscientific or antiobjective, the notion of a human science, if properly understood, helps to deepen and extend the meanings of both science and objectivity. With respect to the latter term it was suggested that the term "accuracy" might be a better expression since it would be less confusing in dealing with the host of non-object-like phenomena that psychology is interested in.

Addendum: Contemporary Natural Science
Is Not a Substitute for the Human Sciences

It might occur to the reader during the course of all these analyses that psychology not only adopted the viewpoint of the natural sciences but it adapted to its own ends the idea of natural science that was held during the late nineteenth century. Since that time the mature natural sciences have developed and changed in a radical way so that the main problem of psychology is one of cultural lag. Thus, if psychology today were keeping completely abreast of the development and theories of today's natural sciences, there would be no basic problem with psychology. Many psychologists maintain this view, which means that psychology's error is not due to the fact that it adopts a natural scientific approach, but to the fact that it has adopted an outmoded natural scientific attitude.

Obviously, we favor catching up with cultural lags and being aware of the latest developments of the natural sciences, but our opinion is that even if psychology were imitating the forefront of physics, or the new wave of biology, etc., there would still be a necessity for the perspective of the human sciences in psychology. In the latter cases psychology would still be *imitating* other approaches rather than defining its field for itself; it would still be merely *accepting* a world view rather than constituting its own world view based upon its intrinsic questions and its own data. Perhaps our position on this point will be understood better after we present our reasons for including the concept of approach in science in the next chapter.

CHAPTER 3

THE NECESSITY OF INCLUDING THE CONCEPT OF "APPROACH" IN PSYCHOLOGY

The Meaning of Approach

One rarely encounters a discussion of the "approach" to psychology in psychological works. Often there are some preliminary remarks about the place of psychology in the hierarchy of the sciences, and then one simply proceeds to a discussion of the methods and then the content of psychology. Our position is just the opposite. Most of our discussion will revolve around the whole question of approach as distinct from method and content. The latter two topics will serve as illustrations of the implications of the approach of psychology as a human science rather than be treated fully in their own right. We have adopted this position because we believe that it is at the level of approach alone that the whole issue of whether or not psychology can be conceived as a human science can be settled. Any attempt to settle this issue in the realm of method or content will immediately lead one outside of these realms to the problem of how one conceives or understands psychology, and what presuppositions one entertains concerning the nature of man. Whether one likes it or not, it is essentially a theoretical problem that implicates a number of philosophical presuppositions. We would like to stress, however, that it is conceivable that this problem of approach will not always receive such an undue emphasis. The apparently excesssive emphasis that the problem of approach will receive here is largely due to the fact that it has been ignored most of the time, and thus it remains ambiguous—although to some psychologists, the questions raised in the realm of approach are merely obvious. That is, ready, stereotyped answers are often given to the questions asked. Secondly, the necessarily theoretical

nature of the approach sometimes turns psychologists away from
its consideration, although this factor is no longer as strong as
it used to be.

What, then, do we mean by approach in this more restricted
sense? By establishing the category of *approach* we mean to take
into account the researcher himself in the enterprise of science.
By approach is meant the fundamental viewpoint toward man
and the world that the scientist brings, or adopts, with respect
to his work as a scientist, whether this viewpoint is made explicit or remains implicit. We also recognize that in a very real
sense this task is inexhaustible. That is, no person could ever
make completely explicit all of the characteristics of his approach. However, we would also maintain that it is worthwhile
to make explicit whatever one can. We would argue against the
position that would say that since one cannot make fully explicit
his presuppositions, or his approach, there is no sense in trying
at all. The very nature of science, or any human effort for that
matter, is such that there is this note of incompleteness in its very
core. Yet, in spite of this incompleteness, we must strive for a
knowledge that transcends the particular and the momentary.
This is where the social aspect of science comes in. From his
limited viewpoint each scientist states the truth as he sees it or
understands it, and then he lets the rest of his colleagues criticize
or modify it until what is true stands and what is false is shed
away. Thus far, it has been the practice to do this with both
method and content; we are merely stating that the same thing
should be done with respect to approach. The reason for the reluctance of accepting the necessity of approach in science is that a
different attitude on the part of psychologists is necessary to cope
with the approach problem adequately and the attitude that is
required does not blend easily with the established ways of dealing with method and content. It is the continuous presence of
approach that makes it so difficult to handle; it is implied when
one deals with problems of method and content, but it must
become explicit when one deals with it in a thematic way, and
yet it can never be completely so. Thus, one must also draw
upon indirect ways of uncovering one's approach.

*The Necessity for Dialogue
Among Approach, Method, and Content*

While we have stressed the necessity for the inclusion of approach, we do not imply that the questions of method and content can be merely brushed aside. Our argument is not so much to do something different from what we are doing already, as it is to do something additional first—although this may imply doing things differently too. Indeed, psychology must move to a level of operating whereby it becomes axiomatic that there is a constant dialogue among the approach, the method, and the content of the phenomenon that is being studied. The way in which this dialogue can take place can be most clearly presented by means of an example. We shall do this presently, but first we wish to point out that one value of including as a necessary category for all psychological research or theorizing the role of approach is that it is a place where psychological theorizing and the theorizing concerning metapsychological or even philosophical problems can take place. It is becoming increasingly apparent that psychology will have to dialogue with, or at least be much more concerned about, the problem of its foundations than it has heretofore. This concern is basic even for those who hold the view that psychology should be more aware of what people in contemporary natural sciences are doing. For example, it is fairly well known that physicists are concerned with how their own operations interfere with the phenomena they investigate (Heisenberg, 1966). Psychology, however, was *never* free from this problem, although it pretended to be when it accepted the model of "independent observer." Thus, by directly confronting some of the presuppositions of its own field, and some of the fundamental attitudes that it carries to its work, both of which would be the proper concern of the approach category, psychology can bring its differences out into the open, and therefore possibly provide a basis for the clarification and resolution of these issues. This would be true even if at times metapsychological and philosophical issues would be involved; after all, psychology hardly fears to cross the boundaries of the natural sciences. And to the extent that it is justified in doing the latter, it should also be justified in touching upon philosophy and other human sciences.

Now we can turn to some examples of the dialogue among approach, method, and content, and indicate how priority cannot be assigned to any one of them at the expense of the others, but that the priority must be given to the entire dialectical process as a whole. Indeed, even though only method and content have been stressed, as a rule, we shall indicate how an assumed approach is inevitably present.

Let us, for example, try to put the priority exclusively on the side of the content, and we shall take the phenomenon of learning as a case in point. We can even take a nonlaboratory example such as learning to drive a car. Thus, we would like to study this phenomenon in a way that will be relevant for the psychology of learning, and we shall place priority on the side of the content. We are immediately faced with the issue of what questions to put to the phenomenon. Data can be derived only if one questions a phenomenon. But this implies a certain stance on the part of the questioner, or it implies a certain approach. Similarly, what method one chooses also implies an approach. For example, does he ask how long it takes to learn, or does he ask the learner how he experiences his task, or both? Depending upon the approach one adopts, any of these alternatives could be used. Thus, it is impossible to place exclusive priority on the side of the content, for the very definition of the phenomenon, the very ability to ask a question of the phenomenon, implies the presence of a researcher with his approach. Similarly, one cannot place exclusive priority on the content in the determination of method, either, because there is never a univocal method for any phenomenon, even within the perspective of a single approach. For example, the method of serial anticipation and the reproduction method are equally acceptable methods for verbal learning researchers, but which particular one may be used depends perhaps less on the content—both are applicable to learning—than on the purpose or the context. Thus, placing exclusive priority on the side of the content does not answer the question of which of several equally plausible methods one should use. Lastly, the determination of any specific method depends to some extent upon one's awareness of the range of methods available. For example, one could not ask a subject who is learning to drive a car to describe for us every movement he made in the entire learning process, even though such knowledge is highly desirable, simply because it is impossible. Thus, this knowledge helps to determine precisely what method might be feasible, even though it may not do complete justice to the phenomenon one is researching. Thus, complete priority on the content or phenomenon itself fails in the sense that the specific research design adopted reflects considerations of approach and method as well as the particular phenomenon under study.

The relationship among approach, method, and content is even more obvious when one tries to place the privileged position with method, because to do so one would have to believe in a universal method, which either becomes patently absurd, or else is at such a high level of generality that it reflects an approach rather than a method. For example, it is not accidental that the methods of serial anticipation and reproduction were developed in the context of learning, and that the methods of limits and constant-stimuli were developed within the context of psychophysics. In other words, methods are always developed in dialogue with the phenomena or content.

What is perhaps less obvious, but equally true, is that methods were also developed only through dialogue with the researcher's viewpoint or approach. For example, when Watson dismissed the relevance of consciousness for psychology, it was not surprising that he did not develop a method for the study of consciousness. Similarly, if a psychologist is a psychophysical parallelist who believes that experiences parallel brain activities, then there is little likelihood that he will develop a method for studying experience directly when there are so many physiological methods available. On the other hand, if a psychologist believes that experience is an irreducible phenomenon, then he will try to develop a method that will study it adequately. In other words, the methods that one adopts are also related to the approach one holds. Consequently, it is not possible to place priority exclusively on the method either.

It should be clear from what has already been said that one cannot place exclusive priority on the approach either. To do so would mean that one would be prejudging both method and content. However, it is clear that one should remain open to the possibility of multiple methods and multiple contents. What has not been equally clear, however, is that one should also remain open to multiple approaches. And precisely because approaches are multiple and not univocal, they should be rendered explicit. Our main point here is that any researcher or scientist, implicitly at least, has certain views about the nature of the phenomena he is concerned with, and that he should permit these views to enter into the public aspects of science rather than trying to keep them hidden or attempting to limit all researchers to the commonly accepted views at any given time. However, to try to place priority exclusively on the side of the approach would be to do just that. No approach can exclusively dictate to its method or content. The most viable approaches are those that evolve after some dialogue with the phenomena, rather than those that are imposed in an a priori manner.

Thus, even though our recommendation may not be as simple nor as parsimonious as the current practice of psychology, it is far truer to the actual state of affairs to realize that the priority is precisely in the dialogue among approach, method, and content, rather than on any single one of them. Consideration of any one always refers to the others.

The Value of the Category of Approach for Psychology Conceived as a Human Science

We have tried to show above that the approach of the psychologist is always present. In the past, attempts to deal with this phenomenon have led to the development of techniques of neutralization. That is, whenever there was an awareness that the approach of the researcher was present, methods were introduced whereby the presence of the researcher could be cancelled. However, these methods did not truly eliminate the presence of the researcher; they merely required him to assume a so-called "neutral" or impersonal attitude. But even a "neutral" attitude is the attitude of a human person. Thus, it means that what has been attempted has ultimately resulted in a change in attitude of the researcher from one of being "personally" present to one of being "neutrally" present. Obviously, when within the realm of the physical sciences, this might not make too much difference; but when dealing with the life sciences and the human sciences, this difference may be critical.

It is for this reason that we believe that another way must be found. We feel that within the context of the human sciences it is essential for the researcher to be present in a human way and not in a neutral way. However, this does not mean that a subjective factor is present in the pejorative sense. The human way in which the researcher is de facto present can be described, both by himself and by the subjects, and the meanings that emerge from these descriptions represent the control, or set the limits, for understanding other data that may have been obtained. Of course, there are limits to description; but there are also limits to the ability of assuming a "neutral" attitude. Yet, the latter works, so why should the former not also work?

However, before we get too far ahead of ourselves, we would like to use the above discussion as an example of why the concept of approach will be useful in psychology. First of all, as shown before, it is always present anyway, and it is better to acknowledge its presence than ignore it. Secondly, by reflecting on the problems that are characteristic of approach—viz., purposes, presuppositions, biases of researchers, theoretical viewpoints, criteria, etc.—one may uncover hidden factors that have been stumbling blocks to progress in the field. Thirdly, one may also clarify operational procedures that have been fruitful without understanding why. Lastly, one may also discover ways of clarifying and describing procedures for tackling new problems and new research projects. The next section will demonstrate in a concrete way the manner in which awareness of, and concern for, the approach can be fruitful for psychology.

*Demonstrations of the Value of Approach
for Psychology*

All of the issues about to be raised in this section are problems
or concerns that we believe properly fall within the domain of the
approach as we have utilized it in this work. Moreover, we feel
that even if these issues have not been explicitly raised in the
past, psychologists have implicitly "lived" answers to these questions. Again, our point is simply that progress in psychology will
be haphazard until the implicit questions are brought out into
the public realm, honestly faced, critically evaluated, and either
accepted, rejected, or modified. This is the basic concern we
would like to communicate, and a fundamental presupposition
of this concern is that it is legitimate to raise these questions
within the framework of science, even though many issues are
fundamental and may also share the concern of philosophers.
In other words, it is not wrong for a scientist to help in formulating and clarifying the very framework within which he will
operate, even if these concerns bring him in touch with metapsychological issues. On the other hand, he need not think that
his word is the last word. The final arbiter will undoubtedly be
a future community of scholars interested in the same issues.

CONCERN FOR THE PRIVILEGED POSITION
IN PSYCHOLOGY

Our thesis thus far has been that psychology, with a few not-
able exceptions, has been essentially conceived along the lines
of a natural science. One of the inevitable corollaries of this
conception is that traditional psychology places the natural
scientific conception of the world in the privileged position. By
privileged position is meant that the ultimate criteria by which
the reliability and validity of psychological phenomena are
tested are drawn from the way in which the natural sciences
conceive the world. To speak of a privileged position is really
to speak of the ultimate court of appeal, and for psychology, this
has always been science, but implicitly it has always meant the
natural sciences.

Indeed, so much has it been taken for granted that science is the ultimate ground of truth that even when it is made explicit that psychology has been implicitly ascribing this privileged position to only a part of science, viz., the natural sciences, there is still not much concern expressed. Undoubtedly, the majority of psychologists agree precisely with this position. Most psychologists simply do not even raise the question of whether or not psychology can be scientific in another way. Many still presume that there is only one way to be scientific, and that is the way of the natural sciences. But this further substantiates our point that this attitude makes a privileged position out of the natural scientific way of conceiving the world.

We have stressed this point because we intend to challenge it. Drawing upon phenomenological philosophical insights, we will maintain the position that the natural scientific perspective is not the privileged position even for the physical world—let alone for psychology—because even the natural scientific perspective presupposes a more primordial experience, namely, the experience of the life-world. The experience of the life-world is more primary than the experience of the scientific world because the latter always presupposes the former. From phenomenal perspective, this fact should never be lost sight of, and it should be weighed every time one is concerned with the activities of the scientist. Since psychology conceived as a human science begins with the activities of the scientist, then it too must be ever mindful of the privileged position of the life-world.

Within a phenomenal perspective, the concept of the life-world is undoubtedly a technical term, and we shall try to clarify its meaning. However, precisely what the life-world means in all of its nuances and connotations is still not completely settled because the term is still undergoing modifications and development. As a matter of fact, Natanson (1964) believes that the concept of the life-world was one of Husserl's operative concepts in the sense used by Eugen Fink, that is, a concept that is frequently utilized but also one that never reaches the level of thematic clarity. Nevertheless, we do not have to remain mute with respect to this concept, and in fact, in general terms, the idea of the life-world has been referred to a number of times, and not just by phenomenological philosophers. Schutz (1962), for example, indicates that for Dewey, the life-world is the social matrix within which unclarified situations emerge which have to be transformed by the process of inquiry into warranted assertibility; and that Whitehead has stated that it is the aim of science to produce a theory which agrees with experience by explaining the thought-objects constructed by common sense through the mental constructs or thought objects of science. These expressions come close to Husserl's idea of the life-world, by which he means man's immediate presence to reality, or that world in which everyday life runs its course. Or again, we could say that the life-world is the world as we encounter it in everyday experience, the world in which we pursue our goals and our objectives, the world as the scene of all our human activities (Gurwitsch, 1966). It is the world as we live it prior to any reflection upon it as such.

However, the significance of the life-world lies in its priority. By priority is meant that the life-world is the first world that we all come to know simply by being born human beings, and all other specialized worlds—such as the world of science, music, sports, or entertainment—are more narrow than the life-world, and they are also the result of specialized attitudes that result in more specific meanings. The life-world must be distinguished from these more specialized universes of discourse—and of course science is almost always· singled out as a specialized universe— because these specialized universes are refined and more specifically conceptualized experience rather than immediately experienced. Ideally, the experience of the life-world should be taken in its original immediacy, that is, as we have it independently of and prior to specialized conceptualization of any kind. The life-world is the fundamental order of existence in the sense that it underlies all other orders including conceptual orders like logic and mathematics. In other words more specialized universes of discourse can be fully understood only in terms of the life-world (Gurwitsch, 1966). Thus I can understand number only because I have experienced discrete objects that can be subsumed under a numerical unity, or I can understand the formula for computing the diameter of a circle because I have experienced circular objects.

However, as Schutz (1962b) points out, the so-called concrete facts of common sense or everyday life are not so concrete as they seem to be. All of our knowledge of the world, both in common sense and in scientific thinking, involves constructs, i.e., a set of abstractions, generalizations, formalizations, etc., specific to a given level of thought organization. Strictly speaking, there are no such things as pure facts. All facts are selected from a universal context by the activity of our consciousness, and hence they are always interpreted facts. This does not mean that we cannot grasp the reality of the world; it simply means that we merely grasp certain aspects of it depending upon the point of view that we adopt. Once again the importance of the viewpoint of the person can be seen.

Thus, we come to see a certain difficulty which is both an advantage and a disadvantage. We want to get back to the life-world and the purity of the contact with the world, but we find that it is already permeated with abstractions and constructs. This introduces a problematic into our description of that experience. On the other hand, this fact also demonstrates that the very kinds of activity that are essential to the production of scientific knowledge are already taking place in a prescientific attitude. Thus, if scientific knowledge has priority, it is not because of the kind of activity of the person who is a scientist. Actually, this demonstrates the priority of the life-world once again, since science itself is possible only because of a refinement of a kind of activity that a person already executes prescientifically. But it also demonstrates that what we know in a "common sense" way is not necessarily obvious. This is precisely Husserl's point, and why he feels that every term or concept we use must be clarified because otherwise we are always laboring in at least partial obscurity. This is also the reason that he can take the problem of the *Lebenswelt* seriously, and why he wants to approach it in the manner of a "rigorous science."

Now then, the significance of the life-world is that it is the ground phenomenon for any of man's activities, including science. This means that while scientists must pursue their aims in ways that are highly specialized and sophisticated, they are never entirely free from life-world activities in their work. They still perceive pointer readings, or watch a rat running in a maze, or get irritated if they have to miss lunch because a subject arrived late, or get emotionally excited when an experiment is going well for them. The significant point is that they write up their reports, or interpret their data, as a rule, only on the basis of their derived specialized perspective, rather than in a more descriptive manner, or in dialogue with the life-world perspective that they are also living. In addition, the more established a science is, the more hidden remain the origins of the methods developed, and the original meanings of certain key concepts.

Gurwitsch (1966) paraphrases the theme of Husserl's "crisis" article and shows how a legitimate, fruitful, and highly successful technique can also obfuscate its origins in such a way that its limits, as a technique, are no longer seen. The example chosen is Galileo's inauguration of modern science and how his method paved the way for Descartes' philosophy. Briefly considered, Galileo inherited traditional Euclidean geometry which he accepted as self-contained, that is, a science having no roots or foundations outside itself. In doing this, Galileo merely presupposed the role of the life-world as a "foundation of sense" for geometry. At any rate, this was the first step in conceiving reality in terms of a thoroughly rational universe accessible to a totally rational science (mathematics). Since geometry is possible because of the process of idealization, i.e., a mental operation by means of which we can construct ideal-limit forms, like circles and triangles, eventually, all possible geometrical figures may be generated by means of constructive operations upon the elementary ideal entities. Thus, geometry provided a method of definitively overcoming the relativism of perceptual experience, and furthermore, the results of this approach must be accepted by all who use the same method. In short, the methods of geometry were interpreted as leading to the discovery of absolute truths, i.e., truths holding for everybody, and to the disclosure of "being as it really is in itself." As the techniques improved and became mastered over the centuries by thousands of practitioners, for whom they even became habitual, the rootedness of geometry in the pregeometrical experience of the life-world was forgotten. As Gurwitsch (1966) expresses it, the complete refinement and development of geometrical techniques is but the last phase of the process of origination of geometry, and yet, the accomplished result to which this process leads is all that is retained. Awareness of the process itself is gone. Geometry taken as thus constituted and established undergoes a certain transformation of sense; it seems to rest on its own grounds and the validity of its results seem self-evident. Because it has been severed from its origin and its context, it cannot be understood as an accomplishment that was achieved only after a long struggle and as being dependent on a more primary way of experiencing the world.

The final paradoxical step is the fact that geometry is then applied to experience in order to discover reality as it is in itself as opposed to the unreliable and varying appearances and phenomena. Thus, through successively ingenious developments the mathematization of nature is completed; space, time, and causality are mathematized, and even qualities of phenomena are correlated with their mathematically understood spatio-temporal dimensions. A universe of ideal mathematical entities related to one another by exact laws is substituted for the life-world which, with all its features, is relegated to the status of a mere subjective phenomenon or appearance. These subjective phenomena have significance only in so far as they may serve as indications of the true, i.e., mathematical, condition of things. According to Gurwitsch (1966), Husserl also considered the abandonment of the principle of determinism in contemporary microphysics and the other departures from classical physics to be, from a philosophical point of view, of less radical significance than they are often presented to be. The reason for this is that all of the innovations in question concern only mathematized nature, i.e., nature as interpreted in terms of mathematical entities and formulas. For Husserl, what is important is that the very existence of the life-world is lost sight of, and its relation to nature as the physicist conceives it is not even seen as a problem. Husserl has also referred to this situation by saying that man originally conceives of the world in terms of a network of ideas, and later he calls that network itself "the real" (Strasser, 1963).

In Merleau-Ponty's (1962, p.71) terminology, we must distin-

guish between the notion of a universe and the world. The universe is a notion or an idea, i.e., a completed and explicit totality
in which the relationships are those of reciprocal determination.
Thus, if I know the sides of a triangle, I can determine the size
of its angles, or if I know the circumference of a circle, I can
determine its diameter. This is because in the realm of geometry
the aspects are related in a reciprocally determined way. But the
world is the open and indefinite multiplicity of relationships
which are of *reciprocal implication*. When we say the experience
of the world implies a subject we do not mean that it determines
the subject; or if we say that any consideration of a subject necessarily implies a world, we do not mean that the subject determines the world. In both cases, the meaning of the implication
has still to be worked out, but the very fact that it is not already
determined and fixed means that there is a degree of freedom or
a certain openness.

The major implication of the fact that there is a difference
between "world" and universe is to make clear that the experience of the world does not follow the norms of a notional
universe. The notion of a universe is possible only because there
exists a prenotional world. While science, up until this time, has
pretended to operate exclusively within the realm of a notional
universe, twentieth-century thought has made it clear that science
must now relate itself to the world as we experience it and as it is
lived with all its open horizons and ambiguities.

As Merleau-Ponty (1962, p.71) explains further, in order to
arrive at a universe, I must detach myself from my experience
and pass to the idea. Like the object of realism, the idea purports
to be the same for everybody, valid in all times and places, and
the individuations of an object in an objective point of time
and space finally appear as the expression of a universal positing
power. I am no longer concerned with my body, nor with time,
nor with the world as I experience them in antepredicative
knowedge, in the inner communion that I have with them. I
now refer to my body only as an idea, to the world as an idea, to
the *idea* of space and the *idea* of time. Thus "objective" thought
is formed—being that of common sense and of science—which
finally causes us to lose contact with perceptual experience, of

which it is nevertheless the outcome and the natural sequel (Merleau-Ponty, 1962, p.71). Thus, the whole significance of the discovery of the life-world as the ground is precisely the rediscov- of the phenomenal, which is the primary contact between man and world. As Merleau-Ponty noted, it does not mean that one does not also experience the life-world in ways that are the direct consequences of idealism and realism, or at least interpret the life-world in terms of those philosophical prejudices; but in spite of these facts, we also experience the life-world as we live it, which is to say, in terms of phenomena. Therefore, the priority of the life-world lies precisely in its phenomenality, which is the fundamental way in which the world is given, and it must be understood as such. Any transformation of phenomena, e.g. into ideas or objects, automatically prohibits a proper understanding of them. As Merleau-Ponty (1962, p.x) states, the real has to be described, not constructed or formed.

Thus, from the perspective we adopt, the life-world is the ground or foundation of all of our other knowledge. The argument is that if all knowledge, however abstract or universal, is based upon how man experiences the life-world, then one must ultimately understand that abstraction or universality in relation to its origins in the life-world. We must not make the mistake of seizing upon an accomplishment and understanding it only in terms of itself if it is in fact the end result of a long process. However, the long process that must be understood and taken into account is nothing other than the activities of the scientist himself, and that is one of the reasons for including the concept of approach in psychology.

More precisely, the significance of the life-world for the approach to psychology is that psychology must account for its phenomena in terms of how they appear, or how they are experienced, and not in terms of some idea of how they ought to appear. We have already seen how science has unwittingly posited certain ideas about the world to be the real world. Again, this is not to say that the positing of these ideas has not been fruitful for man, but these ideas are of limited service, and we must ascertain whether or not they are fruitful for psychology. The important question for us, as psychologists, is whether psychology has been properly aware of the phenomenal origins of its phenomena, or whether it began to study its phenomena with certain preestablished ideas. Since we already know that psychology began by intending to become a natural science, and it borrowed methods, concepts, assumptions and viewpoints from the natural sciences, and we know that science is already a more narrow and specialized world than the life-world, that in fact it is basically a conceptually constructed world, then we become immediately suspicious, and within the perspective of traditional psychology, our suspicions are almost universally confirmed. The process of developing the science of psychology has, from its inception, not been based upon the most primary phenomena it could have been based upon, but rather upon secondary or derived phenomena, i.e., phenomena as they have been interpreted in the world of the natural sciences.

Most of the psychology we have begins from a perspective that is already within science, and little concern is shown for the pre-scientific beginnings, just as in the case with geometry provided by Gurwitsch (1966). Many examples of this could be pointed out but we will limit ourselves to just a few. Bartley (1958, p. xi), for example, in a book on perception, states that his book is:

> . . . written on the supposition that psychology is first of all a science. As a science it is a form of biology and so developed as to take its place in a coordinate way among the other disciplines such as physics, chemistry, zoology, and botany. Much has been done in recent years to circumvent the forthright use of the word biological with reference to psychology. Terms such as life science, behavior science, etc., have been coined. With regard to each of these the author suspects the inventor's lack of the appropriate appreciation for both psychology and biology.

Implicitly such a statement means that psychology must be understood in terms of the understanding of the world as seen primarily through the eyes of biology, with help from physics, chemistry, etc. Thus, the primacy is with other sciences and not with the life-world. Even attempts to break from this perspective are discouraged by Bartley, for he says that a proper appreciation of both biology and psychology will indicate that one should adopt his perspective. Fortunately, from our point of view, Bartley does not stick rigorously to his own formulation, since he often includes examples of everyday perception in his book, but it is equally significant that he does not deem it necessary to formalize this reference to the life-world.

However, there is a more explicit example of this primacy of other scientific disciplines in Hebb (1961). Hebb argues that psychology, as a science, is only in its infancy, and therefore it must seek help wherever it can find it. He mentions, however, only two sources: mathematical methods of analysis and the biological sciences, i.e., two sources that already imply the assumption of a natural scientific attitude. His main concern is with biology; with respect to its relationship with psychological subject matter, we find statements like the following: "Modern psychology takes completely for granted that behavior and neural function are perfectly correlated, that one is completely caused by the other" (1961, p.xiii). In principle, Hebb admits that the above statement is only a working assumption, and might some day have to be rejected, but he also adds that it is important to see that we have not reached that day yet, and that that particular working assumption is a necessary one, and there is no real evidence opposed to it (Hebb, 1961, p.xiii). Again he states: " 'Mind' can only be regarded, for scientific purposes, as the activity of the brain" (1961, p.xiv). Or, "The problem of understanding behavior is the problem of understanding the total action of the nervous system, and vice versa" (1961, p.xiv). And finally, "A philosophical parallelism or idealism, whatever one may think of such conceptions on other grounds, is quite consistent with the scientific method but interactionism seems not to be." In these statements, we see the implicit attitude that psychology must be understood in terms of physiology and other natural sciences; that the natural scientific understanding of the world is primary: and that a philosophy should be adopted in terms of its consistency with the scientific method and not vice versa.

Hebb is a good example for our point because he has later admitted that aspects of the theory he developed in *The Organi-*

zation of Behavior have proved not to be correct (Hebb, 1963). However, Hebb takes pains to point out that it is the specific theory that is wrong, but not necessarily the universe from which it was drawn. He still recommends a *class* of theory that is in line with his original view, and he explicitly states that there is still some vitality in the original *approach* (Hebb, 1963, p.16) (my emphasis). In other words, what Hebb is really affirming is an approach, and more specifically, the natural scientific approach. Theories, facts, methods, and even subject matter can change (Hebb [1963, p. 26], despite the statements in the above paragraph, later admits that psychology cannot be reduced to physiology), but the approach remains constant. Yet, few psychologists, if directly questioned, would be able to affirm that the last point of resistance in their psychological work is the set of assumptions and beliefs that they hold concerning science.

However, lest one think that the primacy of scientific knowledge exists only among reductionistic psychologies, we can turn to Skinner for our last example. One point that behaviorists of the Skinnerian school and phenomenologists have in common is that they both wish to deal with observable phenomena and account for these phenomena in their own terms, i.e., in a way that does not reduce them to physiological substrata. The difference between them is how they go about this task, which depends upon how they observe and identify their phenomena, which in turn, depends upon their respective presuppositions. An analysis of the presuppositions leads us right back to the point at issue here, viz., what is the ground phenomenon or the primary point of departure? What is ground for Skinner emerges very clearly in his famous description of Utopia in *Walden Two*. Let us quote what we believe to be a relevant passage on this point:

"Mr. Castle," said Frazier very earnestly, "let me ask you a question. I warn you, it will be the most terrifying question of your life. What would you do if you found yourself in possession of an effective science of behavior? Suppose you suddenly found it possible to control the behavior of men as you wished. What would you do?"

"That's an assumption?"

"Take it as one if you like. I take it as fact. And apparently you accept it as a fact too. I can hardly be as despotic as you claim unless I hold the key to an extensive practical control."

"What would I do?" said Castle thoughtfully. "I think I would dump your science of behavior in the ocean." . . .

"So long as a trace of personal freedom survives, I'll stick to my position," said Castle, very much out of countenance.

"Isn't it time we talked about freedom?" I said. "We parted a day or so ago on an agreement to let the question of freedom ring. It's time to answer, don't you think?"

"My answer is simple enough," said Frazier. "I deny that freedom exists at all. I must deny it—or my program would be absurd. You can't have a science about a subject matter which hops capriciously about. Perhaps we can never *prove* that man isn't free; it's an assumption. But the increasing success of a science of behavior makes it more plausible." (Skinner, 1948, pp. 213–214)

What is revealed in this discussion is the priority of the science of behavior over the life-world. Castle, speaking from the perspective of the life-world, says that there is an experience of freedom; but the behavioral scientist says that he must deny freedom or else his program is absurd. Thus, in the conflict between a phenomenon of the life-world and a certain idea of what science must be, the latter receives the priority over the former. The whole idea of a science that must remain in tune with, or faithful to, the phenomenon as they are experienced is not raised. The idea of science or its methods remain firm and the subject matter must conform to the idea.

These statements, plus the examples and critiques provided earlier, clearly show that traditional psychology took as its point of departure, or its privileged position, the perspective of the natural sciences. In doing so, they either bypassed the true origins of psychological phenomena and began with a formulation of these phenomena in terms of the perspective of the natural sciences, or they in fact were present to the life-world origins of psychological phenomena but felt that progress meant the transformation of the life-world phenomena into the perspective of the natural sciences. In either case, we feel that true psychologi-

cal progress was hampered. But in any event, the main point is
that we must turn towards the life-world to discover the origins
of psychological phenomena, and they first must be described,
and then significant questions concerning these phenomena must
be formulated, but this time in a human scientific way and not
in a natural scientific way. An attempt to describe how this is
done will be given in the next chapter.

CONCERN FOR THE PROPER UNDERSTANDING
OF THE ORIGINS OF PSYCHOLOGICAL PHENOMENA

Once again we will draw upon phenomenological thought to
help us work through this problem. Phenomenology is concerned
with the constitution of the phenomena of the world and one of
the conclusions arrived at as a consequence of this concern is that
knowledge is in the appearance of phenomena, and not just behind them. We mean to say by such a statement that there is also
truth in the very appearance of a phenomenon; that phenomena
reveal as well as conceal, and that while it is possible to unfold
a phenomenon in such a way that what was originally concealed
can become revealed, the unfolding itself is possible because of
the appearance and not in spite of it. This fact needs reemphasis
today because of the successful use by the natural sciences of
models and constructs which tend to obscure their original
dependence on appearances, on one hand, and the completely
uncritical acceptance of certain phenomena as obvious on the
other. With respect to psychology, these two attitudes have been
influential in terms of the constancy hypothesis and the natural
attitude, respectively. We shall discuss these two factors and see
how they have obscured the presence of phenomena.

The constancy hypothesis refers to the principle which states
that there is a point-by-point correspondence and constant connection between the stimulus and elementary perception (Merleau-Ponty, 1962, p.7). That is, according to this view, perception
is explained in terms of sensation elements, which in turn exhibit
a point-to-point correspondence with stimulus-elements in the
proximal stimulation (von Fieandt, 1966, p.7). While this viewpoint is being increasingly discarded, even by traditional psychol-

ogists, it nevertheless is still residually influential. Bartley (1958), for example, in speaking about the difficulties in trying to determine whether cold and warm experiences are manifestations of a single sense modality, states that two of the factors that tend to lead to the conclusion of separateness of modality are that the thresholds for warmth and cold are not similar and the skin spots for warmth and cold are different in distribution. That is, the same spots are not the foci for the two experiences. This means that the problem is still being conceived in terms of the constancy hypothesis because the type of stimulus employed and the receptor distribution are the means by which the classification of sensory experience will be determined. Same spots and same receptors would mean same sense; different spots and different receptors mean different senses.

However, as indicated above, it has been repeatedly confirmed that the same receptor cells and the same sensory nerve endings can yield many different phenomenal qualities, and this is especially true if one takes the prevailing total situation into account (von Fieandt, 1966). As a consequence, the constancy hypothesis is being abandoned and fresh attempts are being made to understand the nature of sensing (Gibson, 1966; Straus, 1965). But the residual effects of this style of thinking are still making an impact. In fact, Gurwitsch (1964, p.271) has emphasized the firm grip that the constancy hypothesis has had on psychological and philosophical thinking when he pointed out that Husserl's own theory of perception implicitly posits the constancy hypothesis even though in principle phenomenology dismisses the hypothesis. The significant point for us at the moment, is that because of the implicit adoption of the constancy hypothesis, many psychologists ignore the investigation of the phenomenon as such; they ignore what is being experienced, or they bypass what is given precisely as it is given, in order to observe the functioning of the underlying receptors or organs, real or presumed. Or they are more interested in observing the kind of experience that the hypothesis might predict, with an all-or-none attitude, rather than allowing the experiences that in fact took place to emerge. Thus the existence of the constancy hypothesis is one reason why the concern for phenomena has been obscured, and why the phenomenological approach that reawakens this concern would be a positive contribution.

However, we must still consider the other side of the problem, the question of the natural attitude. The natural attitude refers to a particular kind of attitude that one holds with respect to the world. According to Husserl (1962, p.96) we find continually present and standing over against us the one spatio-temporal "fact-world" to which we belong as do all other men found in it. This "fact-world" we find simply to be there, and we take it just as it gives itself to us as something that exists. Even doubting and rejecting the data of the natural attitude leaves the thesis of the natural standpoint untouched. The thesis of the natural attitude refers to the fact that, in that attitude, we simply accept the existential character with which the perceptual world and whatever it contains present themselves. That is, there is implied or involved, the belief in the existence of the perceptual world (Gurwitsch, 1966, p.91). It is given to us as really existing, and in the natural attitude, its existence is simply taken for granted (Gurwitsch, 1966, p.97). As a rule, the existential belief assumes a rather implicit and inarticulate form, but it still underlies our dealings with mundane existents. We naïvely take things as real beings, and we do this precisely because by virtue of certain acts of consciousness, objects present themselves as real, mundane existents (Gurwitsch, 1966, p.170). In fact, in the natural attitude, we conceive of ourselves as mundane existents among other mundane existents. The perceptual world which comprises whatever exists comprises our body and its interactions with other bodies and things, and since we know that physical systems come to be substituted for perceptual things as known in common experience, this also holds for the human body. Thus, a special physical system, the *organism* as conceived in anatomy and physiology, is substituted for the body as given and the way we are familiar with it in the immediate experience of everyday life (Gurwitsch, 1966, p.98). To give just one brief illustration of the natural attitude carried over into psychology in this sense, we shall quote once more from Bartley (1958, p.21).

As has already been said, the psychologist regards man as a part of the physical world, and not apart from it. He obeys all physical laws just as though he were a substance in a test tube or retort. . . . So the psychologist, in relating man to his environment, is obliged to start with the consideration of man as an energy system. What the psychologist understands stimuli to be must conform to the way the physicist would specify them, and what the psychologist understands as the lower-order body processes must be described as the chemist and the physiologist would describe them.

This latter remark with its example makes it clear that not only is the attitude of prescientific life in the perspective of the natural attitude, but so also is the attitude of science. That is, the existential belief which pervades perceptual experience is carried over into the scientific interpretation of the world and it underlies the elaboration of the physical sciences, e.g., in the form of an implicit and unreflecting acceptance of the existence of the perceived world of scientific praxis. Hence, no departure from the natural attitude is involved in the transition from perceptual knowledge and common experience to scientific explanation (Gurwitsch, 1966, p.97).

While we have already discussed the constancy hypothesis, we can point out along with Gurwitsch (1964, p.161) that the constancy hypothesis has its roots in the natural attitude. Since the scientific attitude is also in the natural attitude, and since in that attitude we regard ourselves as mundane existents interacting with other mundane existents, then both stimuli and organismic processes allow themselves to be expressed according to the concepts and language of the natural sciences. From an historical perspective, the constancy hypothesis can then be understood as the first attempt to establish a simple relationship between the stimulation of sense organs on one hand, and on the other, both the aroused physiological processes and the concomitant sensations. However, the constancy hypothesis is but one statement concerning these relationships, and furthermore, it becomes clearer that its validity is based upon the assumption of the natural attitude. That is, sensations as experienced have to be understood in terms of the physical stimulating agents; and it is

not surprising that the first attempts at interrelating these factors were in terms of point-to-point correspondence, which is
what the constancy hypothesis posits.

The main point at this time however is to emphasize the fact
that the natural attitude conceals the world as phenomenon. In
the natural attitude we are too much absorbed by our mundane
pursuits, both practical and theoretical; we are too much absorbed by our goals, purposes, and designs, to pay attention to
the *way* the world presents itself to us (Gurwitsch, 1966, p.427).
The acts of consciousness through which the world and whatever
it contains become accessible to us are lived, but they remain un-
disclosed, unthematized, and in this sense concealed (Gurwitsch,
1966, p.427). By means of the phenomenological reduction, i.e.,
by a change in attitude, the world can be considered as phenomenon. That is, by means of the reduction, the acts which in the
natural attitude are simply lived are now thematized and made
topics of reflective analysis (Gurwitsch, 1966, p.429).

The key to understanding this point is to recognize, once
again, the priority of a more primary or original way of experiencing than objective knowledge provides. As pointed out
earlier, objective knowledge is a derived and secondary way of
knowing the world which is dependent upon the way the world
appears to us in a more practical and preobjective way. This is
true even though, because of our education and training, it may
be difficult to assume the attitude whereby we can catch ourselves
knowing the world in this more primordial or phenomenal way.

According to Merleau-Ponty (1962, p.49), a complete reform of
understanding is called for if we are to translate phenomena
accurately, and for this reason, the objective thinking of classical
logic and philosophy (or actually objective thought in general)
will have to be questioned because it forces the phenomenal
world into categories which make sense only in the universe of
science (Merleau-Ponty, 1962, p.11). Merleau-Ponty consistently
draws our attention to the distinction between the universe of
science or objective thought, and the world of phenomena, and
the latter is always cast in the role of the more primordial. Let us
turn to some of Merleau-Ponty's expression on this point.

Our task will be to rediscover phenomena, the layer of living experience through which other people and things are first given to us; (1962, p.57)

experience of phenomena is the making explicit or bringing to light of the prescientific life of consciousness which alone endows scientific operations with meaning and to which these latter always refer back; (1962, p.58)

to concern oneself with psychology is necessarily to encounter beneath objective thought which moves among ready-made things, a first opening upon things without which there would be no objective knowledge; (1962, p.96)

our image of the world can be made up only in part of actual being, and we must find a place in it for the phenomenal realm which surrounds being on all sides; (1962, p.275)

if indeed we place ourselves within being, it must necessarily be the case that our actions must have their origin outside us, and if we revert to constituting consciousness, they must originate within. But we have learned precisely to recognize the order of phenomena. We are involved in the world and with others in an inextricable tangle. (1962, p.454)[1]

Let us draw out some important aspects of these statements. First of all, in order to arrive at this "phenomenal level" we must pass through two reductions. Ordinarily, we are simply aware of things, or of scientific facts and formulae as such, but we are so only because we live through the phenomena of experiencing them, and if we turn our attention to the "phenomenon of experiencing a thing," we perform a first reduction and open up a phenomenal field because we observe the "experience of the thing" rather than the thing. In other words, we bracket the thing as we "know" it in order to observe our experience of it. The phenomenal field itself, however, becomes a transcendental field when we come to wonder about the "phenomenon of experiencing the thing" instead of merely living through the latter. As Merleau-Ponty (1962, p.63) states it, "the psychologist's self-scrutiny leads us, by way of a second-order reflection, to the

[1] Reprinted with the permission of Humanities Press, Inc. from *Phenomenology of Perception* by Maurice Merleau-Ponty. Copyright © 1962.

phenomenon of the phenomenon, and decisively transforms the phenomenal field into a transcendental one." Merleau-Ponty (1962, p.63) also stresses that phenomenology speaks about a transcendental *field,* indicating that reflection never holds, arrayed and objectified before its gaze, the whole world and the plurality of subjects in it and that its view is never other than partial and of limited power. Thus, although one arrives at the layer of phenomena by means of reductions, there is still an opacity in what remains after the reduction through which the influence of the world on man still enters.

Secondly, Merleau-Ponty's views on phenomena indicate that he starts with the *fact* that there is consciousness of something; something shows itself to man and this is the phenomenon (1962, p.296). For Merleau-Ponty (1962, p.296), "consciousness is neither the positing of oneself, nor ignorance of oneself, it is *not concealed* from itself, which means that there is nothing in it which does not in some way announce itself to it, although it (consciousness) does not need to know this explicitly. In consciousness, appearance is not being, but the phenomenon." But a "phenomenal field is not an 'inner world,' the 'phenomenon' is not a 'state of consciousness' or a 'mental fact,' and the experience of phenomena is not an act of introspection" (Merleau-Ponty, 1962, p.57); rather, Merleau-Ponty (1962, p.377) expresses the view that "through consciousness I discover . . . the simultaneous contact of my own being and the world's being." However, even though the phenomenon is the point of contact between my being and the being of the world, it does not exhaust either. According to Merleau-Ponty (1962, p.318),

. . . each phenomenon, on its appearance, attracts towards the field of existence the whole of my body as a system of perceptual powers. I run through appearances and reach the real colour or the real shape when my experience is at its maximum of clarity.

Further on he states:

. . . what I call experience of the thing or of reality . . . is my full co-existence with the phenomenon, at the moment when it is in every way at its maximum articulation, and the "data of the different senses" are directed towards this one pole . . . appearances are for me appearances of a certain true spectacle. (Merleau-Ponty, 1962, p.318)

Thus, appearances or phenomena are not "the real," but they are the means by which we come to know the real. Or we can express the relationship by saying that a phenomenon is to the "real" what a part is to the whole. This latter expression can help us understand why thinkers have come to distrust appearances, e.g., in the realist or idealist traditions, because appearances, being partial, very often conveyed significance that did not always stand up against a more careful and thorough scrutiny. On the other hand, the statement helps us to understand why phenomenologists can say that knowledge is in the appearance, because one expects to encounter things on the basis of how they appear. Thus, the attitude toward appearances or phenomena is what is ultimately important. If phenomena become *mere* phenomena, then one does not know how to make the leap from what appears to me to what *is* for me; and if one totally ignores phenomena, then he can only discover in the world the ideas that he is willing to find there (Merleau-Ponty, 1962, p.397f). However, by adopting a strictly descriptive approach, we can let the phenomena speak for themselves, and when we do, we discover that whatever appears suggests in its very appearance something more which does not appear, which is concealed. For this reason, a phenomenon can be said to contain significances since it refers beyond what is immediately given (Dreyfus and Dreyfus, 1964, p.xi). Hence, in a more precise sense, the given that is in the appearance of phenomena is "directionality," or "sense," or "significance." In other words, when one experiences phenomena, a direction is offered, or a significance is held out which we either pick up and follow, or turn away from. That is why Merleau-Ponty (1962, p.xx) can state that the "phenomenological world is not pure being, but the *sense* which is revealed where the paths of my various experiences intersect, and also where my own and other people's intersect and engage each other like gears." However, that this sense already reflects a dialogue between man and world and is not merely the product of man's activity can be seen from the fact that the referential character of perception (its sense) cannot be changed at will. Organization is autochthonous to experience as Gurwitsch (1964) forcefully demonstrates, but Merleau-Ponty has also shown how experience can organize itself according to laws not dependent upon explicit consciousness. Sometimes, an experience even leads me to see what I intellectually judge *not* to be the case, as, e.g., in illusions (Dreyfus and Dreyfus, 1964, p.xi).

It seems, therefore, that there are two important consequences of the rediscovery of the phenomenal order and the emphasis of knowledge being in the appearance of things. First of all, it rids us of the notion that emerges from the perspective of the natural attitude that perception is an incipient science and that classical science is a methodical and complete perception (Merleau-Ponty, 1962, p.56f.). Rather, by viewing phenomena unbiasedly, i.e., without any specific ideal of knowledge, Merleau-Ponty (1962, p.57) can claim that

. . . classical science is a form of perception which loses sight of its origins and believes itself complete. The first step would then appear to be to return to the world of actual experience which is prior to the objective world since it is in it that we shall be able to grasp the theoretical basis no less than the limits of that objective world, restore to things their concrete physiognomy, to organisms their individual ways of dealing with the world, and to subjectivity its inherence in history.

In short, all of the ambitions that Merleau-Ponty describes are ways of dealing with the subject-world relationship that have been only implicitly and tangentially utilized by psychologists, but in a phenomenological approach they would be available in a more explicit way.

Secondly, because perception in the traditional view was presented as perception of a *being,* it was not considered necessary for science to undertake a genealogy of being, and science was content to confine itself to seeking the conditions which make being possible. Now since it was seen that phenomena yield "directions" and "significance," the genealogy of being becomes a real possibility, and we are no longer limited merely to the manipulations of conditions in order to see if there is a possible effect on some objective fact or datum. Let us take, as an example, experiments designed to discover the threshold time for subjects to perceive how many dots are on a screen. This experiment is usually described as "perception as a function of time," meaning that the experimenter is interested in finding out how long it takes the subject to perceive what he (the experimenter) already *knows*. Thus, the subject must acquire knowledge and express an objective fact—x dots—and is usually not in any way instructed to relate how he experienced the phenomenon of tachistoscopic visual presentations. The latter factor is simply presumed and never taken into account. However, if one were cognizant of the fact that the phenomenal order provides "directions," the dynamic aspect of our relationships with the world could be stressed as opposed to the static.

One could learn how the "objective fact"—x dots—is arrived at with this particular mode of presentation as opposed to some other type. This is contextual information that is not mere "gravy"; not just a nice addendum, but information and data that is absolutely essential for understanding the very phenomenon under investigation. This fact will be referred to again when we begin integrating in a more direct fashion the characteristics of psychology as a human science.

Nevertheless, what we can say at the moment is that the emphasis on phenomena as the ground of objects and facts means that psychology as a human science cannot ignore the phenomenal level if for no other reason than to find out how to transcend this level. Thus far, science has been explicitly committed to only one way of going beyond the phenomenon, and that is the objective way based upon the natural scientific perspective. However, we have seen that while it is possible to do this in psychology, it is not desirable. Thus, psychology must go back to the phenomenal level in order to rediscover there how the world appears to man, and then to learn how to ask a question about this appearance that will help in understanding how man experiences and behaves in and with respect to the world.

In other words, a properly psychological question can be put to a phenomenon only when this phenomenon is described or understood in the most basic way possible, viz., in terms of the life-world. Of course, the very questioning of the phenomenon will transform the life-world perspective, but this transformation should be different from the way a natural scientific attitude toward the same phenomenon would have transformed it. We hope to elucidate some features of this transformation in the next chapter.

For some time now phenomenologists have been saying that psychology ought to be dealing with phenomena. Sartre (1962b, p.29), e.g., has stated that for the time being, psychology should endeavor not so much to collect the facts as to interrogate the *phenomena,* i.e., the actual psychic events insofar as these are significations, not insofar as they are pure facts, Merleau-Ponty (1964, p.95) has also stated that psychologists have been led to redefine psychological knowledge. This has been due in part to the direct influence of phenomenologies, in part to a diffuse influence of which they were not conscious, and above all to the pressure of the concrete problems with which they had to deal. In a sense, all of the critical studies and articles of the last chapter were responses to pressures of concrete problems. At any rate, Merleau-Ponty concludes by stating that psychology is tending, rather, to rely on a disciplined reading of the phenomena which arise both within one and outside of one and on a resulting grasp of the meaning of human behavior. Both Sartre and Merleau-Ponty agree on the fact that psychology should begin with phenomena; however, they are not very explicit on how psychology should question phenomena, and how psychology should go beyond phenomena so that an understanding of psychological reality is arrived at, although they do implicitly attempt both tasks. We shall also try to make this more explicit in the next chapter.

There is one more point that the above analysis has clarified, but it has remained only implicit and now we want to bring it to explicit awareness. Because we have broken from the natural attitude, which only saw man as a part of the world, i.e., as a mundane reality, we were able to see that there is also a sense in which the world exists for man, a sense in which man is the originator of his world (Strasser, 1963, p.6). However, these statements should not be misconstrued to mean that man merely posits the world in an ideal sense. There are aspects of the world that are not part of man in a literal sense, but what is being affirmed is that no aspect of the world can be spoken about that is not in some sense, however indirect, given or present to man's stream of experience or behavior. Another implication of these statements is the fact that man is both a recipient and a giver of meaning, but again, being a recipient does not necessarily mean man is passive. In other words, because we affirm that we can study man as the originator of the world does not mean that one has to dispose of the dialogue between man and the world. A comprehensive human science, such as we are arguing that psychology must be, would still take such a dialogue as a basic presupposition. Moreover, we are affirming that it is possible to have a human scientific perspective for psychology and also be outside the natural attitude.

Thus, by bringing the problems surrounding the concern for the proper origins of psychological phenomena to explicit awareness, we have uncovered another possible reason for lack of progress in psychology, although the root of the problem is not exclusive to psychology. As Merleau-Ponty (1962) has shown, man's relations with the world *begin* at the phenomenal level even if they do not remain there. This means that things, objects, ideas, events, etc., all have phenomenal origins. However, psychology, in general, has *begun* with things, objects, ideas, etc., believing that they were the points of departure for psychology. The implication of our analysis is that psychology must travel this road for itself; it must go back to the phenomenal realm and then move toward the form of closure that will best define psychological reality. Our point is that this type of closure will not turn out to be thing, or object, or idea, etc., but something entirely different. Undoubtedly, this is a big problem, but we feel that it is one whose solution will be much more fruitful for psychology than many others that are taking up so much of psychology's energies.

CONCERN FOR UNDERSTANDING THE NATURE OF CONSCIOUSNESS, EXPERIENCE, AND BEHAVIOR

Consciousness and experience have always been problem areas for psychology, in spite of the fact that every psychologist is obviously a conscious, experiencing being. Somehow, a large number of psychologists were able to consider this fact irrelevant for a viable psychology. From the perspective of a human science, however, it is essential to come to grips with the phenomena of consciousness and experience. From the life-world perspective these phenomena are constantly referred to and accepted as givens. It is up to a scientific perspective to clarify them and see precisely to what extent common-sense beliefs concerning them are true. Dismissing them as irrelevant and relegating them to the position of secondary phenomena are not solutions so much as evasions. It is time that we squarely confront these phenomena and learn to question them intelligently so that they too may come under scientific study. Our own approach will once again be to draw upon insights from phenomenological philosophy to help us formulate the problems. Of chief value in this analysis will be the concepts of intentionality and meaning.

It is not an easy task to clarify the notion of intentionality, especially for the purpose of relating it to psychology, but we feel that an attempt is necessary. The main difficulty, as with most of the concepts we borrow from phenomenological philosophy, is that the concepts themselves are still undergoing clarification. Nevertheless, some helpful statements can be made.

The idea of intentionality was taken over by Husserl from Brentano, although Husserl gave the term a radically new meaning. For Husserl, intentionality refers to the fact that all consciousness is consciousness of something that is not consciousness itself. Or as Husserl (1960, p.33) expresses it:

Conscious processes are also called intentional; but then the word intentionality signifies nothing else than this universal fundamental property of consciousness: to be consciousness of something; as a cogito, to bear within itself its cogitation.

Gurwitsch (1966, p.124) expresses it in the following way: "Experiencing an act, the subject is aware of an object, so that the act may be characterized as a consciousness of an object whether real or ideal, whether existent or imaginary." An intentional act, therefore, is an act in which a subject is presented an object. In general, then, to every act of consciousness belongs the "object" of which the act conveys consciousness, just as and exactly as the "object" appears, presents itself, is meant and intended through that act. The "intentional object" belongs to the act as its correlate, its sense, or meaning. In its full and concrete sense, the term "intentionality of consciousness" expresses just this correlation of correspondence between acts and their "intentional objects." No description of an act of consciousness is adequate unless allowance is made for its intentional correlate (Gurwitsch, 1966, p.440).

It should not be forgotten that the above statements are all made from a point of view that is outside of the natural attitude. This is mentioned in order to avoid interpreting intentionality as a property belonging to mental states, or as a real quality of acts such as intensity is said to be a quality of all sensory experience. In the phenomenological attitude, consciousness is radically distinct from nature, as traditionally conceived by the natural sciences, and the thesis of the natural attitude is suspended. Thus, to consider consciousness as intentional is to consider it in its presentational function, and it is the discovery of this function, or at least the explicit articulation of it, that has led to the phenomenological understanding of consciousness.

According to Merleau-Ponty (1962, p.xvii), the value of the notion of intentionality is understandable only through the reduction. What distinguishes the phenomenological notion of intentionality is the fact that before being posited by knowledge in a specific act of identification, the unity of the world is "lived" as ready-made or already there. Merleau-Ponty (1962, p.xviii) claims further that this deeper meaning of intentionality is implied by Husserl himself when he distinguishes between intentionality of act and operative intentionality. The former refers to those occasions when we voluntarily take up a position or a stance, and the latter refers to the natural and antepredicative unity of the world and our life as apparent in desires, wishes, etc. In other words, Merleau-Ponty (1962, p.121) claims that the originality of Husserl, strictly speaking, lies beyond the notion of intentionality as such. Rather, it is to be found in the elaboration of this notion and in the discovery, beneath the intentionality of representations, of a deeper intentionality, which others have called "existence." In short, intentionality does not indicate primarily a cognitive relationship but a relationship of being (Kockelmans, 1966, p.64).

In Merleau-Ponty's usage of the term, then, intentionality is a relationship of being. As such, it can also be understood as describing man's openness for, his orientation towards, or his essential directedness to the world. These expressions try to indicate the primordial relatedness of man and world, and from such a perspective, cognitive or strictly conscious relations are a derived or secondary form of "being-in-the-world" (Kockelmans, 1966, p.64).

The relevance of the above insights for psychology is that they offer a way of understanding consciousness and experience that will enable these phenomena to be studied within the framework of psychology. That is, because of its particular perspective and emphasis, phenomenological philosophy has uncovered an irreducible relation, the intentional relation. In general, psychologists have tried to understand consciousness in terms of cause-effect relations, and one of the reasons that consciousness has proved to be so difficult a topic is that it cannot be understood in terms of that relation. It is in terms of the intentional relation that consciousness and experience must be understood. By means of the methods of reflection and description the intentional relation of consciousness can be discovered and important facets of the role of consciousness and experience in the totality of human activity can perhaps be better understood.

The reader will undoubtedly have noticed that so far nothing has been said about behavior. However, the reason that Merleau-Ponty's interpretation of intentionality has been included is precisely so that the notion of behavior can be understood. While, historically speaking, the intentional relation was discovered within the context of consciousness, Merleau-Ponty's interpretation clearly extends it to existence. And as Merleau-Ponty (1963, p.226) himself says, what Watson had in mind when he spoke of behavior, others have called existence; or expressing it another way, what some philosophers call existence, some psychologists call behavior. Thus, what we have been leading up to is that behavior partakes of intentional relations. This means not only that it is impossible to understand behavior solely in cause-effect terms, but the implication is also that the cause-effect relation is not even the most suitable relation to understand the phenomenon of behavior. This is because behavior must not be seen in the context of the movement of a "thing," or the dynamics of an "object," or even as the responses of an "organism"; rather, the primacy is with the behavior itself, i.e., the relation between man and world of which behavior is but an expression or manifestation. It is the intentional relation that is better suited to understanding the phenomenon of behavior, and it is a relation that is irreducible to any other (Strasser, 1965).

While intentionality is the term that is used to describe the ultimately irreducible relation, the way in which the presence of this relation is normally known is by means of the phenomenon of meaning. It is by means of the analysis of meaning or significance that one can uncover the fact of the intentional relation. Again, this implies descriptive and reflective methods. The value of the approach is once again evident, because if one assumes a natural scientific perspective toward meaning, not only does one miss the essential features of that phenomenon but one can never arrive at the deeper intentional relation. For example, psychologists have attempted to measure meaning (Osgood, 1952), which means that they saw it from a strictly quantitative perspective, which also has implications about the nature of meaning, viz., that its chief value lies in being quantified. By now, however, we can easily recognize this type of thinking as being due more to the approach of the investigator than to the essential features of the phenomenon itself.

Rather, what has to be changed is the approach to the phenomenon. We must go back to the origins; we must see how meanings are experienced and lived and then see what perspective will be most suitable for understanding them *as* they are lived and experienced. We must learn what the unfolding and explicitation of meanings lead to; we must learn to understand the values they already have rather than try to superimpose values on top of them. All of this, however, implies a different way of looking, and a way of looking that may go against many habitual modes. Nevertheless, if we are to remain open to the phenomena, there is no alternative.

The relationship between meaning and intentionality is a

complex one, and one that is certainly worthy of more study. In the most succinct way, perhaps we can say that meanings are the traces of intentionality. That is, there are meanings only because there is intentionality. Intentionality is used once again here in the sense of referring to man's being itself, and not just to his awareness. It is in man's living of this fundamental intentionality that meaning originates. Meaning is the result of the encounter between man and the world, an encounter in which both are essentially involved (Kockelmans, 1966, p.63). Moreover, implied in the notion of encounter is the dialogue of the lived-body and the world (Kwant, 1963, p.36). Thus, as consciously living human beings, we *find* certain meanings, i.e., we find colors, oriented space, sexual meanings, etc. However, it is because of man's intentionality that these meanings are present, and to be understood properly, they must be referred back to that relation.

In order to understand a little better the contribution of phenomenological thought on this matter, we can perhaps note how the presence of meanings has been misunderstood. For example, because meanings are also discovered in the world (i.e., reflective consciousness is not the absolute origin of all meanings), there is a tendency to see these meanings as absolutes. Thus realism is inclined to see these meanings as a given reality that is independent of us. Certain forms of intellectualism see them as the projection of absolute ideas that are present in us and uncovered by reflection. What is common to both interpretations is that because the meanings in question are experienced as *given*, they are seen only in their givenness. They are not viewed as constituted within the dialogue between the lived-body and the world. Again, it is a matter of being satisfied with the result of a process, and ignoring the process itself, in this case, the dialogue between the lived-body and the world (Kwant, 1963, p.36).

Thus, the discipline that can articulate more precisely the relationship between intentionality and meaning will be doing a great service for those interested in human behavior. We feel confident that such a task can fall well within the framework of psychology conceived as a human science. Even though the notion of intentionality is used mostly within a philosophical context, it does not mean that it cannot be used within a scientific context as well. In fact, the term had its origin with Brentano in a psychological work. It is only because of the natural scientific bias that psychology primarily adopted during the past one hundred years, that development of the term has been left almost exclusively to philosophy. However, psychology as a human science may make equally valuable contributions to our understanding of this key relationship.

The major implication of the fact that behavior itself is intentional can now be stated. If behavior partakes of intentional relations, and if the route to understanding intentionality comes through the phenomenon of meaning, then it is clear that the relevant question for understanding behavior is to inquire about its meaning—not its measurement. We have already seen that the measurement question has become so habitual in psychology that few realize there are other questions to put to phenomena. Thus, the consistent pursuit of this line of reasoning will lead to a wholly different way of approaching psychological phenomena.

Thus, the concern for the proper nature of consciousness, experience, and behavior may circumvent another stumbling block to progress in psychology. The reason that psychology has had difficulty with these phenomena is that by implicitly studying them within the context of the natural scientific approach, psychologists have been studying them from a viewpoint that is not central to them. That is, they did not derive their approach to them on a truly empirical basis, but rather, they tried to execute an approach to them that was based on an *idea* of how the natural sciences functioned. For these particular phenomena, this proved to be less than desirable.

CONCERN FOR THE PRESUPPOSITIONS OF PSYCHOLOGY

From a human scientific perspective, the presuppositions of a psychologist concerning psychology are of paramount importance for understanding the nature of the psychology he espouses. This is because there is no psychology "in itself," but only for a community of scholars. And if there are differences among scholars in this community, it may be due to the fact that they see different aspects of the total field, which in turn may mean different presuppositions. However, the way to achieve consensus is not by trying to establish *the* presupposition for all viewpoints beforehand, but rather by trying to get the presuppositions that any psychologist holds out into the open so that their relative merits can be assessed. A comprehensive presupposition can grow only out of the presence of many presuppositions; it cannot be established in an a priori manner without any data whatsoever. Once again we shall turn to phenomenological philosophy to help us clarify this problem. Phenomenology is always concerned with trying to describe what appears precisely and exactly as it appears, and this is why it uses the technique of "the reduction" and tries to bracket as much "knowledge about" phenomena as possible. This concern for presuppositions or prejudices regarding phenomena has led to the postulation on the part of phenomenologists of an ideal that can best be described as "presuppositionless knowing." However, it is impossible to achieve this ideal completely and consequently phenomenologists assert that all knowledge is in perspective. That is, if one can never be without presuppositions, the next best thing is to clarify those presuppositions that one has. The constellation of presuppositions then defines the perspective that one is in.

To say that all knowledge is in perspective essentially means that every stance that we take up with respect to the world opens up some possibilities and closes off others. The possibilities that are closed off become limits for what we can say about the phenomenon that we want to describe, and they indirectly impose presuppositions on what we want to say, in the sense that we can only speak about what is directly revealed and its horizon of given possibilities. The establishment of the fact of perspectivity thus rules out any stance that can be all-knowing, and in effect, this rules out the possibility of an absolute stance—and this applies to a phenomenological perspective as well.

That an absolute stance is impossible is clearly seen when we remember that man is an intentional being, and as such, is directed always toward the world. However, in being directed toward the world, man experiences that he apprehends only aspects of that world—space and time being obvious limits to man's relation to the world. There are always limits to the fulfillment of intentions. If man intends to "know all," he experiences the fact that this simply cannot be fulfilled. And if man adopts a stance which contains an intention that is capable of being fulfilled, he will note that it is directed toward something limited. Even if we set the intention to "know something in general," it is a limitation because it means that we do not know it specifically; or if we try to know something "comprehensively" it is a limit because we do not know it in detail. Consequently, if the *fact* is that man cannot form a workable intention without at the same time setting limits, i.e., without at the same time being in perspective, then the ideal of an absolute stance is what should be discarded, and we should try to form theories of knowledge that are more in line with this fact. The fact of perspectivity is the main argument against all theories that posit absolute positions.

However, the above argument should not be misconstrued to mean that there is a complete arbitrariness with respect to perspective that one can adopt toward phenomena. This really raises the issue of the privileged position. Is there one point of view that is more adequate with which to approach phenomena? Again, this question cannot be answered without bringing into consideration the fact of intentionality. If we do bring in intentionality, then we would argue that there are some positions that are privileged with respect to any *given intention*. For example, if one wants to examine an object in detail, a "close" perspective is surely better than a distant one, so that at least part of the privileged position for observing things in detail is the fact of "closeness," however it may be defined. More importantly, however, the question of the privileged position brings out more explicitly the fact that the intention of the scientist, or the thinker, or the researcher is a prime factor in constituting a privileged position. This in turn reemphasizes the point we have been making all along, that the approach of the scientist is at least as important as the method and content he deals with, and should be formally communicated in scientific reports and discussions just as the latter two are. Of course this is often done implicitly, but the explicit acknowledgment of it would sharpen the communication. The awareness of the intention of the scientist, if made explicit, has another advantage in that it demands another attitude, one that requires the articulation of a frame of reference, or of a context that would circumscribe the zone of validity or effectiveness of the scientist's work, which, by the way, is there already because of perspectivity. This could be another contribution of making the approach explicit.

One could say that the problems of perspectivity and privileged positions were at least implicitly seen by many traditional psychologists in the sense that hardly any psychologist ever believed that the proper domain of psychology should be the whole of man in every sense. There was always room for other perspectives, but one of the difficulties was that within the psychological perspective itself, there was not much room for freedom because of the unspecified philosophical positions that were adopted. In a sense, then, empiricism or behaviorism recognized the *fact* of perspectivity, but they handled it poorly because they tried to define an absolute position rather than delineate a privileged position. For example, when psychologists say that only observable behavior is the subject matter of psychology (Morgan and King, 1966, p.4), they are not so much saying that other phenomena do not exist, as saying that they do not exist for the science of psychology. This way of limiting really implies an awareness of perspectivity, but it is not made explicit, and hence the relationship between a certain kind of content (observable behavior) and the attitude of a viewer (limiting oneself to methods of dealing with observable behavior) is also not made explicit. In other words, reductionism is an exaggeration of the fundamental truth of perspectivity—that man must delimit in order to function effectively in the world. A more balanced way of expressing this problem is in terms of a "privileged position" which implies both that other positions are possible, and that the relationship between the researcher and the corresponding "field" that is in his purview are taken into account.

One of the values of the reemphasis on perspectivity lies in the fact that it permits us to see experience as "person-related." That is, all of our experiences are based upon our *actual* viewpoint; we are partial toward the world. But partiality here does not mean that we purposefully act from a definite standpoint we have chosen; it means being party to what is taking place, being involved in what is happening (Linschoten, 1968, p.113). It becomes clear then that a subject in an experiment has his own perspective on things and events that more often than not are different from the psychologist's, and it is important that the experience be understood from the standpoint of the subject. In addition, precisely because of perspectivity, psychology should be the study of experience and behavior *as it is* experienced and behaved, and not studied according to a certain idea of how it is experienced or behaved. In other words, perspectivity would dictate that we study experience as it is experienced for it characterizes a person with his perspective. It is precisely here where psychology has run into so much trouble because "ideas" of experience and behavior that have been "depersonalized" and that have a range of applicability far broader than the *phenomena* of experience or behavior have replaced the latter. The phenomena themselves are tied to the person much more closely. However, for a human psychology this tie-up with the person's involvement is not only desirable but essential. It has not been emphasized by natural scientific psychology because of its priority on universality. For example, in traditional psychology a certain "idea" of what sensation must be was investigated rather than studying how sensing persons experience aspects of their world. While the movement toward universality may have been fruitful for the natural sciences, it is not immediately obvious that the human sciences partake of the same kind of universality. Moreover, the human sciences did not go through their own history and arrive at the idea of experience that might best represent the phenomenon of experience. This is precisely what is lacking; they have begun with universal notions as a presupposition. This is why under the concept of approach we are interested in clarifying presuppositions. Moreover, we feel that progress in psychology can be enhanced by more considerations of this type.

In effect, the reason that we feel that uncovering of presuppositions can be valuable for psychology is that, because of its history in trying to imitate the natural sciences, a host of natural scientific assumptions are hidden, and if our thesis is correct that a fundamental error was made in trying to adopt a natural scientific posture, then the uncovering of these presuppositions can only be an advantage. Again, some of them may prove to be valuable for limited purposes, but it would still be a gain to be able to specify or circumscribe the area within which such assumptions are valid.

CONCERN FOR THE INEVITABLE PRESENCE OF THE SCIENTIST IN SCIENCE

Under the concept of approach, all of the problems dealing with the inevitable presence of the human researcher in his own research are considered. It is not that others have been blind to this fact (e.g., Rosenthal, 1966; Heisenberg, 1966); it is just that very few have seen the need to account for this presence in a consistent and thorough way. Certain writers (e.g., Brody and Oppenheim, 1967) admit that the researcher has to be an experiencing person, but then this fact remains a mere presupposition and in no way influences how the research is practiced and interpreted. Others may admit that it is a problem, but then use this fact as an argument for using "objective" methods.

However, as we saw above, "objective" methods do not remove the presence of the researcher, they simply make him present in another way. The presupposition is that the objective approach is better than any other approach—but, we would add, for what intention? It is conceivable that a "neutral" presence may be the best attitude for the experimenter to assume in certain situations. But the problem is that most traditional psychologists (1) absolutize this presence, and (2) speak of it as a nonpresence. That is, they believe that it is an attitude that is universally valid and that, in a literal sense, the researcher is independent of his experimental situation. Thus, to state that the researcher is present not only initially but throughout the entire course of research, including interpretation and writing, is to introduce many problems. However we feel that the introduction of these problems constitutes an advance because previously they were not absent, but present in a hidden way. Perhaps now we can work towards the solution of some of them.

First of all, let us try to demonstrate the way in which the re-

searcher or theorist is constantly present. Let us first take a research situation. Everyone agrees that a laboratory situation is
an artificial situation. But what does that mean? It means that
the laboratory situation exists in a way that is not found naturally in the world. But how did the laboratory situation get
that way? Precisely through the activities of the experimenter. He
is the one who structured it. He constituted the experimental
situation by his selection of equipment, his definition of variables,
his selection of stimuli, etc. In other words, the laboratory situation is artificial because it is a *human artifact;* it, more than an
everyday situation, is the result of a single human person's intervention. Surely, the experimenter draws upon general principles
and accumulated knowledge, but the specific variables that are
chosen are still selected by him, the number of subjects are
determined by him, the procedures used to analyze the data are
determined by him, and so on. In other words, rather than
being independent of the researcher, the artificiality of the
laboratory situation means that more so than many other situations, it represents the viewpoint of *one* other person using the
media and knowledge of a community of persons. Human
presence cannot be defined by sheer physical presence; it is a far
more contextual matter than that. Let us pursue the matter to
the stages of data collection, interpretation and writeup. If experiments simply generated objective, independent facts, there
would be no need for the organization of the facts, nor for a
discussion of them. The simple truth would be there for all to
see. However, no published reports ever present merely raw
data. The data are always summarized or organized in some
fashion and there is always a discussion of them. The discussion
tries to indicate the significance of the facts, and it relates them
to relevant theories and points out the hypotheses and interpretations that the data support and oppose whenever this is
possible. If there were "objective" facts with univocal implications, none of the above would be necessary. In other words,
organization and discussion of data are not just pleasant activities
a scientist indulges in, but they are necessary to complete the
research. That is, human intervention is once again necessary;
there is no "reality-in-itself" that man merely registers; he ac-

tively participates in the constitution of what he calls "the real" (Boulding, 1967).

Lastly, we can point out that in the case of human subjects, the experimental situation ultimately must *exist for them,* and there is never any guarantee that the way it exists for them is the way the experimenter intended it (Giorgi, 1967). More important, however, is the simple fact that the experimental situation exists *for* the subject. This means that the situation is once again charged with human significance, and that the primary frame of reference for understanding the data should be the relation between the subject and the situation. One implication of this fact is that it will not be possible to account for results with expressions like "behavior as a function of stimuli" or "differences in behavior as a function of conditions" because they are not accurate (they may be acceptable as shorthand expressions, but it would be better to avoid them so that misinterpretations are not communicated). They are not accurate because the "conditions" or the "stimuli" are constituted in part by the subjects (not necessarily reflectively); it is not in terms of world versus subject or subject versus world that the results must be understood, but rather what kind of change in the subject-world relation is necessary to change any given subject-world relation. This latter terminology already implies human presence.

Note, we have not stated that because laboratory situations are artificial, they are not valuable; indeed we would hold the opposite. What we are simply trying to point out is that the reason that laboratory studies are valuable can be understood in a more adequate way. It is not because they uncover a "truth-in-itself" or because an "objective" attitude eliminates the presence of man from the research. These are not adequate explanations, because laboratory studies are inventions of men and because they are constantly being supported by human activities and awareness. Obviously something right is being done in laboratory situations, but we can still clarify these situations further. The implication we would like to stress, however, is that it is not simply an obvious platitude that science is constructed by man, but rather a highly relevant fact for both scientific understanding and praxis.

For example, if by means of an analysis such as we have just completed, one discovers that an "objective" attitude, in the traditional sense, does not really remove the presence of the observer, and that it is not a universal desideratum but merely describes one way of being present, one way of conducting research, the possibility of other ways of being present immediately presents itself. In other words, might there not be stiuations in which other ways of being present might be more fruitful? We believe there are, and especially when it comes to dealing with specifically human modes of behavior. The obvious question here is the one of circumventing the bias of the researcher or investigator. How is this to be done? Our answer, just as in the case of presuppositions, is that if biases cannot be eliminated, then they should be included. The reason is simply that they are part of the data that belong to a situation. Moreover, the mode of presence of the researcher is not limited to his own interpretation of it; wherever possible the subjects should also report on *how* the researcher was present. The presence of the bias limits the generality of the data, but this is precisely why a scientific perspective would want this information. An objective attitude is also a biased presence. By means of relating the results of a study with the biases (or perspectives) of a researcher, one would be able to circumscribe the context within which certain results would be valid. This *is* the way science progresses, and levels of high generality are achieved only after a long time. Sciences do not begin with universality, they arrive there; and it must be kept in mind that psychology is a young science. That sciences progress by carefully circumscribing areas of competence and validity is succinctly summarized by the Nobel Prize physicist Eugene Wigner as cited by DuBos (1965, p. 16):

The regularities in the phenomena which physical science endeavors to uncover are called laws of nature. The name is actually very appropriate. Just as legal laws regulate actions and behavior under certain conditions but do not try to regulate all actions and behavior, the laws of physics also determine the behavior of its objects of interest only under certain well defined conditions but leave much freedom otherwise.

Thus, when we discover that the bias of the observer or researcher sets a certain limit to the generality of his finding and therefore circumscribes the area or context within which the findings are valid, we are simply following the general aims of science. The only way to discover the limits of a human attitude or bias is to get it out in the open where all can see it. The assumption of an attitude or viewpoint that is somehow above or beyond either limits or biases is simply no longer tenable.

Thoereticians are no less exempt from being constantly present to their subject matter than are practitioners, and this is because ideas also obey the laws of relevancy to context. We discussed above how Husserl indicated that Galileo conceived of understanding things and events in their spatio-temporal dimension and that this led to consequent mathematization of nature and ultimately to the conclusion on the part of some scientists that nature *is* this network of mathematical relations. Since it was generally believed in scientific circles that nature was best understood from a quantitative perspective, psychology, in trying to be scientific, also presumed that the quantitative question was the most relevant one. In other words, it was forgotten that this was only one way of conceiving nature; it was taken to be the way nature was.

Another example of this can be seen in the very attitude many psychologists hold toward psychology. For example, many psychologists who adopt the view that psychology is a natural science, simply state that psychology *is* a natural science (Giorgi, in press), implicitly assuming the realistic position that science is something existing "out there." On the other hand, we have been careful to stress that we are speaking of psychology conceived as a human science. Psychology can be *conceived* as either. Our argument has been that psychology conceived as a human science will be far more fruitful for the understanding of human phenomena and the solution of human problems than psychology conceived as a natural science and that, moreover, the human scientific conception should take priority because psychology conceived as a natural science implicitly intended to accomplish the same task as human scientific psychology, but it chose the wrong means. But a second advantage of human scientific psychology is that it *admits* that it is *one way* of conceiving the science of psychology. This is an advantage both of the concept of approach and of the admission of the presence of the scientist in the constitution of his field. The implication is that the scientist's mode of conceiving is constantly part of the dialogue in constituting the science. Perhaps a method may be inadequate, or perhaps a phenomenon is misunderstood, but also, perhaps the scientist's way of conceiving the problem is in error. The latter is an equal plausibility because of the theoretical admission of the scientist's presence. When one says that psychology *is* a natural science, then the probability of questioning one's most fundamental assumptions is very remote. The awareness of presupposition and biases must precede their questioning; but if an ideology is present that states that one has *the* way of doing research, then questioning of implicit but equally relevant factors becomes much more difficult. Again, obviously, many traditional psychologists in their everyday praxis do challenge assumptions and presuppositions, etc.; the only problem is that such processes rarely get mentioned, let alone formalized. Our position is that if this is what most scientists *do*, then it must be an important facet of scientific activity and it should be systematized. A more careful description of precisely what goes into the making of science, in our eyes, is no small achievement.

Summary

We have covered certain problems that we feel that the introduction of the concept of approach has made possible. We do not feel that we have exhausted the problems that the consideration of the approach will permit; we have merely covered five that we feel are highly germane to psychology. Moreover, while we feel that we are still a long way from the completely successful solution of all of the problems that we have introduced, we do believe that we have broken a psychological logjam and that solutions of the sets of problems we have introduced will be conducive to the advance of psychological knowledge in a significant way.

Let us summarize what we have covered. In speaking about the problem of the privileged position, we saw that traditional psychology wanted to be a natural science and that it took (often implicitly) as its primary frame of reference or point of departure the approach and methods of the natural sciences. We pointed out, however, that even the natural sciences have a more fundamental point of departure, the life-world, and we suggested that psychology look for its roots directly in the life-world rather than by going through the natural scientific perspective or simply using the latter as its ground without raising the question of its roots.

This led immediately to the consideration of the proper origins of psychological phenomena. Our analysis revealed that traditional psychology often used ideas borrowed from the natural scientific perspective as the best representatives of psychological phenomena, or else it often treated psychological events as possessing thing-like or object-like properties. This latter feature is of course common to all of Western culture and not just a characteristic of psychology. Nevertheless, we suggested that one would have to assume a different attitude in order to open up the phenomenal realm and first describe and understand psychological processes as phenomena, and then work towards closure (e.g., in terms of psychological meaning) but in a way that does more justice to the psychological realm than either object-like closure or thing-like closure.

The third consideration was for the adequate understanding of the nature of consciousness, experience and behavior. Psychologists, with the possible exception of some of those whom we called precursors of human scientific psychology, have always had difficulty with these phenomena. Implicitly, however, we feel it was because these phenomena were compared against criteria that came from a natural scientific perspective. However, we felt it was necessary to assume a phenomenological attitude in order to understand these phenomena correctly. We also argued that it was possible to assume such an attitude and still stay within the realm of a scientific perspective, assuming that a human scientific perspective was understood. The phenomenological attitude would then permit one to understand the world, or a situation, as it existed *for* consciousness or a behaving subject. A careful study of the latter point leads one to posit as a priority the relation between man and his world rather than either understood as an isolated datum.

The fourth concern dealt with presuppositions. Implicit presuppositions that psychology had adopted were ideas of a world "in-itself," aspects of the approach of the natural sciences, and an a priori notion that there could be a universal viewpoint for all psychological problems. Our concern for presuppositions led to the explicit admission of perspectivity for any human endeavor, including science, and this led to the idea that initial universality as an ideal could be very misleading. Rather, universality was seen as an ideal-limit, but perhaps one that is never actually realized. This led to the more realistic notion that psychology should be content, at least for a while, to deal with generalities and that just as much, if not more, headway could be made by accurately circumscribing the context within which the generalities were valid. It was also seen that the intention of the scientist was a key factor in circumscribing a valid context.

The last problem considered was the one dealing with the inevitable presence of the scientist in the making of science. Psychology has been emphasizing this fact recently, but the full implications of this insight have not as yet filtered down to praxis. Thus we still see psychologists, with varying degrees of awareness of the problem, trying to execute the idea of an independent observer with the corollary assumption that an "objective" attitude kept the scientist out of his own situation. We took more seriously the fact that the ideal was not achievable and interpreted the objective attitude as meaning a certain type of presence that was never without influence. Our suggestion for controlling such varying modes of presence was to have them included as data. Thus, each scientist must include as much as possible his assumptions, biases, intentions—both as they appear to him and to others— in all his reports. In this way a body of data on the researchers *and* their findings will be accumulated, and one can then see more adequately the kinds of situations and the kinds of purposes for which the findings have greatest relevancy.

In effect, then, we feel that our viewpoint leads to an opening up of psychology. We have uncovered certain attitude or pre-suppositions that we feel have been blocking progress in psychology. The major difficulty for most psychologists, as we see it, is that the direction of the alternative suggestions we have made seem either to be beyond the realm of science or seem to demand a belief based on little or no data. But both of these difficulties presuppose perspectives that we challenge. Perhaps the clearest way of communicating our intention is to state that, in Kuhn's (1962) terms, psychology needs another paradigm. We feel that the paradigm within which psychology has been laboring has reached the limits of its usefulness, and that it is time to find a new paradigm. However, we are still in an age of transition; we are in a position where the insufficiencies of the older paradigm are readily apparent, but the articulate expression of the new paradigm is not yet known either. In this dilemma, we choose to leap into the unknown and try to work out the visible features of the new paradigm rather than to try to shore up the notches and gaps in the old one. Undoubtedly not all psychologists will agree with us. All we ask, however, is the freedom to state our case, so that those who may choose to participate in this vision may do so. Unfortunately, we feel certain that this period of psychological history will be filled with those activities that characterize transitions from one paradigm to another: resistances, debates, exaggerations on both sides, polemics, squabbles, etc. However, since these activities have not been entirely missing from psychology thus far, and since they are certainly not new in the history of man, we are inclined to accept them as undesirable but necessary accompanists to the development of human thought. It simply demonstrates what a human activity the making of science is.

CHAPTER 4

ON THE WAY TOWARD A HUMAN SCIENTIFIC PSYCHOLOGICAL PARADIGM

WHILE WE CONCLUDED THE LAST chapter by stating that we were working toward another paradigm for psychology, there is also a sense in which we could say that psychology is in its preparadigmatic stage of development with respect to an adequate and generally acceptable paradigm. Only this fact can account for the multiplicity of theories, viewpoints, tensions, and premature system building that very often characterizes our science. Watson (1967) has recently listed some of the polarities that have de facto guided the development of psychology, and Heidbreder (1933) saw as one of the positive features of the "schools" of psychology the fact that, in so many words, they served as paradigms for the earlier phase of psychology's history. However, the very fact that there were so many of them indicates that they were narrowly conceived and that no single one was able to "corner the market" so to speak. Moreover, we have James's statement quoted above that psychology is still waiting for its Galileo or Lavoisier.

In any event, we would assert that with respect to peculiarly human phenomena, psychology is definitely in its preparadigmatic phase. There is as yet no science that has fully articulated and expressed paradigms for the systematic and disciplined study of peculiarly human phenomena. This is simply another way of expressing the fact that the human sciences are lagging behind the natural sciences in development. But it is time that the human sciences as a group worked towards the development of their own identity independently of the activities and superior successes of the natural sciences. That is why it is important for some member of the human sciences to confront this issue squarely and to attempt the beginning of a resolution. We feel that psychology is at least as well qualified as any other human science, so that it certainly should be one of those making the attempt. For this reason, in this chapter, we shall try to articulate some features of the paradigm of psychology conceived as a human science.

We have been using the term "paradigm" as employed by Kuhn (1962), meaning the set of rules, theories, facts, problems, etc., that guide the research activities of scientists in the pursuit of normal science. From what we have said about the value of approach in the previous chapter, it perhaps can be seen why we would argue that the paradigm for a psychology of any conception, if it is to arise, can only come from the type of questioning and problems that are dealt with in the approach, and not from either method or content. For one thing, we have already seen that there exists within contemporary traditional psychology an approach that implicitly guides what is and what is not acceptable to psychologists. Consequently, we are not introducing a wholly new category, but rather merely trying to raise to explicit awareness something that is already present. Secondly, it is precisely the approach that deals with rules, theories, presuppositions, constitution of significant problems, and so on, which are also the very same topics that are of concern for paradigms. Hence, there is a very close similarity to Kuhn's usage of "paradigm" and our use of "approach," but they are not identical. The difference is that for us a "paradigm" is the articulated aspect of an approach; the term "approach" would include an explicit paradigm but also the nonarticulated sources of the paradigm itself. It is for this reason that we will concentrate primarily on approach and only secondarily on paradigm. The latter cannot be clarified without a better description of the former.

Our earlier analyses have revealed that what is presently guiding psychology is the approach of the natural sciences, which is an idea of science that is based upon how the natural sciences are practiced. But the whole point of this work has been that psychology ought not to have imitated or adapted the praxis of the natural sciences. Rather, the human sciences as a group, and psychology conceived as a human science in particular, should have gone to life-world phenomena in a more direct fashion and formulated its questions, problems, methods, and procedures independently of what the natural sciences were doing. Only after the human sciences have done this, and have applied and tested their own concepts and methods, can one come along and see to what extent the human sciences and the natural sciences have methods, concepts, and answers in common. But to start with their communality is a gratuitous assumption and goes against the spirit of science itself. Consequently, in this chapter, we shall attempt to articulate the approach, and indirectly the paradigm, of psychology conceived as a human science, by considering only matters that arise within this project itself. Obviously, however, we are not ahistorical; we are not even naïve with respect to psychology; we cannot even fully explain why the particular stand we take is more agreeable to us than a number of other plausible stands that we could assume. Our major responsibility, however, is to make clear as much as possible what this stand is—i.e., what our approach is—and this we shall proceed to do.

Before starting, however, it should be appreciated that the full articulation of the approach of any science, however critical it is, is not something that comes *first* in the process of practicing science. Rather, initially one is guided by a vision, in the sense of Strasser (1963), that is at first indeterminate and consists equally of gaps and ideas. The approach itself, however, is clarified in the very process of investigating specific phenomena by specific methods. Thus, at the same time that a vision is adopted, just as with a paradigm, it is *presumed* to hold until the evidence proves otherwise. It is with such a notion in mind that we begin, in the next section, an articulation of some of the characteristics of the approach of psychology conceived as a human science. While the precise way in which they are articulated here may not be the way such factors may ultimately be adopted, we are convinced that something similar to these factors will have to be dealt with in any truly authentic human scientific psychological paradigm.

*Some Characteristics of the Approach
of Psychology Conceived as a Human Science*

Where the characteristics are repetitious from earlier discussions, they will simply be stated here. Discussions will deal only with new characteristics. The minimum characteristics of the approach are listed below.

THE PRIVILEGED POSITION
OF HUMAN SCIENTIFIC PSYCHOLOGY

With respect to privileged position, the life-world is the most basic frame of reference from which psychology must take its point of departure and with which it must be in constant dialogue. Psychology does not remain within the attitude of the life-world. It must develop its own specialized attitude, which also must be clarified, but it begins with life-world phenomena and must dialogue with them constantly so that it is not cut off from its source of raw data.

ORIGINS OF PSYCHOLOGICAL DATA

As implied earlier, psychology must return to the phenomenal origins of any psychological process and then more toward closure if it is to be understood adequately. One corollary of this assumption is that psychological phenomena are essentially dynamic and they must be understood in their temporal aspects. A second one is that there must be a constant dialogue among the approach, the method and the phenomenon (or content) in any specific research or theoretical project as discussed earlier.

A related presupposition is also raised by this assumption, but it is a difficult one and it will require a lengthy discussion. This is the problem of the terms to be employed to express both the phenomenal origins of a psychological process and the mature phase of the same process, or the point at which sufficient closure has resulted for it to be established as a relevant psychological datum or reality. We propose to use the term "structure" to speak of the phenomenal origins, and for the lack of a better term, we shall use the term "psychological meaning" for the matured phase of the process. By the latter term we simply mean the best way of interpreting and expressing psychological reality. As we have indicated, our position implies that we must come to grips with the meaning of behavior as a uniquely psychological phenomenon.

Far more complicated is the understanding of the term "structure." We adopt Merleau-Ponty's usage of this term. Merleau-Ponty (1963, p.47) defines structure as follows:

> . . . [structures] are defined as total processes which may be indiscernible from each other while their "parts," compared to each other, differ in absolute size; in other words the systems are defined as transposable wholes. We will say that there is form whenever the properties of a system are modified by every change brought about in a single one of its parts and, on the contrary, are conserved when they all change while maintaining the same relationship among themselves.

Thus, "structure" is a comprehensive term that nevertheless implies an invariant meaning based upon relationship of discriminable parts. One of its values for us is that it is precisely structure that is the reality that one responds to at the phenomenal level. Merleau-Ponty (1962, 1963) has argued this point convincingly by showing the priority of structure as opposed to either elements, things, objects, ideas, etc. Over time, as one moves toward concretion, i.e., toward objects, things, or ideas, the structural context does not disappear, but rather it is transformed. Thus, there is still *some* context, but the total situation is no longer best described as a basically structural one as understood at the phenomenal level. For psychology, then, one must move from an understanding of a phenomenon in its structural sense to its "psychological meaning," which would seem to be the best type of concretion or closure for psychology. It should be noted that this is a very different kind of progress from beginning with a natural scientific idea of a psychological phenomenon and attempting to move toward a more properly psychological understanding of it.

Merleau-Ponty speaks about the distinction between structure and idea in another passage which may help clarify our point. He (Merleau-Ponty, 1962, p.429) states:

> . . . what constitutes the difference between the Gestalt of a circle and the significance "circle," is that the latter is recognized by an understanding which engenders it as the abode of points equidistant from a center, the former by a subject familiar with his world and able to seize it as a modulation of that world, as a circular physiognomy. We have no way of knowing what a picture or a thing is other than by looking at them, and their significance is revealed only if we look at them . . . from a certain *direction,* in short only if we place, at the service of the spectacle, our collusion with the world.

Thus, we can see that the context or frame of reference for significance is far more specifiable than that for structure; it is somewhat like the distinction we reported earlier that Merleau-Ponty makes between world and universe. Universes can be specified far more readily than worlds, but they are ultimately dependent upon and intrinsically related to the life-world. For a proper human scientific psychology, a progress akin to the movement from the life-world to a universe is also necessary. We simply wanted to clarify, however, that one must at least begin with structures if one is to return to the phenomenal level.

Merleau-Ponty has elucidated the meaning of structure in another way that is highly revelant for psychology conceived as a human science. Merleau-Ponty (1963, p.184) distinguishes three orders of structure, which are not powers of being but what he calls "three dialectics"; they are the physical, the vital, and the human orders. The physical structure is an equilibrium that is achieved with respect to the forces of the milieu; the vital structure is a stability that is achieved for itself by an organism based upon needs and instincts; and the human structure is a third dialectic whereby "signification" is the chief means of achieving stability. Another way that Merleau-Ponty expresses these orders is in terms of the following pairs: for the physical order we have "stimulus-reflex"; for the vital order, "situation-instinctive reaction"; and for the human order there is "perceived situation-work." These three orders are irreducible to each other. If these orders are accepted, and they are by us, then one can see more clearly the difficulties of trying to account for man in terms of stimuli and reflexes, or of even trying to account for him in terms of needs or drives. Rather, the challenge facing a human scientific psychology is that of trying to establish concepts, categories, techniques, and methods that will enable us to work with the dialectic "perceived situation-work." In other words, one of the primary responsibilities of psychology conceived as a human science is that it remains strictly within the human order. Except for some implicit breakthroughs, traditional psychology has not generally worked in this realm nor conceived of its problems in these terms.

Finally, another reason we feel that the term "structure," which emerges precisely because of the concern for origins, is valuable is because of its integrational possibilities. We have especially in mind here the possibility of integrating both the external and internal viewpoints that have caused so much difficulty in psychological history. The value of the concept of approach comes to the fore again because it should be understood that we are speaking about internal and external viewpoints and not methods or contents. In first trying to understand the internal viewpoint adequately, psychologists spoke about "inner contents" and the whole idea that what the self was present to were private data soon became prevalent (although this idea certainly antedated the existence of psychology). This idea is so strong that it exists to the present (e.g., Brody and Oppenheim, 1966). However, this idea could not persist so strongly if there were not a confusion between the internal viewpoint and internal contents.

Similarly, there has been confusion between the internal viewpoint and internal methods. Thus, for example, introspection has consistently been characterized as a method of internal observation. In fact, however, it is assuming an external viewpoint towards oneself. It can be called a "method of inner observation" only if one first believes in "inner contents"; but it really means stating the facts about oneself as any other person would do *if* he could be observing what the introspector happens to be observing. This means that the introspector must ignore his personal viewpoint and his unique proximity to his own

experiencing. This is why it can be classified as an external attitude or viewpoint toward oneself.

Consequently, it must be emphasized that this value of structure is in the integration of internal and external *viewpoints*.
That both viewpoints are necessary for the proper growth of
psychology is clearly attested to by the history of psychology. The
tension concerning the proper subject matter of psychology has
always implied the tension between internal and external viewpoints—those preferring an internal viewpoint defining psychology as the study of consciousness, and those preferring
an external viewpoint defining it as the study of behavior (this
does not imply that in all cases either consciousness or behavior
was properly understood). An examination of the act versus
content controversy can serve as an illustration of the necessity
of both viewpoints (see Boring, 1950). The act school held that
regardless of what the content of a conscious act was, an *act* was
necessary to have any content whatsoever. Therefore, they defined psychology as essentially being an investigation of the acts
of consciousness, or consciousness in general. But what turned
out to be embarrassing for this viewpoint were acts whose sources
were not conscious, plus various types of habitual behavior.
Thus, the total range of topics of interest to psychologists could
not be subsumed under this viewpoint. The content theorists, on
the other hand, stress the fact that regardless of what the act is,
a *content* is given to someone and what is important is the relationship between the content and the conditions in which it
was produced. Thus, their investigations led to systematic variation of conditions which were held to be more valid because they
were in the public realm and easily accessible to any observer.
However, what is a constant source of difficulty with this viewpoint is the factor of "experimental error" or the variance that
accompanies any experimental situation. In addition, it has been
demonstrated that one can keep stimuli constant and obtain
different responses, or one can vary stimuli and obtain the same
response; thus, the subject's response to some extent at least also
depends on the subject's viewpoint on the situation. Therefore,
in either case, one reaches the limit of the viewpoint without ex-
hausting all the possible topics of interest to psychology. Clearly,

then, a complementarity is suggested by these facts. But it is not a case of a simple side-by-side complementarity, but a dialectical one because it will be necessary to have internal and external viewpoints with respect to the "same situation" in some meaning of that term. We feel that the concept of structure of behavior will allow us to do this because Merleau-Ponty's idea of it implies that behavioral structures contain an intrinsic intelligibility—or its parts are internally related—and this type of relation is accessible from an internal viewpoint. On the other hand, behavioral structures are not wholly private phenomena, but on the contrary, they are also visible to the external viewpoint because they are also in the perceptual world. In other words, it is just as difficult to completely hide one's behavior—i.e., to be totally inexpressive—as it is to be completely open about oneself. Thus, by adopting a descriptive approach, Merleau-Ponty unveils behavior as the ambiguous phenomenon that it is, and he implicitly challenges the criteria of full clarity that we have been taught to expect about phenomena, as well as challenging the "either-or" notions of public and private.

In addition, Merleau-Ponty also shows that the whole problem of viewpoints is far from settled. The assumption is often made that an internal viewpoint must refer back to the self, and that an external viewpoint must refer to an other. However, this distinction is too simplistic. It is too simplistic because it presupposes that all viewpoints are limited to being mere passive attitudes. However, in assuming an active stance, which a reflective act is, a subject is able to grasp the meanings of experience or behavior, whether they be his own or another's. In other words, a reflective attitude is neutral with respect to the distinction between internal and external experience (Merleau-Ponty, 1964, p.65). Moreover, another complication comes in when we consider that the distinction between internal and external is often ambiguous. Does internal or external refer to the attitude, or to the object that is being attended to? If we consider that it is the former, then it should be emphasized that one may take either an internal or an external attitude toward oneself; or an internal or external attitude toward the other. While the proper explanation of this ability may be lacking, the fact that it can be done is

an experiential given. Otherwise, the method of introspection
would not be possible. Even though it is not a complete explanation, the process seems less mysterious if one remembers that an
external viewpoint is really a *highly specialized internal viewpoint* in the sense that it is still the viewpoint of *one,* or a position that that *one* must be capable of assuming. For example, I
can approximate the viewpoint that my wife might assume with
respect to a certain house, and I have some idea of what the earth
must look like from the moon. In both cases the viewpoints are
not naturally mine, but I have access to them. In other words, we
constantly move from internal to external viewpoints in the
course of everyday living; but this also means that an internal
viewpoint may not be as inaccessible as it is often assumed to be.
This does not mean that we know an internal viewpoint wholly
or *exactly as* the other knows it, but as we said above about behavior, it would be just as difficult to know nothing about it.

These are the kinds of problems that the concern for origins
initiates. Our position is not so much a concrete solution as the
offering of a direction in which certain key problems may receive
more precise articulation which ultimately will lead to concrete
solutions.

SOME KEY PRESUPPOSITIONS

There are at least three key presuppositions for psychology
conceived as a human science. They are presented below.

FIDELITY TO THE PHENOMENON OF MAN AS A PERSON   We mentioned previously that for any science the priority should be with
the relationships among the approach, the method and the content. We still agree with this position, but what we want to emphasize here is that within the context of such a trialogue, a human scientific psychology would stress fidelity to the phenomenon
of man as a person. This would be stressed, first of all, to counter
any reductionistic tendencies that may be prevalent. This is
especially important when operating within a scientific perspective because there is a strong bias in our culture that believes
that a human person cannot be studied scientifically. However,
the problem usually arises when one simply assumes the current
cultural meaning of science as indicating primarily the natural

sciences, and then one is left wondering how to fit man as a person into that context. Our aim, however, is to broaden the understanding of science by trying to devise ways in which to study man as a person rigorously and systematically. It is for this reason that fidelity to man as a person is a constant concern. In our understanding of the term, "person" includes all the specifically human characteristics attributed to man in the life-world as well as any other type of behavior that has been recorded and observed whether for good or evil.

SPECIAL CONCERN FOR UNIQUELY HUMAN PHENOMENA We mentioned earlier that one of the insights from phenomenological philosophy was that all positions were perspectival. If so, what is the special intention guiding our own approach that opens up possibilities that are worth pursuing? More than anything else, we would say that the concern for understanding uniquely human phenomena in a psychologically rigorous and valid way is the prime motivating factor. However, while we began with this intention, our understanding of it has expanded in a way we had not anticipated. That is, while initially we thought that problems of freedom, choice, destiny, death, etc., would be paramount, it became increasingly evident that far more areas than we originally were willing to allow were also relevant. This was one consequence of the introduction of the notion of human order by Merleau-Ponty. If the human order is irreducible, and if it consists of the dialectic "perceived situation-work," then many more processes that could have been considered more or less autonomous, or as belonging to a range of organisms rather than just to man, suddenly also become "uniquely human." Thus, Merleau-Ponty's thought opens up considerably the array of researchable human phenomena.

Nevertheless, as with all perspectives, some possibilities are closed off too. The chief domain that remains untouched by our approach is that of animal psychology. This is not to demean that area; it is simply a matter of recognizing legitimate limits of our approach.

THE PRIMACY OF RELATIONSHIPS The third presupposition we adopt is the primacy of relationships as opposed to seemingly independent units and entities. This is, of course, one of the fundamental insights of phenomenology, and it specifically refers to the primary relation of man and world. In practice this means that one is hard pressed to put a priority on the side of the world conceived independently of man, or on the side of man conceived as existing prior to his engagement in the world. Consequently, whatever phenomenon is considered has to be understood as already involving both man and world. The challenge facing human scientific psychology is the one of realizing this "primacy of relationships" in a concrete way and of being able to express its variables as the "related" variables they de facto are. Of course, there is an awareness of this fact within traditional psychology, but we feel that this notion has to be emphasized even more than it is and it must be formalized in a more systematic way.

A good example of the primacy of relationships is provided by Berger (1963). Berger speaks against the myth that in courtships some irresistible force can strike a person from anywhere and attract him toward "anyone." He points out how sociological investigations reveal "patterns" of courtships and uncover a complex web of motives related in many ways to the entire institutional structure within which an individual lives his life, e.g., class, career, geography, economic ambition, aspirations of power and prestige, etc. In such analyses, the "miracle of love" begins to look very synthetic or fictional. In short, these complex relationships preceded and even guided the awakening of "love" which from the point of view of the individual was an "individual phenomenon arising almost spontaneously from nowhere."

However it is not just with social or cultural phenomena that the importance of relations are being recognized. Rock (1966, p.260), for example, speaking of perception, writes:

. . . assuming the existence of bounded and shaped things, the relationship of their images to one another corresponds very closely to the relationship of the things themselves to one another in the real world. Thus relative orientation, position and size and the intra-figural or object-relative aspect of shape are all directly given by the relationship of the retinal images of objects to one another.

The fact that relations among objects in the real world are reflected in the relations among their corresponding images provides, in my opinion, one major explanation for the veridicality of perception.

While we do not necessarily agree with all of the expressions in the above paragraph, it does show how there is an increasing awareness of the role of relationships as an explanatory factor. In other words, what Rock is saying is important is not the relation between object and image, but the relation between the relationship among objects and the relationship among images. This also shows that there is a more explicit movement on the part of psychology toward the contextual, a matter we shall discuss shortly. In any event, by beginning our analyses with the concept of structure, we simultaneously presuppose the priority of relations in this sense.

SOME CHARACTERISTICS OF THE ATTITUDE OF HUMAN SCIENTIFIC PSYCHOLOGY

The attitude toward psychological phenomena will be different in a human-scientific psychology. There are two particular characteristics of the attitude we would like to discuss.

NECESSITY OF A BROADENING OR OPEN ATTITUDE   We have already indicated the distinction between a universe of discourse and the world, and how science functions by attempting to delimit the world in such a way that a universe is constituted. Operationally, this task has been simplified by setting up, as one of the restrictions, the analysis of only those events that have been completed, or in other words, of *past* events. When an event is past, it is closed, and even if one cannot know all of the factors determining an event or a phenomenon immediately, one can at least be sure that new factors cannot interfere. Consequently, if one can replicate conditions perhaps one can take closer and closer looks at the phenomenon until its enigmatic aspects disappear, or at least until the investigator is satisfied that he has coped with this phenomenon adequately.

The attitude of closure, or a constant narrowing or zeroing in on a phenomenon, is an attitude that is adequate for trying to understand "past" events or "closed phenomena." However, once a human being is introduced into a phenomenon as a constitutive

aspect, a "closing" attitude is no longer adequate; rather, if we
are to be able to stick to the primary criterion of our approach,
viz., fidelity to the phenomenon, then we shall have to utilize an
attitude that is more open, more indeterminate and consisting of
gaps as well as "filled" sections. Not so much because these factors are desirable in themselves; but simply because they are
there, and we want to note what actually happens. But then one
may object: is this still science?

Our answer would be that it may not be natural science, but it
is the attitude that one must use for a human science, and indeed,
such an attitude is incompatible only with the articulate views
of existing natural science, but not necessarily against the idea of
a human science, if for no other reason than that it has not as yet
been articulated. It should be evident to the reader that this is a
problem of *approach,* and therefore one that is not ordinarily
explicitly articulated within the realm of psychological science.
What makes the set of criteria for which we are arguing difficult
to reconcile with the idea of science is that the latter is supposed
to yield certitude, be a basis for prediction, operate deterministically in the sense of assuming a closed system of causal factors,
etc. But these are characteristics of the approach to natural
science, and not necessarily science per se. It still remains to be
seen what list of characteristics a human science would consist of.
An analysis of the human science characteristics *and* those of the
natural sciences might yield a deeper and more clarifying view of
what science as a whole actually is. However—and this is the
main point we wish to establish in this section—it is clear that
whatever else is necessary, an attitude that requires an opening
up rather than closure, one that allows for future possibilities as
well as past facticities, and one that does not foreclose the reality
of indeterminacy and ambiguity, will be a necessary point of
departure—because, to repeat, the main emphasis is fidelity to
the phenomenon as it appears, including processes, and *not* to an
idea of science that has been developed in a different context.
The essential point is that an "open" or "expansive" attitude
should not be judged against the criteria of the approach of the
natural sciences, e.g., predictability, certitude, etc. Rather, the
key factor to consider is whether or not an "open" attitude can

lead to the establishment of "actual happenings" or facts in a rigorous way. It is our assertion that it can and we hope to demonstrate this point in the next section.

THE NECESSITY FOR AN "ENGAGED" ATTITUDE   We have spoken at length above about how an objective attitude was not really a removal of the presence of a scientist, but rather a special kind of presence. Once that point is clarified the question of whether or not the objective attitude still remains the best possible attitude for all situations can then be raised. Our answer to the question is that it is not, and that for psychology conceived as a human science, a fully engaged attitude is required. By this is meant that if attempts to keep man, as a researcher, out of the situation fail, then perhaps the solution is to put him completely in it. Similarly, instead of trying to have human subjects respond unidimensionally, a better procedure might be to let the subject be completely in the situation. The idea here is to catch man more totally "engaged" rather than being present in more limited ways that are not spontaneously constituted by him. We must learn to delineate an attitude that reflects precisely man's involvement with the world. This necessity applies to both the experimenter and the subject, but in different ways, because their thematic presence is different. The experimenter's engagement is in the pursuit of science, and in specifying situations in such a way that subjects who behave more or less "normally" reveal patterns or styles of living that are presumably typical for those situations. Nevertheless, once the data are obtained, they are organized, interpreted, and written up according to the researcher's view of the situation. The major protection against bias is for the viewpoint itself to be made explicit, so that its validity may be circumscribed. It is not the sheer presence of a bias that vitiates data, it is the extension of limited biases to situations where they are not relevant and thus they lose their fruitfulness. Precisely because man is always in a limited situation, in a perspective, we feel that an engaged attitude which acknowledges such a perspective is a more accurate description than an "objective" one, and thus we feel that a more accurate understanding of why research situations have validity may be achieved.

What should be thematic for subjects of research is that they respond to the situation according to the instructions they are given. However, they too are engaged in the situation, and it would be wrong to think that they could be merely "objectively" present. Any experienced researcher knows that instructions can be interpreted in a number of ways, and this means that it is the subjects who actually complete the constitution of a research situation. In other words, they are engaged. If this is actually what takes place, then it must be described and understood as such.

Thus, we have a researcher who is engaged in the project of pursuing scientific psychology, partially constituting a situation that he believes will help clarify his understanding of a certain psychological phenomenon coming together with other persons (subjects) who also partially constitute the situation and who are engaged in the project of responding to certain instructions in what they believe to be typical ways. Any research situation in psychology is always a place where the engaged projects of two different attitudes intersect, even if it is only one subject responding to a stimulus. If we keep in mind what we have said about the primacy of relations and the necessity of contexts, it becomes apparent that the change in terminology is not just a semantic difference, but one that points to a more accurate description of a research situation in psychology. Anything that will throw light on the "projects" of the two attitudes, or on their respective theories, will help in understanding the situation better. That is why the notion of engagement is potentially so valuable. Moreover, the above description once again points out that psychology is essentially an intersubjective science.

THE SUBJECT MATTER OF PSYCHOLOGY CONCEIVED AS A HUMAN SCIENCE

In this section we shall try to clarify more sharply what we conceive to be the subject matter of human scientific psychology. We shall do this by discussing attitudinal differences and then by trying to clarify the phenomena of experience and behavior.

HUMAN SCIENTIFIC PSYCHOLOGY: THE DISCOVERY OF THE ACTUAL IN ORDER TO LEARN THE CONTEXTUAL Within the perspective of psychology conceived as a human science, the main con-

cern is to discover the actual, by means of description, in order
to learn about the structure of the situation as a whole, which is
done by revealing the context. The full psychological meaning
of the event is also uncovered by this process. This approach
emphasizes the youthfulness of psychology, where there are still
so many relevant findings to be discovered, as opposed to the
emphasis in the natural sciences whereby, because of their
maturity, they are able to "create" their data (Mead, 1964) by
structuring a situation and then observing if their *ideas* about a
phenomenon or theory are correct. The natural sciences are
mature enough to have many specific and precise ideas about
their experiments; but with human scientific psychology the
researcher has only some vague anticipations or expectations
about what to observe, and his attitude must remain more open-
ended and general, and his precision is directed toward a description of the actual occurrence rather than to any kind of treatment of the actual. Thus, the difference in emphasis we are
articulating is that, because of its subject matter, human scientific psychology remains open to the emergence of the *actual* and
tries to capture it as faithfully as possible so that *ideas* of it may
be formed. In the natural sciences, the research paradigm is
mostly (but not exclusively) one where a researcher tries to test
his *idea* of the phenomenon. This is another reason why direct
imitation of contemporary natural sciences is an erroneous procedure, because for the most part they are at a more developed
phase of their history. Psychology might even be better off trying
to imitate the *beginnings* of the natural sciences; but curiously
enough, that would involve an historical analysis which would
once again put us in the realm of the human sciences.

The above discussion concerned a difference in emphasis, but
now we want to speak about an essential difference between
human scientific psychology and the natural scientific approach.
In the natural scientific approach, methodologically speaking,
once a unit or a whole is established the analytic process is then
usually applied, which means that the whole is broken down into
elements or parts and then the whole is understood in terms of
this analysis. In a human scientific approach, we are suggesting
that once the unit or whole is established it is then conceived to

be merely a constituent of a larger-structured context, and through the process of explicitation (Giorgi, 1966) precisely how the constituent under consideration is related to the whole becomes known and its meaning can be ascertained. In other words, in this perspective the discovery of the actual (understood as what is present, but not necessarily limited to its physical aspects) is the point of departure for uncovering relationships, contexts, and meaning. This is necessary because the latter types of information are far more valuable for the human sciences than mere facts, physical dimensions, or quantitative expressions. While the exact procedures used in the process of explicitation can still undergo further clarification, our position is that they can be applied as rigorously, in principle, as any analytic procedures.

An example of the application of this method is provided by Colaizzi (1967) who was interested in discovering how nonsense syllables changed in their appearance during the course of learning. Consequently he interrupted subjects during their learning at various phases of the process in order to obtain descriptions of their experience. One interruption took place after a single exposure of the ten syllables and we shall concentrate on this phase to demonstrate our point. First of all, the fact emerged that not one subject was able to repeat a single syllable correctly, although he was asked to do so. Secondly, if one were to ask about the facts that were discovered, one would find a seemingly uncorrelated array: some subjects spoke about the apparatus, some mentioned the instructions, some talked about the experimenter, some spoke about the shock of being interrupted, some mentioned unfamiliar items or letters, etc. These were the facts that the descriptions produced. With the method of explicitation one tries to understand the actual context within which the facts emerge. Consequently one continually studies the protocols in order to see what is common or typical about the context that would permit precisely these facts to appear. One looks for the meaning that relates these specific facts to the context, as parts to a whole, that would render them all intelligible. Colaizzi concluded that awareness of the learning *situation* is the functional or lived contextual unity that co-relates the seemingly disparate facts that emerge after the experience with a single learning trial.

Thus, while subjects reported different facts—the experimenter, the apparatus, unfamiliarity—the reason that these particular facts were able to emerge was that they were related in a functionally significant way (i.e., meaningfully) to the experience of the situation as the initial phase of a learning process. Thus, more accurately, one could say that the subjects experienced "the-apparatus-as-*part*-of-the-learning-situation," or "the-unfamiliarity-as-*part*-of-the-learning-situation," etc., rather than merely the apparatus or unfamiliarity as such. At this phase of the process the *context itself is experientially figural* even though *parts* of it serve as the vehicle of expression. Moreover, it should not be forgotten that the items themselves were what were sought, and eventually do emerge, at the end of the process. Descriptions reported from different phases of the process reveal different facts, contexts and meanings that can be ascertained in the same manner.

The above example of explicitation may clarify the notion somewhat, but it probably will not silence all questions. Colleagues will surely ask about its validity, reliability, objectivity, etc. At this stage of our experience with this method, we can only reply with the following comments: (1) Undoubtedly, we admit that the method can stand further clarification, articulation, and refinement. (2) One must be careful not merely to superimpose the criteria of the natural scientific approach on this method. It is more a matter of discovering its own internal criteria. (3) We can point to the fact that this method *does* work even though we cannot as yet fully state *why* it works. But this is very often the case in science; certain things work and just why they do is something that emerges only after years of experience with the technique. The real difference is that this method does not *look scientific* according to the expectations of the natural scientific approach. That is why we feel that it is important to overcome this prejudice and allow the development of methods that look different, as they should, when different phenomena are being studied and different questions are being asked. All of this implies a different outlook on science and this in turn explains why we insist on the relevance of the approach. In any event, we are not claiming that human scientific procedures are already in existence and ready for use, but only that they are possible.

THE DELINEATION OF EXPERIENCE AND BEHAVIOR   One of the major tasks still confronting psychology, and this includes human scientific psychology, is the proper understanding of experience, of behavior and of the relationship between the two. Our position is that a structural approach offers a good possibility for such an understanding, although whether or not it will ultimately be the most fruitful approach will of course depend upon how well it fares. At any rate, a structural approach makes possible the study of experiential-behavioral dialectics, which for us is the subject matter of psychology, from a unified point of departure (Giorgi, 1967). Many other psychologists have stated that both experience and behavior are necessary for psychology, but very frequently this is understood in a side-by-side manner. That is, familiar objective techniques are used for studying behavior, and familiar introspective methods are used for the study of experience. The difficulty is that both methods already imply a disruption of experience and behavior; they have developed from viewpoints that considered either behavior or experience as self-enclosed entities. It is our position that behavior and experience are related in an intrinsic way that has not as yet been fully captured.

The way we would propose to attempt this—and we admit that this is still only an attempt—is by trying to understand the experiential-behavioral dialectics in terms of a more comprehensive concept such as structure or situation. As implied above, heretofore one tried to center on either experience *or* behavior, but by making either one figural, the other was implicitly cut off and then one could relate them only externally. Our position is that behavior and experience are best understood in terms of internal relationships.

We will again draw upon a phenomenological perspective to help us formulate the problem. Van Kaam (1966) has spoken of understanding behavior in terms of intentional-functional relations, and Gurwitsch (1964) has restressed the presentational function of consciousness or experience. We propose to utilize these ideas to come up with a framework for understanding the experiential-behavioral dialectics. Our proposal is that these dialectics can be understood by considering them in terms of the following pair of relations: (a) intentional-functional-fulfilling relations, and (b) intentional-presentational-fulfilling relations. First, a general comment about the relations themselves is in order. We interpret these to be internal relations, i.e., intrinsic ones that are discovered over time by a process of unfolding or development. Moreover, both sets of relations occur simultaneously in an even larger context than we are considering, so in that sense, there are limits to the usefulness of these relations in understanding human behavior and experience, but the precise limits cannot be known until much more experience in their application is accumulated. Lastly, we have used a more comprehensive set of relations precisely because of our concern for contexts and the primacy of relations. For example, in the history of psychology, there have always been functional schools and structural schools, but they have always been defined too narrowly. Functionalism usually means stressing the functions or activities of organisms, but then these functions were always related to experience or the world in an external way. Similarly, structural schools usually stressed the invariant features of content, but then tried to relate these contents back to the organism or to the conditions of research in an external way. That is why the approach adopted is so important; it helps to establish the fact that the *way* in which one views phenomena is what is so important. In this context it is precisely the internal viewpoint that has been misunderstood so often.

Hence, van Kaam's idea that behavior should be understood in terms of intentional-functional relations is an important breakthrough, but we feel he stopped short. It is not only the sources (intentions) of behavior that must be understood in terms of internal relations, but also their consequences (fulfillments, implying also their lack). However, a human person is so complex that it is difficult to comprehend him solely in terms of one set of relations. Thus, capitalizing upon Gurwitsch's reemphasis on the presentational function of consciousness, and also recognizing that it, too, has sources and consequences (obviously

Gurwitsch does too but he does not express it in this way), then we can also try to understand man in terms of intentional-pre-sentational-fulfilling relationships.

It should not be forgotten that these analyses are always performed within the context of a more comprehensive structure or situation. This point is essential because it is the only way in which the unity of experiential-behavioral dialectics can be understood. In other words, it is not the same situation seen *first* experientially and *then* behaviorally; rather, it is one situation *containing* experiential and behavioral *aspects*. Experience and behavior are not sheer substitutes for each other, one known to the actor and the other to the observer. The problem is more complicated because experience and behavior literally reveal different aspects of a given situation *at the same time that they overlap* each other. They are different kinds of "openings" to a situation that neither exist merely "side-by-side" nor are reducible to each other. The internal viewpoint (actor) is the *privileged position* for unveiling experience, and the external viewpoint (observer) is the *privileged position* for access to behavior, but neither the internal viewpoint nor the external viewpoint is limited *exclusively* to either experience or behavior. Both viewpoints have access to both phenomena, but not equally so. Consequently, once one adopts a structural or situational viewpoint, one sees that the experiential-behavioral relation is a unified action on or response to a situation that is complementary precisely because different aspects of the situation are revealed by either side of the relation. This is the real danger of trying to reduce one to the other; it inevitably reduces the situation and the phenomenon under investigation. Thus, it is necessary to adopt attitudes that will comprehend the entire situation (and this process overcomes the problem of the two sciences of psychology because one is still bound by the *unity* of the situation or structure), and then within that attitude intentional-presentational-fulfillment relations will help to clarify the internal viewpoint and the experiential aspects, and intentional-functional-fulfilling relations will help to clarify the external viewpoint and the behavioral aspects of the situation.

Still another point implicit in all these discussions should be made explicit, otherwise some of the value of enlarging the horizons in the way we have suggested may be lost. It is most important to realize that from a human scientific perspective the "actual" or the real cannot be reduced to physical presence. However we ultimately come to understand the presence of contexts or relationships, it is clear that they are experientially given and not in a physical sense. Once again we would follow Merleau-Ponty (1968) here, this time in the direction that his notions of the visible and the invisible suggest. Merleau-Ponty points out how man, as embodied subjectivity, is the perceivable perceiver, the touchable toucher, the sensible sensor; and he generalizes this under the notion of the visible and the invisible. The point is that the real consists precisely of a dialectic between these two and not of just one half. Moreover, that which is visible is not understood in precisely the same way as the one who is doing the seeing, and vice versa. In other words, phenomena are constituted by both halves of this dialectic, and it is only because of empiricistic and positivistic biases that we are surprised to discover that the real consists of more than just the sensory or physical. Applied to the discussion at hand, we would say that from an external viewpoint, experience is the invisible aspect of a situation in which the behavior is visible; and that from an internal viewpoint, behavior is the invisible aspect of a situation in which the experience is the visible. However, these should not be conceived as dichotomous or in an all-or-none sense. As implied before, we affirm that the internal viewpoint is the privileged position for access to experience and that an external viewpoint is the privileged position for access to behavior, but that these are not exclusive. Merleau-Ponty also holds not only that the two perspectives of visible and invisible are not exclusive, but that they do imply each other, and overlap, and "encroach" upon one another. They meet within the lived-body, and it is difficult to tell where one leaves off and the other picks up. We would say the same about experience and behavior. They intersect within the lived-body, and without the latter notion— a valuable contribution of Merleau-Ponty—it would indeed be difficult to locate the point where behavior and experience intersect.

PSYCHOLOGY'S SUBJECT MATTER REQUIRES A NEW CONCEPT OF
NATURE We mentioned earlier that in speaking of consciousness, experience, or behavior, intentional relations are always
involved, and thus trying to understand these phenomena within
a cause-effect paradigm or in terms of external relations (or, in
short, with a strictly naturalistic viewpoint) is not an adequate
approach for psychology conceived as a human science. Insofar
as the natural scientific approach in its theoretical formulations
explicitly, and in its praxis almost exclusively (there are some
implicit deviations), considers man as *part of the world*, it studies
him without reference to his intentional relations *to* the world.
But man is also one *for whom the world exists* and this side of
him hardly ever receives explicit reference within the natural
scientific viewpoint. Psychology as a human science especially
wishes to do justice to the latter aspect—not to detract from the
former, but to integrate it.

Perhaps the difference between our approach and the natural
scientific approach can best be understood in these terms. We
follow Merleau-Ponty's (1963) line of reasoning here. It is not
that the natural scientific approach to psychology yields nothing
or deals with phenomena that are nonexistent. Rather, it deals
with the behavior of man at levels that are lower than his most
integrated functioning. Most of its theories, concepts, hypotheses,
definitions, etc., are derived from or refer to the vital level of integration and not yet to a more properly human structural level.
Many of these phenomena are found with pathological cases or
with traditional laboratory studies, both of which, for different
reasons, allow only a reduced level of functioning to appear
(Merleau-Ponty, 1963). The difficulties in communication between the two viewpoints is perhaps greatest just at this point.
Because the human scientific viewpoint is holistic it asserts that
when one is interested in studying man at his highest level of
functioning, at the level of the unequivocally human, then facts
obtained at lower levels of functioning are not necessarily relevant as such. They may or may not be, depending upon the
extent to which a human context was implicitly present. Natural
scientific psychologists often interpret this attitude as a mere
dismissal of their data; human scientific psychologists, however,

intend to communicate caution because they realize that crossing contexts uncritically can be just as misleading as comparing data when methods differ. We feel that the caution is justified because it is not merely a matter of adding up such facts in order to build a human order, nor is it simply a matter of interpreting the "same" facts differently; it is literally a matter of trying to determine what the relevant facts at the human level would be. Thus, to integrate the "naturalistic" aspects of man literally means a transformation of them. On the other hand, when such "naturalistic" behaviors appear, one can also assume that the person to whom they belong is not behaving in the most integrated fashion possible vis-à-vis his particular situation. This is why we must learn to conceive of research situations in such a way that the higher levels of functioning are given at least an equal chance of appearing. Only in this way will facts concerning them be discovered and understood.

The above comments lead to a direct confrontation with the problem of the meaning of nature. We do not intend to resolve this complex issue here, but we feel that some minimal clarification is in order. Because of the aim of the human sciences to study systematically the human level as it is lived, and the fact that man is also a creature for whom the world exists, the natural scientific conception of nature is not adequate. Within the latter perspective Cartesian influences are dominant, and nature came to be defined in opposition to consciousness and vice versa. Thus, as Merleau-Ponty (1963) states, nature came to mean the reference to a multiplicity of events external to each other and bound together by relations of causality. To the extent that psychology has attempted to be a natural science, it has remained faithful to realism and to causal thinking (Merleau-Ponty, 1963), and our own analyses have indicated how often psychology has expressed such an ideal.

However, Merleau-Ponty (1963, p.3) himself does not accept this definition of nature, but because many practitioners of science are often guided by such a concept, he wishes to bring its meaning to the level of explicit awareness, in order to show how theories of nature must be brought into better harmony with the facts. The long history of success in the natural sciences has made most of us uncritical with respect to all of its aspects, and thus many provisional conceptual formulations of science are often accepted as absolute ones. Thus it is not surprising that the natural scientific understanding of nature was almost universally accepted. Due to the prevalence of this conception of nature, then, one must either state that man is in part nonnatural in order to comprehend him adequately, or the concept of nature itself must be broadened so that *all* aspects of *human* nature can be included. Either choice is fraught with difficulties, but we prefer the latter alternative. In either case, however, the natural scientific conception of nature is not adequate for the phenomenon of man as a person. Primarily this is because it was conceived too narrowly, and because it neglects to take into account the complex relationships that the phenomenon of consciousness introduces. The last statement, of course, presupposes that the study of man can be undertaken without necessarily assuming the historical dichotomy between consciousness and nature understood in its more narrow sense.

It is also important to realize that one does not have to leave the realm of science in order to try to understand the complexities that consciousness introduces, or the fact that the world also exists for man; one must simply go beyond the realm of the sciences of nature as they have been traditionally understood. In other words, the *aim* of the human sciences is similar to the *aim* of the natural sciences, namely, to observe, describe, and try to render intelligible all of the phenomena that man experiences or is capable of experiencing. But the implementation of human scientific psychology must differ because the way human phenomena reveal themselves also differs; the way man relates to the phenomena of the physical world and the way he relates to, *and is related to by,* the phenomenon of man, is radically different in the life-world. It is this difference that we take seriously and try to systematize into a scientific viewpoint. It is possible to achieve this scientific ambition because we must remember that seeing the phenomena of the world in terms of cause-effect relations, in an objective way or in thing-like categories, is ultimately due to a certain *attitude* toward the world (Kockelmans, 1965); and in order to see human phenomena in terms of intentional relations or in terms of a human category system, one must also assume a certain *attitude* toward those phenomena, but not the same attitude in both cases. All that is necessary is that science admit more than a single attitude into its domain, and this it already does. It seems to us that what should characterize a scientific perspective is the relevancy and the fruitfulness of the attitude that science assumes with respect to a group of phenomena, and the rigor with which it is applied, but not the absolutization of a single attitude or of a single technique for being rigorous. One would be more conscious of these distinctions if more attention were paid to the role of approach in science.

One can certainly understand the desire of natural scientific psychology to attempt to place the totality of phenomena within one unified perspective or under one concept. Such a unity is the constant striving of man be he scientist, philosopher, poet, or mystic. Our objection is not to the intention so much as to the specific concept or perspective that purports to be all-encompassing. We feel that the specific conception of nature being offered as the basis for unity is too narrow, too one-sided, and unduly influenced by the perspective of the natural sciences. As we indicated above, we also feel that the very understanding of science itself has been too closely associated with the praxis of the natural sciences. That is why our own approach is more open-ended—why we would argue for a broadened conception of nature, so that inputs from different perspectives could be readily assimilated. Precisely because we do not know the exact meaning of nature, it is for us still a problem to be solved, rather than an answer to be defended. We do know, however, that the answer to the meaning of nature being offered by the natural scientific perspective would exclude many legitimate psychological phenomena, and that is too heavy a price. Because of our insistence that the life-world is the ground for science, and especially the source of its raw data, we turn the problem around. We assert that the proper investigation of many concrete psychological problems, if they are formulated precisely as they reveal themselves, will put increasing pressure on established psychological concepts and theories to cope with them. The result of this confrontation between the concrete problems and the established theories, we believe, will be the broadening of the theories, including their concept of nature.

To say that our approach is open-ended also means that we have no specific commitments as to what the answer to the problem of nature should be. If the study of all of the phenomena that man can experience demonstrates that they are all of one nature, and can be subsumed under one concept yet to be defined, that is agreeable to us. If, on the other hand, the above described phenomena can only be understood by positing multiple natures, then that is also agreeable. The only alternative we would not permit is the achievement of unity at the price of the exclusion of some phenomena for whatever reason. The discovery of phenomena that upset man's categorical systems have more often than not proved to be rewarding for man. Hence, we argue for the broadening of concepts rather than the delimiting of phenomena.

One last point. While we have been mostly arguing against a natural scientific approach in this section, these arguments should not be interpreted as arguments for an opposite mentalistic position. As with Merleau-Ponty (1968), we do not wish to choose sides with respect to the classical antinomies, but we prefer to emphasize the embodied human person in the most comprehensive sense, so that a means of integrating the truths of "naturalism" and "mentalism" may be found in a way that goes beyond the excesses of either.

THE INEVITABLE PRESENCE OF THE SCIENTIST IN THE CONSTITUTION OF SCIENCE

This notion has been discussed at length but there are two more implications we would like to emphasize.

THE CONTEXT FOR INVESTIGATING MAN AS A PERSON CANNOT BE LESS THAN THE CONTEXT FOR UNDERSTANDING MAN THE INVESTIGATOR This is an extremely significant point that is often neglected—partly because it is not as problematic within the context of the natural sciences, partly because it is recognized in theoretical discussions but not necessarily carried through in practice, and partly because it can be justified by claiming that science must limit in order to function. Obviously, we agree with the latter principle; the only question at issue is the type of lim-its that are set. The point at issue is that man as subject of research can in no way have assumptions attributed to him that one would deny to man as researcher. Stated positively, one would have to assert of man as subject of research all the as-sumptions and attributes that one holds concerning man the re-searcher. And even more importantly, one would have to *con-duct* research within the context of these assumptions. Probably many psychologists would object that the imposition of such demands would make research in psychology impossible, or they would try to argue that such demands are unnecessary because there is obviously a lot of successful research currently being conducted outside the context we recommend. However, we must remember that such objections come from within the context of the natural scientific approach, and the assumptions that are valid in that context do not hold within our perspective. Un-fortunately, one of the major difficulties of conceiving psychology as a human science is that it is simultaneously the problem of conceiving of the proper functioning of the human sciences themselves. In other words, there are few precedents to go by, and because of this, many of the notions that are introduced seem to be "far out" or absurd, but we feel that they can only be com-petently judged by criteria that have yet to be devised, and cer-tainly not by the present standard criteria.

In any event, we would posit that the investigator and the sub-ject are equals with respect to basic assumptions about their humanity. What does differ, as we explained before, is their *thematic presence* in a situation. This is true whether one is speaking of an experimental situation or a therapeutic one. This way of describing psychological situations once again reveals the radical intersubjectivity of psychology conceived as a human science.

A NON-MANIPULATIVE PARADIGM IS NECESSARY This is a di-rect implication of the above point. Understanding human psy-chological research in terms of cause-effect analyses or in terms of "a function of x variables," etc., will no longer be desirable. The relationship between experimenter and researcher will have to be based upon appeal and cooperation and understood in that sense as well. Moreover, research designs will always have to be open-ended so that the final closure can be made by the subject himself. When the closure is accomplished, data are obtained, but now they are obtained from a perspective that includes the subject's more spontaneous participation. In short, if one truly believes that humans should not manipulate other humans, then it seems to be absurd to try to build a human science on the basis of a paradigm that violates this essential point. Obviously here we are referring only to the direct or indirect manipulation of other humans and not to the manipulation of the physical environment.

Implications of the Characteristics of Human Scientific Psychology for Its Paradigm

In this section we will merely try to articulate a direction rather than come up with definitive answers. Earlier we characterized the approach to natural scientific psychology as being empirical, positivistic, reductionistic, objective, analytic, quantitative, deterministic, concerned with prediction and largely operating within the genetic bias and with the assumption of an independent observer. All of these factors have operated in such a way that the paradigm of natural scientific psychology was structured primarily to ask a measurement question and to reveal the quantitative dimensions of reality. It also favored a paradigm that sought specificity and explanations that were within the context of cause-effect relations. This, in turn, has led to designs that favor isolation of variables with the assumption of a constant relation between specific variables and the conditions of the experiment, but this constancy is understood as being due to external relations between man and the world.

From what we have said thus far, it is readily apparent that the paradigm for conducting research within the context of psychology conceived as a human science will be very different. The approach of the human sciences may be characterized as being concerned with meaning, description, qualitative differences, the process of explicitation, investigating intentional relations, dealing with human phenomena in a human sense and in a human way, articulating the phenomena of consciousness and behavior within the context of a broadened conception of nature, and assuming the privileged position of the life-world, the primacy of relations and the presence of an involved scientist. These characteristics will have to lead to a paradigm that is far more dialectical than the traditional paradigm, one in which the implications of every decision that the researcher makes will have to be pursued and one in which the precise meaning of the researcher's presence will have to be ascertained. It implies a paradigm that must be far more open-ended than the traditional paradigm, and one that will allow the presence of indeterminateness and generalities because such phenomena exist in research situations. It will be more open-ended also because subjects are seen as co-constituting the closure of the paradigm with the meanings *they* bring to the situation. Consequently, because of the last two reasons, precisely what variables were operating in the experiment or research situation can be ascertained only *after* the research is completed—not before. This fact clearly indicates that while a human scientific psychology is not empiricistic or positivistic, it is *empirical* (based on experience) and *positive* (it affirms a reality). This is also why we feel we can include this project within the context of a science, because it is the aim of science to be faithful to experience and to unravel the mysteries of the world. The only problem with empiricism and positivism is that these philosophies defined experience and the real too narrowly, and by means of certain *ideas* of experience and the real which brought closure too rapidly. Consequently, this is why we argue that the approach is absolutely vital, and why an approach must be characterized as including the vague, the general, and the indeterminate. First of all, existentially speaking, they are *there*. Secondly, as Merleau-Ponty (1962) asserts, they are positive phenomena. We must not see them as merely the lack of specificity, but as contexts and horizons that give the specific objects, things, and ideas their meaning. Lastly, the difficulty is not so much with experience and the real, as with our formulated ideas of them. Thus our ideas of these phenomena must change, and this can only be done by turning away momentarily (bracketing) from the established ideas, then by trying to be present to experiences and the real in a fresh way, and only then trying to formulate more accurate ideas about them. Only after the newer ideas have emerged can they be compared to the older ones. But all of the above implies an openness for new attitudes and a tolerance for new styles of thinking—especially when they are in their beginning phases.

The last sentence might be interpreted as a plea, and perhaps it is. Undoubtedly, to argue for a new paradigm means that one is essentially dissatisfied with the existing one. It also means that many supporters of the older paradigm will have to disagree with the newer one if only for the simple reason that the existing paradigm is for them fruitful. Our only concern is that the suggested new paradigm be judged according to intrinsic criteria rather than in terms of the criteria of the older paradigm. Thus, it would be wrong to state that the new paradigm we suggest is erroneous because it violates the principle of determinism. It is precisely the principle of determinism applied to human phenomena that helped to create the need for a new paradigm. This is why the concept of approach had to be introduced. In a sense, it deals with the whole problem of the criteria of criteria, which cannot be irrelevant for the conduct of science. Still, there will be problems in trying to establish the idea of a human science in general, and we would like to speak to some of these problems in the next section.

Problems in the Establishment of a Human Science

Undoubtedly there will be difficulties associated with the establishment of a whole new division of science in a radical way, and there will be objectors, detractors, etc., but we feel that none of the objections can really overcome the positive advantages of articulating and developing both the intention and the practice of a human science. Nevertheless, some of the difficulties are real, and anyone who expects a "completed program" is really judging the *project* of a human science from the vantage point of its completion and it simply is not legitimate as yet to do so. An analogy would be to say that science cannot meet with success because it has not yet discovered the cure for cancer or because science still does not fully comprehend the workings of the central nervous system. Other difficulties to the establishment of a human science are misunderstandings about its intentions. Consequently the purpose of this section is to discuss both misunderstandings and real difficulties.

A HUMAN SCIENCE IS **NOT** THE EXTENSION OF A THERAPEUTIC ATTITUDE

Many objections to psychology conceived as a natural science come from clinical psychologists and therapists who find the natural scientific model of man irrelevant for their concerns and problems. We can agree to their objections but we feel that to substitute "therapy models" for "mechanical models" is another opposite, but equal, error. Both attempts reflect the desire to fill the void created by the lack of an authentic human psychology, but both turn out to be extensions of a more restricted viewpoint. We are not saying they do not contribute to psychological knowledge, but merely that they overextend themselves to meet the void of an authentic psychology. Rather, a rigorous approach to the study of the human person has to be developed so that he can be studied sheerly for the purposes of understanding him, i.e., within a context that is not as restricted as therapeutic or clinical psychology, nor in a context that has left out the essentially human.

IS THERE A NECESSITY FOR A HUMAN SCIENCE?

Perhaps the most serious difficulty in the way of a legitimate human science will be the burden of demonstrating that it is needed. Unlike research in outer space, psychology has no lunar landscapes or distant galaxies that lie unclaimed and uncharted, waiting only for the bold explorers to come to them. The provinces of knowledge with which we are dealing, like all the land and waters on the earth, are all claimed. Consequently, the domain that the human sciences must deal with has to be carved out of areas that already have owners, and cause must be shown why the human sciences have a superior right or a priority on such claims even though it is the human sciences that are the late-comers. Obviously, the two pretenders are natural science and philosophy. Thus far, most of science has claimed to be natural science; only recently has the notion been introduced that a human science ought to be conducted radically differently from natural sciences. On the other hand, the claim is still definitely that it is science we are speaking of and not philosophy. Unfortunately, it has become commonplace for philosophers to claim the whole human domain as their prerogative, and for some, even the exclusive rights to the method of reflection. Psychologists, on the other hand, have often been only too willing to surrender the method of reflection to the philosophers because of the biases inherent in empiricism (a particular philosophy) and also because it smacked of "arm-chair" psychology to sit and reflect on a problem. However, after our first chapter, it is clear that what psychology wanted to break from was *speculation* but not necessarily reflection. However, in order to be sure that they were not guilty of speculation, psychologists threw out the proverbial baby with the bathwater.

In other words, the struggle to establish a separate category of knowledge will have to go through a kind of battle that science itself went through to break away from philosophy, except that the problem is compounded by the fact that now there are *two* establishments instead of only one. With respect to philosophy, on this point we agree with the British philosopher and commentator on Dilthey, H. A. Hodges (1944, p.50), who has a somewhat lengthy, but trenchant analysis of specifically this point:

It may be suggested that the human studies and philosophy are now in much the same position with regard to psychology as philosophy once was with regard to natural science. Philosophy was concerned from the beginning with questions whose solution required some knowledge of the system of nature. But since in those days the method which has made modern science possible had not been discovered, the philosophers were compelled to do their physics and astronomy as best they could for themselves. It was amateurish stuff, but it had to last until the coming of a proper scientific method took these questions out of the philosophers' hands, and then their speculative constructions were over-taken and shattered by the progress of genuine scientific discovery. Philosophy is still reeling from the blow. Some modern philosophers are trying to recover their balance by claiming the study of the higher mental functions as their peculiar province. They man the frontier between the "psyche" and the "spirit" and hurl defiance at the psychologists on the other side. The psychologists refuse to recognize the frontier, and surely they are right. It is here as it was with natural science. Philosophy and the human studies have been carrying on with an amateur psychology of their own, or rather with innumerable amateur psychologies, one for each separate student, because the genuine psychology which could do their business had not arisen. It had not arisen in 1894 and it has not in 1943, and while we are waiting there is no harm in the philosophers and humanists doing the best they can with an understanding-psychology of their own. They are wrong if they think it will not ultimately be overtaken by real psychology, but when that happens it may not be so thoroughly shattered as philosophical physics was. It, or the best of it, may rather be absorbed.

Thus in assuming Hodges' position we are saying that philosophy, because of its intent to speak about all that is, has, in fact, done so—and it has spoken for man as well. However, the manner in which it has spoken for man very often is in an overextended way. What is needed is a more limited and specific way of discovering the facts about man, about how he actually lives in the world and goes about his chores in it. In order to accomplish this end the psychologist must reflect on the nature of his problems and he often must obtain, although not necessarily, the reflections of his subjects. These facts, however, do not prohibit the philosopher from reflecting upon the data obtained by the psychologists; only he would do so with a philosophical perspective rather than a psychological one.

Another way of expressing this dilemma is by noting the distinction that is often made in philosophy between the philosophy of nature and the philosophy of man. The curious thing, however, is that the primary data for both aspects of philosophy come essentially from a "science of nature" perspective, because of the dominance of the natural scientific approach in recent centuries. Obviously the expression "sciences of man" has been used, but more often than not it has meant the natural science of man and not the human science of man. In principle we do not rule out a possible integration of these two perspectives, except that we feel that such an integration is still far in the future. The human science of psychology has to get off the ground and yield some significant findings before an integration is even conceivable.

Thus when we emphasize the human science of psychology as distinct from philosophy it is because we feel that a scientific perspective can do more justice to the specific aspects of the phenomenon of man. Those philosophers who claim the whole of human reality as their exclusive subject matter, in our opinion, have overextended themselves. Anyway, de facto, they depend upon the contributions of psychologists, but psychologists who follow a natural scientific bent. We are claiming no more than to provide better data for the philosophers to work with; we have no interest in interfering with their legitimate concerns. In a certain sense, the philosophers, too, rushed in and filled the void that the lack of an authentic psychology has created.

On the other hand, human sciences are not sciences in the sense of natural sciences. They are sciences because they participate in the aims of a science; but they are not natural sciences because they are not conducted in the same way. The differences in how the two are conducted flow primarily from the fact that the subject matters differ, and from the concern of the human sciences for fidelity to the phenomenon of man as a person. The study of the physical sciences, physics and chemistry, essentially has to deal with the relationships between two inanimate factors as they are apprehended by man. Consequently, the assumption of a closed system and a description of the totality of factors that may operate within a well-defined situation are legitimate ways of pursuing such an end. Biological sciences usually deal with the relationship between a life organism and some inanimate reality, or between life organisms, as they are apprehended by man. But to say that something, or someone, has life, is not the same as saying that it participates in human culture—however difficult the precise line may be, it is clear that there are also important distinctions. Lastly, a human science deals essentially with a relationship between a human being and an inanimate reality, or a biological organism, or another human being, also as apprehended by man. The complexity that enters here is apparent, and even if, in the end, one were to show that there is a continuity among all these orders of existence, to *approach* all of them as if this were an already established *fact* is a prejudice that should be avoided. Such a view posits an answer where many others see a problem because of the level of complexity and organization that man possesses. Remember the key phrase in all the relationships described above: "as apprehended by man." Man apprehends himself at least as being cultural and therefore more complex than other animals. Thus, because of the level of organization that man clearly demonstrates, if for no other reason (and there are many others), the conduct of a human science would have to proceed differently from the conduct of a natural science. The reason that biological and scientific approaches toward man also work is that man can be understood as merely an objectified thing or a biological organism. We would even affirm that this is valuable knowledge for specific contexts, but that man as a person cannot be best understood by projecting this knowledge upwards. Our argument is for the inclusion of a direct approach to the study of man as a person. Thus, we conclude with our point that psychology is a science, and not a philosophy, and it deals with the subject matter of man as a person, which differentiates it from the practice of the *natural* sciences.

COOPERATION AMONG HUMAN SCIENCES

If it is true that human sciences are to be conducted differently from the natural sciences, then it seems that psychology should be far more interested in what happens among social sciences than the natural sciences. Thus far, the emphasis has always been for the relevance of mathematics and the physical sciences for psychology, but now it becomes clear that perhaps, from the point of view of the human sciences, much more relevant information could be obtained by studying political science, anthropology, sociology, economics, and history, granted that these have also liberated themselves from the natural scientific perspective. De facto, very often they are liberated, although ideologically, they often speak as if the idea of performing an experiment just the way physics does would be ideal. In any event, if psychology majors were required to take a majority of human science courses, and only a minority of natural science courses, the freedom to operate within the perspective of the human sciences might be much better. As it is now, the very equation of science with the natural sciences almost makes the move to consider psychology as a human science impossible. Mead (1964) has commented on how the communication to be scientific almost exclusively means to be impersonal or inhuman, and this implicit meaning undoubtedly prohibits progress in all of the human sciences. As we pointed out earlier, the double problem facing us is that of communicating the idea of a human science itself plus the notion that psychology should be among the human sciences. Any help that can be obtained from other human sciences would be most welcome, but in order to receive such help we must be better informed about their approaches, findings and methods.

THE MEANING OF HUMAN

The last factor we shall consider with respect to the problem of initiating a human science is the problem of resolving the meaning of human. Would it be unfair to say that such clarification comes at the end of our efforts? Surely we are guided by some idea of what it means to be human or to be a person, but it is not definitive, and precisely for the reason that it has not been investigated in either a thorough or adequate way. Just as the idea of what it means to be a scientist is clarified by the pursuit of science, the idea of what it means to be human will be clarified as the investigations get underway. One may begin, if he so chooses, by defining human and then proving that his definition holds up against the data he collects; but that is only one method. Our method is to accept the notion that the meaning of human is an ideal that is yet to be achieved and we are concerned with *all* that man does, even if it turns out to be "inhuman." As a psychologist, one would still have to account for the fact that a man can treat his fellow man inhumanly even if such behavior goes against the grain of one's personal philosophy. Again, one can point to all sorts of "borderline cases"—the Wild Boy of Aveyron, schizophrenics, people who are in a coma, etc., and legitimately raise the question: are they still human? But the very question itself presupposes some idea of being human that is obviously missing in such cases; we do not go around and make such queries of the average person we see walking down the street. Thus, at some level what we are seeking to explain or understand in a clarified way to which we are *living* an answer, and the major problem, as Straus (1966) so often remarks, is precisely to understand the obvious. In any event, we can point to "obvious" cases of human beings, and we shall let those be our guide. After we begin to achieve some clarity on the problem of the meaning of human, we can begin to apply those criteria to the "borderline" cases and see just in what sense they are or are not "human."

One implication we do want to avoid, however, is the notion that in order to study humans adequately one must restrict himself to idiosyncratic data. The notion of structure obviates this difficulty because it is already general, though not universal. It is true that one must go *through* idiosyncratic data to arrive at structure, but one must not misunderstand this by implying that one considers the data in its idiosyncracy. Because human existence is structured, there is also something general about it, and thus it is a phenomenon that can be studied in a rigorous or systematic manner. That is, it can be studied scientifically.

Some Examples of the Approach of Human Scientific Psychology in the Practice of Traditional Psychology

If our thesis concerning the human sciences in general is correct, viz., that the concept of approach is vital to the understanding of these sciences because the kinds of questions and problems that are subsumed under this concept are always at least implicitly present, then it would seem that we should be able to find these factors in the writings and researches of traditional psychology even if traditional psychologists themselves do not mention them. In this section, we propose to demonstrate precisely this point by means of some selected examples.

THE PRESENCE OF A REFLECTIVE METHOD

Our earlier discussions have implied that psychology ought to come to grips with the problem of the correct utilization of a reflective method. First of all, it should be kept in mind that reflection is not speculation; the former is always directed towards the actual and is based upon it, while the latter takes its point of departure from the actual and attempts to speak about the plausibility of certain types of possibilities. It was because of the latter that psychology wanted to break away from philosophy, even though some psychologists today still justify speculation for certain limited purposes (e.g., Osgood, 1957, p.115).

In any event, we are simply trying to render explicit the fact that psychologists do employ reflection during their professional work, and we are trying to foster the utilization of this process along with all of the other methods that are available to us. Examples of the application of a reflective method are the discovery, in our work, of the "approach" of natural scientific psychology, or Watson's (1967) discovery of the polarities that existed in psychology, or Boring's (1950) description of the system of any psychologist.

The only way such information could be arrived at is to examine what other psychologists have written, reflect on the meaning of what they have written, record it, and after most of the meanings have been listed, reflect again, and then draw out the implications of these meanings. In such a manner, one is arriving at a conclusion without experimenting, and without following all of the criteria for the approach of the natural sciences. Moreover, almost all psychologists do something like this when writing an interpretation or discussion section of an experiment. In analyzing what other psychologists have written, the aim may be slightly different, but the process is no different from drawing out the implications of the results of an experiment by reflecting on them. This is an important point because it shows that reflection can lead to truth, or significant conclusions, even if it can also stray (but there are also bad experiments —the sheer fact that one has conducted an experiment does not guarantee its validity; *how* it was conducted is equally relevant) and the implication of this is that one can reflect on a subject's protocols as well as on what other psychologists say. To deny this is the same as undermining the whole texture of communication. If a psychologist can communicate to another psychologist, then surely a subject can communicate to an experimenter. Nor should the problem of interpretation be confused with that of determining meaning. Certain units of meaning can be clear even if the total Gestalt lends itself to multiple interpretations. Moreover, the number of interpretations that are possible are limited and not infinite, so that at least a range of meanings can be established. Psychology is permeated with reflection. We are simply admitting the fact of the matter and then trying to be more rigorous by introducing this fact as deserving of methodological considerations.

PRESENCE OF THE HUMAN ORDER IN PSYCHOLOGY

While natural scientific psychology has not emphasized the personal, it has not excluded it either, although its presence is almost always there only by implication. But precisely because it is there by implication, psychologists have felt that they could get along without its usage. However, it is the purpose of this section to indicate how psychologists really do assume a human order and human functioning at least as a presupposition somewhere in their work.

No one has seen this point more clearly than Erwin Straus (1963). One of Straus' famous dicta is: "Man thinks, not the brain." By means of this dictum Straus intends to state that human functions ought to relate back to the human person, and not back to some physiological or anatomical aspect of man. By doing the latter, a human function is attributed to the nervous system, and the fact that a human person must necessarily be present is hidden. Straus (1963, p.134), for example, draws out all of the implications of the fact that an observer, after watching a rat run a maze, can make the simple statement, "animals learn." First of all, he indicates that this is anything but simple optical registration. It implies that the experimenter can compare the actual route taken by the rat with all of the possible routes he could have taken; it implies the apprehension of spatial and temporal relations; it implies the powers of differentiation, comparison, distinction, summarization; it implies the understanding of repetition and the presence of the experimenter as an historical person. All of these factors are implied in the simple observation of a rat learning a maze, and they are all human functions. Or as Luijpen (1960) says, to see is to see meanings, and for a human being it means human meanings.

Rock provides another example. In discussing the theoretical aspects of perceptual adaptation he states (Rock, 1966, p.251):

With continued exposure to the optically altered image, however, traces *congruent* with the *new* stimuli take the place of the *original* traces. Since the relationship between retinal images has not been altered, the necessary information about size or shape or *orientation* is conveyed just as in the past. This information can be supplied either by (a) direct sight of the body, (b) movement of the observer, or (c) the *presence* of *familiar* objects whose size, orientation or shape is *known*. An association, therefore, is formed between the *new proximal* stimulus and the *relevant properties* of the *distal* stimulus. . . . As *comparisons* with the *pre-experimental* traces begin to be replaced by *comparisons* with the *new* traces, perceptual adaptation will be evidenced. The optically transformed image now leads to normal perception because *traces* of the transformed image *have been associated* with *veridical* information about the properties of objects. (My emphasis.)

All of the emphasized words in the above paragraph have at leas an analogous reference to a human presence, either to the experimenter *as a person,* or to some anonymous person presumed to be functioning within the nervous system. Who can determine congruence but a human being? The notions of "new" and "original" imply a history, and only experiencing beings, not their parts, have histories. Orientation is a phenomenal datum (i.e., there is no way to describe orientation without implying an experiencing being), not a characteristic of a biological system as such. Precisely what does it mean to say that the brain is a depository of knowledge? Similarly, "near" and "far" are phenomenal (experimental) characteristics. How and what does the brain experience (as opposed to being stimulated)? Lastly, man is the proper reference for terms such as familiar, presence, relevancy, comparisons, associations, etc. All of the above, of course, does not even question the existence of traces and how they are formed, although there are certainly good reasons for doing so (Straus, 1966). The main point here, however, is the hidden presence of human functions that are somehow transferred to the brain or nervous system; or if it is argued that they are only used analogously, then lack of explicit reference to a human subject who is the source of all these activities hides the fact of the necessity of a human presence. This is all we wanted to point out in this section.

Perhaps one last example will help. Broadhurst (1963, p.17) states:

> . . . it is generally agreed nowadays among psychologists and other behavioral scientists that awareness, or consciousness, and indeed all mental processes, are dependent upon physical *structures* and chemical *changes* in those structures—that is, the nerves and the brain. Now lower animals have nerves and brains, and the control which they exercise over behaviour is not detectably different from that found in humans. The *messages* pass to and fro along the different nerves in the same way. . . . (My emphasis.)

Now, this text was not quoted because of its reductionistic tendencies, but simply to show the inevitability of a human function. According to Merleau-Ponty (1962) structures can only be perceived and perception implies an experiencing creature. How can changes be detected except ultimately by being aware of time? What does it mean to say that nerves carry "messages"? Of course, the term is being used analogously. Messages really only take place between experiencing beings. Once again, there is an attempt to account for mental processes in terms of the brain and the nervous system, and what happens is that the researcher must inevitably invoke or refer to specifically human modes of functioning to complete the description or explanation. We feel, along with Merleau-Ponty (1963), who has described this refer-

ence to the phenomenal, and ultimately to the human order, as
inevitable, that it would be far more accurate, descriptively
speaking, to make this inevitable presence to human modes
count. That is, the presence of man must be seen as relevant and
necessary for understanding all of those psychological phenomena that utilize uniquely human modes and yet ignore them in
their explanatory systems. Thus, psychology has not really gotten
by without referring to uniquely human powers, only its theories
have.

THE INEVITABLE PRESENCE
OF THE PHENOMENAL LEVEL

While many psychologists overtly condemn and disclaim reductionism, the impact of reductionism is still so strong that its
effect is constantly present and it is utilized even by disclaimers.
A perfect example of this is provided by Kagan (1967). Kagan
speaks about how we must break away from a psychology
that is absolutistic and intolerant of ambiguity. We agree.
Therefore, there is no conflict in aims. When he stresses that
attention must be acknowledged as a critical factor to understand the phenomenon of learning, we can also agree. But when
it comes to explaining how attention is to be understood, then
we must part company from Kagan, and this is where we see the
reductionistic bias enter. Kagan argues that conceptual ideas for
mental processes must be invented, but, as though coiling from
potential criticism, he immediately apologizes and states that his
comments should not be interpreted as calling for a return to
undisciplined philosophical introspection. He searches for clues
to help us understand attention and its role in learning, and he
comes up with factors such as cardiac and respiratory rate as
indices of attention, and other neurophysiological variables such
as evoked potentials. His main ideal is still limited to seeking
promising strategies of measurement.

This is a classic case of the influence of reductionism, and our
objection to this is as follows: Kagan speaks of autonomic varia-
tions as being indices of attention. Now then, why must the
phenomenon of attention be sought or apprehended only
through "indices"? Why can it not be apprehended more di-

rectly, according to any means that will permit a direct apprehension of it? That is, why can attention not be apprehended precisely as a phenomenon? Because Kagan is still responding according to the criteria of the natural scientific approach to psychology. This means that the priority is given to the measurement perspective, and in order for something to be measured, only its tangible aspects can be apprehended, and thus the "indices" of a phenomenon become more important than the phenomenon itself.

Furthermore, such an approach implicitly accepts the reality of the phenomenal, for it says that the way the phenomenon appears is not satisfactory; we must transform it in such a way that it is acceptable to science. But this already implies a response to the phenomenal, otherwise what is there to be transformed? Similarly, if one is correlating evoked potentials or cardiac activity with attention, one is still implying a presence to the phenomenal or experiential, otherwise the correlation itself makes no sense. One could object, however, that there is no phenomenal order really, and the layman's use of the word "attention" is simply an error, and that the index of the phenomenon *is* the phenomenon. But, then, one could no longer say that increased cardiac activity is correlated with attention, nor could one really say that attention is increased cardiac activity, because that would be either meaningless or redundant; one could only say there is increased cardiac activity. Psychologically speaking, however, such a statement is meaningless unless it is related to an experiential or behavioral event. Can "cardiac activity" in this undifferentiated sense really be classified and replace words like perceiving, attending, emoting and learning? To even attempt such a thing is not the making of psychology, but its demise. In other words, to create an authentic psychology, one must admit the presence of the phenomenal order. Even more seriously, the person who tries to identify the index of a phenomenon with the phenomenon has the problem of explaining what guided his index-recording operations in the first place. To deny any such phenomenal guidance is tantamount to saying that in producing the index he created the phenomenon. This kind of statement leads to the implication that the scientist deals only with the phenomena he creates on his own, and in such a case, there is no reason to believe that they have anything to do with the phenomena he encounters in the life-world as a layman.

It seems to us that the difficulties in trying to avoid the phenomenal layer (even if possible) are more insurmountable than those involved with trying to confront it directly. That is why we feel that a real breakthrough in psychology will be achieved when we learn to study the phenomenal domain in its own terms and in a rigorous and systematic manner. In any event, we simply wanted to indicate in this section how the phenomenal domain is of necessity constantly present.

PRESENCE OF THE SCIENTIST IN SCIENCE

We have already indicated how some psychologists have interpreted the assumption of an objective attitude as meaning that the researcher was independent of the research situation. First of all, even the fact that one stresses the necessity of an objective attitude already indicates that the presence of an investigator can bias a situation. However, there is also recent evidence indicating that even an objective attitude does not really mean that the investigator is not biasing his results (Rosenthal, 1966). It is interesting, however, how this is interpreted. The essential frame of reference for handling these questions of bias is still one of trying to keep the bias *out* of the situation, as opposed to our earlier suggestion of getting the bias completely *in* the situation and then circumscribing the limits within which the biases are fruitful. Plutchik (1968), for example, on the basis of Rosenthal's work, suggests three ways of controlling experimenter bias: (1) minimal contact between experimenter and subject, (2) double blind procedures, and (3) replication of the experiment by different investigators.

It should be apparent, however, that none of the suggested solutions truly solves the problem. We have already explained how the physical presence of the experimenter is not necessary for him to influence the experimental situation in a meaningful way. The double blind situation may in the end introduce even more variability because instead of having subjects and experimenter varying along a single theme, they will be varying among a number of themes because of the ambiguity of the situation. This simply means that the experimenter's presence is more varied, not eliminated. Lastly, the replication of experiments with rotating experimenters simply will indicate how various experimenters are present, but not eliminated. Even if the effects of two experimenters cancel each other out, it still means that two types of presences were such that their influences were complementary, but not absent. Consequently, despite many ways of handling the situation, the presence of the scientist in the making of his science is a way of life in psychology.

We could go on with many more examples, but we feel that our major point has been sufficiently established. We have indicated that the types of factors and problems that we want to enter into the very domain of science itself under the concept of approach are already present in the lived activities of psychologists. The only difference is that these factors now operate in random ways because they are not always explicitly recognized, and no attempt is being made to make them explicit and to try to cope with them in a rigorous and systematic way. As a rule, the latter effort is lacking because of the dominance of certain preconceived notions of science. With the introduction of the concept of approach, and within the context of a human science, the last named factor should no longer be a stumbling block.

The Approach of Psychology Conceived as a Human Science and the Contemporary Critiques of Traditional Psychology

Earlier in this work we listed a number of critiques levelled at psychology by some contemporary members of the field. These critiques are contemporary in the sense that we limited ourselves to contemporary authors, but our historical survey also indicated that many of the same objections to psychology were also made earlier in our history. The question we raise here is, how does our own approach fare vis-à-vis these same criticisms?

We had enumerated seven themes earlier, and we singled out

as the most important one the criticism directed against psychology's direct imitation of the practices of the natural sciences. By now it is obvious that we took this criticism seriously, since we directly challenged it and came up with the alternative that psychology ought to be conceived as a human science. The sixth criticism was that psychology was not doing justice to uniquely human phenomena. This criticism, too, is handled by our approach, since the primary aim of a human science is to do just that. The seventh theme was the one that said that traditional psychology did not dialogue sufficiently with the life-world. We have openly advocated such a dialogue and have asserted that the life-world is the ground for the human science of psychology.

The fourth criticism stressed the fact that meaningful psychological phenomena were not being studied in a meaningful way with the implication that psychology was not ascertaining the proper perspective with respect to its phenomena. Closely related to this point was the fifth critical theme, stating that psychology lacked holistic methods. We feel that we have met the demands of these two criticisms. Within a human scientific perspective, because of the priority placed upon dialogue with the life-world, the gap between psychological research and theory on one hand, and problems as they are lived in the life-world on the other, should never get too great; there can thus be a meaningful relationship between the two. Moreover, we have emphasized the idea that for a human scientific psychology the more proper question to put to behavioral phenomena was precisely to ask about their meaning and not their measurement, and we feel that data yielded by such a perspective will be more relevant to the implicit questions that most people have concerning psychology, and therefore also more meaningful. In brief, we feel that the existence of this critique is due to the fact that the natural scientific approach to psychology was both too narrow and off-center with respect to a proper understanding of psychological phenomena, and our emphasis upon the qualitative aspects of phenomena, a descriptive approach, and the insistence on the relevancy of contexts and relationships have all been attempts to broaden and center the perspective of psychology. The latter point also reveals why holistic methods have been sought, and for us, the method of explicitation is a holistic method. It is an attempt to go from the "given" to its actual context, which is equally present, and this knowledge will make the psychological event more comprehensive and more comprehensible. Thus, again we feel that at least in principle we have met the objections about the lack of meaningfulness in psychology, both with respect to methods and phenomena studied.

The remaining two criticisms dealt with the problems of unity and direction. We feel that the idea of structure and the notion of experiential-behavioral dialectics as a unified but differentiated relation to the situation offer much promise for solving the chronic problem of the unity of psychology. This problem has escaped solution in spite of repeated attempts in the past. It was even difficult to see just how many of these past attempts have missed, and that fact leads us to believe that perhaps the solution is more obvious than we realize. We believe that perhaps the differentiation of the relations in terms of viewpoint, method and content may make an advance towards this crucial problem. Finally, the problem of direction was handled by insisting that the proper domain for psychology is the realm of the human sciences. We are aware that this may cause difficulties for both philosophers and natural scientists, but we thought the advantages to be gained were worth the effort. It should be clear from the context of this work that our argument is for the introduction of psychology as a human science as another realm of thought and *not* as a substitution for either philosophy or the natural sciences. Thus, in our opinion, we have been able to conceive of psychology in such a way that many of the objections and criticisms that have been present in its history could, at least in principle, be met.

Of course, the last statement in no way implies that the thoughts contained in these pages cannot be proven wrong. Indeed, this writer is only too well aware of the fact that much further growth and formulation, and therefore change, even of a radical sort, is possible. Rather, what we would like to affirm more than anything else is the necessity for a change of direction for psychology. It is time for psychology to construct a new and more adequate paradigm, but this time one that is grounded within the frame of reference of psychology itself. The second thing we are convinced of is the necessity to introduce the concept of approach or something like it in psychology in order to be able to construct an adequate paradigm. This task simply cannot be done within the context of method and content alone, and if we do not contribute to its construction, the task will be done for us by others who are not within our discipline. We strongly feel that psychologists should have a role, even if not an exclusive one, in the construction of the frame of reference within which they are to work.

Lastly, we are very much aware that this is just the first step. We do not feel that the task will ultimately be accomplished by polemics, debates, arguments, etc., but simply by hard work and by attempting to extend the insights contained in the approach articulated in this work to the realms of method and content. All we ask is the freedom to execute this project.

Conclusion

Our conclusion is that far from being a contradiction, the project of establishing psychology as an empirical human science is distinctly feasible. To be scientific, according to criteria that emerge from the way science is practiced, psychology must deal with the experiential-behavioral relationships of man in a detailed away, and it must arrive at intersubjectively valid truth among a group of men who are qualified to judge the data and facts arrived at. To be objective, or accurate in our terminology, the psychologist must be able to arrive at intersubjectively valid knowledge; he must be able to assume a specifiable attitude toward his phenomena; and he must be open to himself, others and the world in such a way that he allows what is present to him to be the way it presents itself. To be empirical, psychology must be based upon phenomena that are given in experience. To be human, it must have as its subject matter the human person and he must be approached within a frame of reference that is also human, i.e., one that does not do violence to the phenomenon of man as a person. The last point does not necessarily imply a lack of rigor or discipline.

The fact that the above description is mostly prescriptive and programmatic does not alter the fact that it is a realizable project. Moreover, we have pointed out earlier that traditional psychology has also operated in part in a prescriptive manner. What is needed more than anything else are the workers who will transform this possible project into an actual achievement. But the project itself is not less empirical, objective, scientific, or psychological than psychology conceived along natural scientific lines. It simply reflects a different conception of those terms.

REFERENCES

ALLPORT, G. W. Scientific models and human morals. *Psychol. Rev.*, 1947, **54**, 182–192.

ALLPORT, G. W. *Becoming.* New Haven: Yale, 1955.

ANGELL, J. R. The place of experiment and measurement in psychology. In Robinson, E. S. & Robinson, F. R. (Eds.), *Readings in general psychology.* Chicago: The University of Chicago Press, 1923, 7–8.

BAKAN, D. The mystery-mastery complex in contemporary psychology. *Amer. Psychologist,* 1965, **20**, 186–191.

BARKER, R. Explorations in ecological psychology. *Amer. Psychologist,* 1965, **20**, 1–14.

BARTLEY, S. H. *Principles of perception* (2nd ed.). New York: Harper & Row, 1969.

BERGER, P. L. *Invitation to sociology: a humanistic perspective.* New York: Doubleday, 1963.

BINSWANGER, L. Freud's conception of man in the light of anthropology. In Needleman, J. (Ed.), *Being-in-the-world.* New York: Basic Books, 1963a.

BINSWANGER, L. Freud and the Magna Charta of clinical psychiatry. In Needleman, J. (Ed.), *Being-in-the-world.* New York: Basic Books, 1963b.

Bonner, H. *On being mindful of man.* Boston: Houghton Mifflin, 1965.

BORING, E. G. *A history of experimental psychology* (2nd ed.). New York: Appleton-Century-Crofts, 1950.

Boss, M. Anxiety, guilt, and psychotherapeutic liberation. *Rev. of Exist. Psychol. and Psychiat.,* 1962, **2**, 173–195.

BOULDING, K. E. Dare we take the social sciences seriously? *Amer. Psychologist,* 1967, **22**, 563–567.

BROADHURST, P. L. *The science of animal behavior.* Baltimore: Penguin, 1963.

BRODY, N. & OPPENHEIM, P. Methodological differences between behaviorism and phenomenology. *Psychol. Rev.,* 1967, 74, 330–334.

BUGENTAL, J. F. T. Humanistic psychology: a new break-through. *Amer. Psychologist,* 1963, 18, 563–567.

BUGENTAL, J. F. T. *The search for authenticity.* New York: Holt, Rinehart and Winston, 1965.

BUSS, A. H. *Psychopathology.* New York: Wiley, 1966.

BUYTENDIJK, F. J. J. The phenomenological approach to the problem of feeling and emotions. In Ruitenbeck, H. M. (Ed.), *Psychoanalysis and existential philosophy.* New York: Dutton, 1962.

CALKINS, M. W. Common ground in contemporary psychology. In *9th International Congress of Psychology: Proceedings and Papers.* Princeton, N.J.: The Psychological Review Co., 1930, 108–109.

CATTELL, J. McK. Objective observation. In Robinson, E. S. & Robinson, F. R. (Eds.), *Readings in general psychology.* Chicago: The University of Chicago Press, 1923, p. 18.

COLAIZZI, P. An analysis of the learner's perception of learning material at various phases of a learning process. *Rev. of Exist. Psychol. and Psychiat.,* 1967, 7, 95–105.

DILTHEY, W. Selected passages from Dilthey. In Hodges, H. A. (Ed.), *Wilhelm Dilthey: An introduction.* London: Routledge, 1944.

DREYFUS, H. L. & DREYFUS, P. A. Translator's introduction. In Merleau-Ponty, M. *Sense and non-sense.* Evanston: Northwestern University Press, 1964.

DU BOS, R. Humanistic biology. *Amer. Scientist,* 1965, 53, 4–19.

EBBINGHAUS, H. Early obstacles to progress. In Robinson, E. S. & Robinson, R. F. (Eds.), *Readings in general psychology.* Chicago: The University of Chicago Press, 1923, 7–8.

FEARON, A. D. *The two sciences of psychology.* Englewood Cliffs, N.J.: Prentice-Hall, 1937.

FERNBERGER, S. W. Behaviorism versus introspective psychology.

In Skinner, C. E. (Ed.), *Readings in psychology*. New York: Holt, Rinehart and Winston, 1935, 36–38.

GAGNÉ, R. M. & FLEISHMAN, E. A. *Psychology and human performance*. New York: Holt, Rinehart and Winston, 1959.

GIBSON, J. J. *The senses considered as perceptual systems*. Boston: Houghton Mifflin, 1966.

GILLESPIE, C. C. The nature of science. *Science*, 1962, 138, 1251–1253.

GIORGI, A. Phenomenology and experimental psychology I. *Rev. Exist. Psychol. and Psychiat.*, 1965, 5, 228–238.

GIORGI, A. Phenomenology and experimental psychology II. *Rev. Exist. Psychol. and Psychiat.*, 1966, 6, 37–50.

GIORGI, A. The experience of the subject as a source of data in a psychological experiment. *Rev. Exist. Psychol. and Psychiat.*, 1967, 7, 169–176.

GIORGI, A. Psychology: a human science. *Social Research* (in press).

GURWITSCH, A. *The field of consciousness*. Pittsburgh: Duquesne University Press, 1964.

GURWITSCH, A. *Studies in phenomenological psychology*. Evanston: Northwestern University Press, 1966.

GUSTAFSON, D. F. (Ed.), *Essays in philosophical psychology*. Garden City: Doubleday, 1964.

HEBB, D. O. *The organization of behavior*. New York: Wiley, Science Editions, 1961.

HEBB, D. O. The semiautonomous process: its nature and nurture. *Amer. Psychologist*, 1963, 18, 16–27.

HEIDBREDER, E. *Seven psychologies*. New York: The Century Co., 1933.

HEISENBERG, W. *Philosophic problems of nuclear science*. Greenwich: Fawcett, 1966.

HODGES, H. A. (Ed.). *Wilhelm Dilthey: An introduction*. London: Routledge, 1944.

HODGES, H. A. *The philosophy of Wihelm Dilthey*. London: Routledge, 1952.

HUSSERL, E. *Cartesian meditations*, trans. D. Cairns. The Hague: Martinus Nijhoff, 1960.

HUSSERL, E. *Ideas,* trans. W. H. B. Gibson. New York: Collier, 1962.

JAMES, W. *Principles of psychology.* New York: Holland Co., 1890.

JAMES, W. A plea for psychology as a natural science. *Philos. Rev.,* 1892, **11,** 146–153.

JAMES, W. *Psychology.* New York: World Publishing, 1892 and 1948.

JASTROW, J. The conflict of the psychologies. In *9th International Congress of Psychology: Proceedings and Papers.* Princeton, N.J.: The Psychological Review Co., 1930, 235–236.

KAGAN, J. On the need for relativism. *Amer. Psychologist,* 1967, **22,** 131–142.

KAHN, M. W. & SANTOSTEFANO, S. The case of clinical psychology: a search for identity. *Amer. Psychologist,* 1962, **17,** 185–189.

KANTOR, J. R. *Principles of psychology,* Vol. 1. New York: Knopf, 1924.

KANTOR, J. R. *The scientific evolution of psychology,* Vol. 1. Chicago: Principia Press, 1963.

KIMBLE, G. A. & GARMEZY, N. *Principles of general psychology,* (2nd ed.). New York: Ronald, 1963.

KING, H. C. *Rational living.* New York: Macmillan, 1906.

KLUBACK, W. *Wilhelm Dilthey's philosophy of history.* New York: Columbia, 1956.

KLÜVER, H. Supplement: Contemporary German psychology. In Murphy, G. *A historical introduction to modern psychology.* New York: Harcourt, Brace & World, 1929.

KOCH, E. Epilogue. Some trends of study I. In Koch, S. (Ed.), *Psychology: A study of a science,* Vol. 3. New York: McGraw-Hill, 1959.

KOCH, S. Psychological science versus the science-humanism antinomy: Intimations of a significant science of man. *Amer. Psychologist,* 1961, **16,** 629–639.

KOCKELMANS, J. *Phenomenology and physical science.* Pittsburgh: Duquesne University Press, 1966.

KOCKELMANS, J. Husserl's original view on phenomenological psychology. In Kockelmans, J. (Ed.), *Phenomenology.* New York: Doubleday, 1967.

KOFFKA, F. *Principles of gestalt psychology.* New York: Harcourt, Brace & World, 1935.

KUHN, T. S. *The structure of scientific revolution.* Chicago: The University of Chicago Press, 1962.

KWANT, R. *The phenomenological philosophy of Merleau-Ponty.* Pittsburgh: Duquesne University Press, 1963.

LEWIS, D. J. *Scientific principles of psychology.* Englewood Cliffs, N.J.: Prentice-Hall, 1963.

LINGIS, A. *Before the visage.* Mimeographed Notes, 1964.

LINSCHOTEN, H. *On the way toward a phenomenological psychology.* Giorgi, A. (Ed.). Pittsburgh: Duquesne University Press, 1968.

LUIJPEN, W. *Existential phenomenology.* Pittsburgh: Duquesne University Press, 1960.

LYONS, J. *Psychology and the measure of man.* London: Free Press, 1963.

MACLEOD, R. B. The phenomenological approach to social psychology. *Psych. Rev.,* 1947, **54,** 193–210.

MACLEOD, R. B. The teaching of psychology and the psychology we teach. *Amer. Psychologist,* 1965, **20,** 344–352.

MASLOW, A. *Motivation and personality.* New York: Harper & Row, 1954.

MASLOW, A. *The psychology of science: A reconnaissance.* New York: Harper & Row, 1966.

MAY, R., ANGEL, E. & ELLENBERGER, H. F. (Eds.), *Existence: A new dimension in psychiatry and psychology.* New York: Basic Books, 1958.

MAY, R. *Psychology and the human dilemma.* Princeton: Van Nostrand, 1967.

MCCALL, R. J. *A preface to scientific psychology.* Milwaukee: Bruce, 1959.

MCCURDY, H. G. William McDougall. In Wolman, B. J. (Ed.), *Historical roots of contemporary psychology.* New York: Harper & Row, 1968.

MCDOUGALL, W. *Outline of psychology.* New York: Scribner, 1923; London, Methuen & Co. Ltd.

MCDOUGALL, W. *Body and mind.* London: Methuen, 7th ed., 1928.

MEAD, M. *Anthropology: A human science.* New York: Van Nostrand, 1964.

MERLEAU-PONTY, M. *Phenomenology of perception,* trans. C. Smith. London: Routledge & Kegan Paul Ltd, 1962; New York: Humanities Press, 1962.

MERLEAU-PONTY, M. *The structure of behavior,* trans. A. Fisher. Boston: Beacon Press, 1963.

MERLEAU-PONTY, M. Phenomenology and the science of man. In Edie, J. (Ed.), *The primacy of perception.* Evanston: Northwestern University Press, 1964.

MERLEAU-PONTY, M. *The visible and the invisible,* trans. A. Lingis. Evanston: Northwestern University Press, 1968.

MILLER, G. A. *Psychology: The science of mental life.* New York: Harper & Row, 1962.

MORGAN, C. T. & KING, R. A. *Introduction to psychology.* New York: McGraw-Hill, 1966.

MULLER-FREIENFELS, R. *The evolution of modern psychology.* New Haven: Yale, 1935.

MUNSTERBERG, H. *On the witness stand.* Garden City: Doubleday, 1908.

MURPHY, G. *An historical introduction to modern psychology.* New York: Harcourt, Brace & World, 1929.

MURPHY, G. *A briefer general psychology.* New York: Harper & Row, 1935.

MUSE, M. B. *A textbook of psychology.* Philadelphia: Saunders, 1939.

NATANSON, M. The Lebenswelt. In Straus, E. (Ed.), *Phenomenology: Pure and applied.* Pittsburgh: Duquesne University Press, 1964.

NEEDLEMAN, J. (Ed.), *Being-in-the-world.* New York: Basic Books, 1963.

OSGOOD, C. E. The nature and measurement of meaning. *Psychol. Bull.,* 1952, 49, 197–237.

OSGOOD, C. E. A behavioristic analysis of perception and language as cognitive phenomena. In *Contemporary Approaches to Cognition.* Cambridge: Harvard, 1957.

PERVIN, L. A. Existentialism, psychology, and psychotherapy. *Amer. Psychologist,* 1960, 15, 305–309.

PLUTCHIK, R. *Foundations of experimental research*. New York: Harper & Row, 1968.

POLANYI, M. The potential theory of adsorption. *Science,* 1963, **141,** 1010–1013.

POSTMAN, L. & EGAN, J. P. *Experimental psychology: An introduction*. New York: Harper & Row, 1949.

RANCURELLO, A. *A Study of Franz Brentano*. New York: Academic, 1968.

RICKMAN, H. P. (Ed.), *Meaning in history*. London: G. Allen, 1961.

ROCK, I. *The nature of perceptual adaption*. New York: Basic Books, 1966.

ROSENTHAL, R. *Experimenter effects in behavioral research*. New York: Appleton-Century-Crofts, 1966.

RUBIN, E. Psychology regarded as a positive science. In *9th International Congress of Psychology: Proceedings and Papers*. Princeton, N.J.: The Psychological Review Co., 1930, 310–371.

RYLE, G. Phenomenology I. *Proceedings of the Aristotelian Society,* Supplementary Vol. XI, 1932, 68–83.

SANFORD, N. Will psychologists study human problems? *Amer. Psychologist,* 1965, **20,** 192–202.

SARTRE, J. P. *Sketch for a theory of the emotions,* trans. P. Mairet. London: Methuen, 1962.

SCHÜTZ, A. Concept and theory formation in the social sciences. In *Collected Papers,* Vol. 1. The Hague: Nijhoff, 1962a.

SCHÜTZ, A. Common-sense and scientific interpretation of human action. In *Collected Papers,* Vol. 1. The Hague: Nijhoff, 1962b.

SEASHORE, C. E. *Introduction to psychology*. New York: Macmillan, 1925.

SKINNER, B. F. *Walden two*. New York: Macmillan, 1948.

SNYGG, D. The need for a phenomenological system of psychology. In Kuenzli, A. (Ed.), *The phenomenological problem*. New York: Harper & Row, 1959.

SONNEMANN, U. *Existence and therapy*. New York: Grune and Stratton, 1954.

SPIEGELBERG, H. *The phenomenological movement,* Vol. 1. The Hague: Nijhoff, 1960.

SPRANGER, E. *Types of men,* trans. P. J. W. Pigors. Halle: Niemeyer Publishing, 1928.

STERN, W. *General psychology,* trans. H. D. Spoerl. New York: Macmillan, 1938.

STRASSER, S. *Phenomenology and the human sciences.* Pittsburgh: Duquesne University Press, 1963.

STRASSER, S. Phenomenologies and psychologies. *Rev. Exist. Psychol. and Psychiat.,* 1965, **5,** 80–105.

STRAUS, E. *The primary world of the senses.* Glencoe: Free Press, 1963.

STRAUS, E. The sense of the senses. *Southern J. of Phil.,* 1965, **3,** 192–201.

STRAUS, E. *Phenomenological psychology.* New York: Basic Books, 1966.

SULLIVAN, J. J. Franz Brentano and the problems of intentionality. In Wolman, B. J. (Ed.), *Historical roots of contemporary psychology.* New York: Harper & Row, 1968.

TAYLOR, R. G., JR. Qualitative vs. quantitative methods in scientific research. *Human Potential,* 1968, **1,** 85–87.

TITCHENER, E. B. *A primer of psychology.* New York: Macmillan, 1904.

TITCHENER, E. B. *An outline of psychology.* New York: Macmillan, 1910.

ULRICH, R., STACHNIK, T. & MABRY, J. (Eds.), *Control of human behavior.* Glenview: Scott, Foresman, 1966.

VAN KAAM, A. *Existential foundations of psychology.* Pittsburgh: Duquesne University Press, 1966.

VAN LAER, P. H. *Philosophy of science. Part I.* Pittsburgh: Duquesne University Press, 1966.

VON FIEANDT, K. *The world of perception.* Homewood, Ill.: Dorsey Press, 1966.

WARREN, H. C. & CARMICHAEL, L. *Elements of human psychology.* New York: Houghton Mifflin, 1930.

WATSON, J. B. Psychology as a natural science. In Skinner, C. E. (Ed.), *Readings in psychology.* New York: Holt, Rinehart and Winston, 1935a, 810–811.

WATSON, J. B. The failure of psychology as a mental science. In

Skinner, C. E. (Ed.) *Readings in Psychology*. New York: Holt, Rinehart and Winston, 1935b, 809–810.

WATSON, R. I. Psychology: A prescriptive science. *Amer. Psychologist*, 1967, **22**, 435–443.

WEISS, A. P. Shall psychology revise its fundamental postulates? In *9th International Congress of Psychology: Proceedings and Papers*. Princeton, N.J.: The Psychological Review Co., 1930, 478–479.

WEISS, A. P. The differentia of behaviorism. In Skinner, C. E. (Ed.), *Readings in psychology*. New York: Holt, Rinehart and Winston, 1935, 811–812.

WICKENS, D. D. & MEYER, D. R. *Psychology*. New York: Dryden Press, 1955.

WOLFLE, D. Preface. In Koch, S. (Ed.), *Psychology: A study of a science*, Vol. 3. New York: McGraw-Hill, 1959.

WOLMAN, B. J. *Contemporary theories and systems in psychology*. New York: Harper & Row, 1960.

WOODWORTH, R. S. *Contemporary schools of psychology*. New York: Ronald, 1931.

WUNDT, W. Principles of physiological psychology, trans. E. B. Titchener. In Rand, B. (Ed.), *The classical psychologists*. New York: Houghton Mifflin, 1912, 683–696.

WUNDT, W. *Elements of folk psychology*, trans. E. L. Schaub. New York: Macmillan, 1916.

WUNDT, W. Contributions to the theory of sensory perception. In Shipley, T. (Ed.), *Classics in psychology*. New York: Philosophical Library, 1961, 51–78.

YERKES, R. M. Value of psychology. In Robinson, E. S. & Robinson, F. R. (Eds.), *Readings in general psychology*. Chicago: The University of Chicago Press, 1923, 26–28.

NAME INDEX

SUBJECT INDEX

Lived-body, 31, 160, 197, 202
Life-world (Lived-world), 85–87, 102, 110, 133–144, 177, 178

Manipulation, 203 f.
Mathematics, 11, 16
      See also Measurement; Quantification
Meaning, 32, 83 f., 159–161, 179
Measurement, 9, 16 f., 64–67, 118, 218 f.
Medical model, 75–79
Mental life, 18, 59
Metapsychological, 127
Method, 14 f., 18, 62 f., 96 f., 113, 125, 127 ff.

Naming as intentional achievement, 118 f.
Natural attitude, 146–148
Natural laws, 14 f., 19

Objective, 39, 46, 60 f., 166–171, 189 f.
Objectivism, 112–122
Operative concepts, 109
Orders of structure, 180 f.

Paradigm, 105–109, 175–177, 206
Perceived situation-work, 180f., 185
Performance, 32
Person-related perspective, 93, 184 f.
Personalism, 33 f.
Perspective, 162
Phenomena, psychological, 39, 83 f., 139, 144–145, 178
Phenomenal level, 139, 149
Phenomenal origins, 178 ff.
Positivist, 61, 63
Praxis, 118, 120
Predictive, 62, 63, 75
Presence of the scientist in science, 128, 130 f., 166–171
Presence to consciousness, 120–122, 194–197
Presuppositions, 39, 142 f., 161–166, 184 ff.

Privileged position, 47, 64, 71 f., 86, 132 ff., 133, 163, f., 178, 196
Psychoanalysis, 72–76
Psychophysics, 9
Purposive, 34, 35, 38

Qualitative, 65–69
Quantification, 16, 46, 59, 60, 62, 63–69, 75, 170

Realism, 112
Reduction, phenomenological, 148 f., 157, 162
Reductionistics, reductionism, 61, 63, 204, 218 f.
Reflective method, 158, 183, 214 f.
Relationships, primacy of, 185–187
Revolutions, scientific, 6, 104–109
Role of researcher, 97 f., 109, 126, 202–204

Scholasticism, 27
Significance, 151, 159
      See also Meaning
Situation-instinctive reaction, 180
Stimulus-reflex, 180
Stream of consciousness, 30
Structure, 25 f., 178–184, 191 ff., 213, 217
Subjectivity, 32, 112–122

Technique, 71
Thematic concepts, 109, 203
Transcendental field, 149 f.

Unconscious, 74
Understanding, 26, 32
Unity, lack of, in psychology, 80 f., 223

Viewpoints, 181–184
Visible and invisible, 197

Weltanschaunng (world-view), 23, 108

Zeitgeist, 19, 49, 52